✕▤✕▤✕

*Plains Indian
History and
Culture*

Plains Indian History and Culture

Essays on Continuity and Change

BY
JOHN C. EWERS

FOREWORD BY
WILLIAM T. HAGAN

University of Oklahoma Press

NORMAN AND LONDON

ALSO BY JOHN C. EWERS

Plains Indian Painting (Stanford, 1939)
Gustavus Sohon's Portraits of Flathead and Pend d'Oreille Indians
   (Washington, 1948)
The Horse in Blackfoot Indian Culture (Washington, 1955)
The Blackfeet: Raiders on the Northwestern Plains (Norman, 1958)
(Editor) *Adventures of Zenas Leonard, Fur Trader* (Norman, 1959)
(Editor) *Five Indian Tribes of the Upper Missouri* (Norman, 1961)
Artists of the Old West (Garden City, 1965)
(Editor) *George Catlin's O-kee-pa* (New Haven, 1967)
Indian Life on the Upper Missouri (Norman, 1968)
(Editor) *Indians of Texas in Eighteen Thirty* (Washington, 1969)
Plains Indian Sculpture (Washington, 1986)

Library of Congress Cataloging-in-Publication Data

Ewers, John Canfield,
    Plains Indian history and culture: essays on continuity and change / by
John C. Ewers; foreword by William T. Hagan.
        p.   cm.
    Includes bibliographical references and index.
    ISBN: 0–8061–2862–3 (alk. paper)
    1. Indians of North America—Great Plains—History. 2. Indians of
North America—Great Plains—Social life and customs. I. Title.
E78.G73E928   1997
978'.00497—dc20   96–34648
                                                                        CIP

Text design by Cathy Carney Imboden.
The text is set in Times.

1 2 3 4 5 6 7 8 9 10

✕≡✕≡✕

Contents

CONTENTS

✕ ▬▬ ✕ ▬▬ ✕

Illustrations

FIGURES

MAPS

TABLES

Foreword

BY WILLIAM T. HAGAN

THERE CAN BE no more rewarding or pleasant way to be introduced to the subject of the Plains Indians than to read this collection of essays by John C. Ewers. He has worked in this area for over half a century, and all of us who have followed him are indebted to this outstanding scholar. We have been informed by his exhaustive research, which has been presented always in clear, jargon-free prose. Moreover, he has never allowed abstract theory to shape his findings or encumber his text.

Ewers's preparation for his lifework was somewhat unorthodox. For a year after graduation from Dartmouth in 1931, he attended art school in New York City. He then enrolled at Yale as a graduate student in anthropology and studied with, among others, Clark Wissler, Edward Sapir, and Leslie Spier. Wissler was his major professor for his M.A. thesis, a study later published as *Plains Indian Painting: A Description of an Aboriginal American Art*. This was not only a thesis that got published, a rare thing; it also was recognized as an outstanding publication by the American Institute of Graphic Arts.

Ewers left Yale without further graduate work and served for several years at various locations as a field curator in the National Park Service. Clark Wissler helped obtain his initial appointment, to a southern historic site. The local citizens, Ewers remembers, took a dim view of Yankees sent south to teach them their history.

A major turning point in Ewers's career came in 1941 when the Bureau of Indian Affairs chose him to supervise development of an arts and crafts center, combined with a museum of the Plains Indian, in Blackfeet country at Browning, Montana. He and Margaret Dumville Ewers, his charming, able colleague and cherished spouse, sought out elderly Blackfeet informants and drew heavily on their expertise in designing the programs and preparing the exhibits for the new museum and arts and crafts center. Service in the navy in World War II interrupted Jack's work at the museum, but Marge continued the project. While she worked with the Blackfeet, he commanded naval detachments that manned guns aboard ships of the merchant marine. Ewers does not remember fondly his relations with the civilians who ran those ships.

After his discharge from the navy, the Ewerses moved to Washington, D.C., where he had taken a position as associate curator of ethnology at the National Museum of the Smithsonian Institution. It was the beginning of a mutually beneficial association that saw him serve subsequently as planning officer of the National Museum and then as assistant director and director of the Smithsonian's new Museum of History and Technology. His career climaxed with his appointment as senior scientist of the National Museum, a post Ewers held until 1979 when he retired as ethnologist emeritus. He has retained an office at the Smithsonian, however, and has continued to be a productive scholar. Ewers's many honors include the first Exceptional Service Award granted by the Smithsonian, an honorary Lld. from the University of Montana, the presidency of the American Society for Ethnohistory, and the Western History Association's prize for distinguished writing. He also was awarded a Gold Medal by the Buffalo Bill Historical Society of Cody, Wyoming, and a medal for service to museums by the American Association of Museums. The awards for outstanding performance in history, anthropology, and museum administration are testimony to the recipient's versatility.

Despite heavy responsibilities in administration and the design and construction of exhibits, Ewers's publications have been numerous and of a consistently high quality. From the beginning he demonstrated an eagerness to exploit all possible sources when researching a subject. Today he is recognized as a founder and practitioner of ethnohistory. Indeed, R. David Edmunds of Indiana University likes to quote the unnamed historian who, unable to provide a precise definition of ethnohistory, defined it as what John Ewers does.

In the late 1950s and early 1960s, some anthropologists and a few historians were attempting to formulate ethnohistory, an approach to the study of Indians about which there was increasing discussion. The use of scholars from both disciplines as expert witnesses before the Indian Claims Commission had given Indian studies new prominence. It was inevitable that the growing number of people in the field would lead to conferences. From two of these in 1952 emerged the forerunner of the American Society for Ethnohistory. Ewers was involved in the organization early on and took a prominent role in the attempts to clarify what ethnohistory really was.

In the fall of 1960 at the Symposium on the Concept of Ethnohistory held at Indiana University, Ewers was one of the two commentators on the papers presented. He took the opportunity to stress the need for multiple approaches to research topics involving Indians. One of the sources he believed to have been underutilized was tribal lore, which he thought should be employed whenever possible, always measuring it critically against other forms of evidence. He pointed out that the abundance of documentary sources was a blessing to those seeking to write about aspects of Indian-white relations, cautioning, however, "that there was much more to Indian life than meeting in solemn councils, dickering with traders, and fighting 'paleface' settlers." He insisted that to write good ethnohistory, scholars must go beyond field studies and library resources and include museum holdings in their search.

Well before the 1960 symposium, Ewers's own work had demonstrated that he was prepared to practice what he preached. Reflecting in the early 1980s on a half century of work in the field, he cited his booklet *Blackfeet Crafts* (1944) as an example of his approach. To write it he had drawn on the available literature, the work of artists going back to the early nineteenth century, museum collections, and Blackfeet informants. The last source had been for him the most valuable as he had the good fortune to be able to interview members of the last generation to have personally experienced the culture based on the horse and the buffalo. It was what Ewers learned from the lips of these elderly Blackfeet that led him to reject the opinion of his major professor, Clark Wissler, that "from a qualitative point of view the culture of the Plains Indian would have been much the same without the horse." In 1955 he put to rest any lingering acceptance of the Wissler thesis with his much-acclaimed *The Horse in Blackfoot Culture*, which has been reprinted in the Smithsonian Classics in Anthropology series. William N. Fenton, the dean of Iroquois studies, declared that it "fulfills Leslie Spier's dictum that a book on material culture should enable the reader to reproduce the technology described." It indeed provided a vividly detailed guide to Blackfeet activities from loading a packhorse to erecting a lodge.

Although his study of the Blackfeet resulted in two books and numerous articles, it represents only one of many areas in which Ewers has enlightened us. As the fraction of his oeuvre presented here reveals, he has a remarkable wide-ranging intellectual curiosity. In this volume he discusses such diverse topics as intertribal warfare, southern plains women's clothing, the impact of the fur trade on the Indians, and their drafting and using maps. To all of these subjects he brings an inquiring mind and the energy and persistence to exploit all sources. His felicitous presentation holds our attention with insightful comments on the evidence as he finds new ways to look at it and fresh questions to ask.

Ewers does not drift with the prevailing winds but hews to the course that his research opens to him. His Indians are not the pawns of the fur companies; they are smart shoppers whose tastes in trade goods no company could ignore. When he discusses the impact of epidemics he is not content to deplore the tragic losses; based on his knowledge of Indian societies, he speculates on the possible effects of the diseases on tribal political and social organization and practices. A quarter century ago Ewers scotched the idea that Indians who guided and fought alongside U.S. troops were mere mercenaries; as he makes clear, they had their own agendas based on alliances and enmities many generations old. Nor is he reluctant to offer us novel insights on the motives and actions of the white men that shaped their own portrayal of American Indians.

This is ethnohistory at its best. Read on and be entertained and informed.

×≡×≡×

Preface

NEARLY THREE DECADES AGO I approached Savoie Lottinville, then Director of the University of Oklahoma Press, with the suggestion that his organization consider reprinting in book form a number of selected articles I had published over a period of years on aspects of the history of the Indian tribes of the Upper Missouri region. The press agreed to try it, and the project resulted in the volume *Indian Life on the Upper Missouri*, published in 1968. This work was well received by reviewers and readers. It is still in print after some twenty-seven years.

In 1995 I again approached the University of Oklahoma Press, offering another group of selected papers on Plains Indian history that I had published in various journals and books since *Indian Life on the Upper Missouri* went to press. These papers dealt with a wide variety of aspects of Plains Indian history that had not been considered in the earlier volume. Most were delivered initially as lectures at scholarly meetings of historians or anthropologists and at the invitation of the organizers of those meetings. All reflected a multifaceted approach to researching problems in Indian history that developed from my lifelong fascination with American history, my professional training in anthropology, and many decades of experience as a field-worker and museum man. This approach involved the search for pertinent written sources, published and in manuscript, interviews with elderly Indians on western reservations, and the examination of Indian-made artifacts and drawings as well as pictures of Indians that were taken by non-Indian artists and photographers known to have had firsthand contact with Indians in the field and that were preserved in widely scattered museums and archives in this country and abroad.

Again my suggestion was accepted by the press, and we are now offering it in a book of a dozen chapters bearing the title *Plains Indian History and Culture*.

Chapter 1, "When Red and White Men Met," is the banquet address I delivered to the members of the Western History Association at their annual meeting in Reno, Nevada, on October 9, 1970. It was published in their journal, *Western Historical Quarterly* 2, no. 2 (April 1971): 133–50. I am grateful to the current editor of that journal, Clyde A. Milner II, for permission to reprint this essay.

Chapter 2, "Indian Views of the White Man Prior to 1850: An Interpretation," was delivered at the invitation of Daniel Tyler and Clyde D. Dollar, organizers of the Viewpoints in Indian History Conference at Colorado State University in August 1974. In 1976, Pruett Publishing Company of Boulder, Colorado, published it on pages 7–23 of the book *Red Men and Hat Wearers: Viewpoints in Indian History*, edited by Daniel Tyler. I thank Marykay Scott, Editor, Pruett Publishing Company, for permission to reprint it.

Chapter 3, "The Influence of the Fur Trade upon the Indians of the Northern Plains," was delivered as the banquet address to the Second North American Fur Trade Conference held at Winnipeg, Manitoba, in 1970. It was published in the book *People and Pelts: Selected Papers of the Second North American Fur Trade Conference*, edited by Malvina Bolus, by Peguis Publishers of Winnipeg in 1972, 1–26. I am grateful to Mary Dixon, Publisher, for permission to reprint this essay.

Chapter 4, "The Use of Artifacts and Pictures in the Study of Plains Indian History, Art, and Religion," was an invited paper given at the Research Potential of Anthropological Museum Collections seminar organized by Anne-Marie Cantwell, James B. Griffen, and Nan A. Rothschild under the auspices of the New York Academy of Sciences in New York City in 1981. It was edited by the organizers of that conference and in 1981 published in *The Research Potential of*

Anthropological Collections, Annals of the New York Academy of Sciences, vol. 376, 243–66. I am indebted to Bill M. Boland of the New York Academy of Sciences for permission to reprint this essay.

Chapter 5, "The Influence of Epidemics on the Indian Populations and Cultures of Texas," was first presented in a session on epidemics among the Plains Indians at the annual meeting of the Western History Association in Omaha, Nebraska, in 1972. It was published under the same title in *Plains Anthropologist* 18, no. 60 (1973): 104–15. I thank the editor of that journal, Marvin Kay, for permission to reprint the article.

Chapter 6, "Symbols of Chiefly Authority in Spanish Louisiana," was delivered at a conference entitled "The Spanish in the Mississippi Valley" held at Southern Illinois University, Edwardsville, in 1970, and in 1974 the University of Illinois Press, Urbana, published it as pages 272–84 of a volume entitled *The Spanish in the Mississippi Valley, 1762–1804,* edited by John Francis McDermott. Thanks are due Cynthia M. Mitchell, Permissions Editor, University of Illinois Press, for permission to reprint this essay.

Chapter 7, "Climate, Acculturation, and Costume: A History of Women's Clothing among the Indians of the Southern Plains," was first delivered as a lecture in a series devoted to methods in the study of material culture offered by the Anthropological Society of Washington, D.C., in 1977. It was published under the same title in *Plains Anthropologist* 25, no. 87 (1980): 63–82. I am again grateful to Marvin Kay for permission to reprint this essay.

Chapter 8, "Folk Art in the Fur Trade of the Upper Missouri," originally was published in *Prelude: The Journal of The National Archives* 4. no. 2 (Summer 1972): 99–108. It is reprinted with the addition of a painting of Fort Union not known to me at the time of original publication and with the kind permission of Henry J. Gwiazda, editor of *Prologue.*

Chapter 9, "Intertribal Warfare as the Precursor of Indian-White Warfare on the Northern Great Plains," was first published as an article in *Western Historical Quarterly* 6, no. 5 (1975): 397–410. I received the Oscar O. Winther Prize of the Western History Association for this paper in 1946. I am again grateful to the current editor of *Western Historical Quarterly*, Clyde A. Milner II, for permission to reprint this essay.

Chapter 10, "The Making and Uses of Maps by Plains Indian Warriors," was first published in *By Valor and Arms: The Journal of American Military History* 3, no. 1 (1977): 36–43. That journal is no longer published, but I am grateful to Mike Koury, its former publisher, for permission to reprint this essay.

Chapter 11, "Women's Roles in Plains Indian Warfare," was an invited paper in a session on Plains Indian warfare at the annual conference of the Plains Anthropological Society at Wichita, Kansas, in 1988. Douglas W. Owsley, Curator of Physical Anthropology, U.S. National Museum, heard that presentation and asked me to include it in a volume he and Richard L. Jantz were editing which would include several papers on evidences of warfare as revealed by mutilated human remains found archaeologically on the Great Plains. So this essay was first published in the volume *Skeletal Biology in the Great Plains* (1994), edited by Owsley and Jantz, pages 325–32. I am grateful to Catherine Jones, Editor, Acquisitions and Permissions, Smithsonian Institution Press, Washington, D.C., for permission to reprint this essay.

Chapter 12, "The White Man's Strongest Medicine," was my contribution to the conference celebrating the centennial of the Missouri Historical Society in St. Louis on March 31, 1967. It was published in the *Bulletin of the Missouri Historical Society* 24, no. 1 (1967): 36–46. For permission to reprint this essay, I am grateful to the current editor of that society, David Miles.

The illustrations that appear in this volume were selected with great care, and I am grateful that the institutions and individuals who own them granted me permission to publish them here. Each illustration is acknowledged in the caption appearing below it.

I cannot forget my debt to the many museums, libraries, and archives in which I have found information helpful to these studies over many years. I must thank them all. I am especially grateful to the staffs of the libraries at the Smithsonian Institution and the Library of Congress.

For many years my wife, Margaret, assisted me in research in this country and abroad. I am grateful to my daughter, Jane Robinson, for her recent assistance in preparing this volume for publication.

≡≡*

*Plains Indian
History and
Culture*

CHAPTER ONE

When Red and White Men Met

I AM AFRAID I must begin with an apology. For it is more than a bit incongruous for me—a refugee from an ivory tower on the mall in Washington—to stand before you academic folks—you veterans of the campus battlefields and assaults upon halls of ivy—to talk about *confrontation*. Nevertheless, I think it is much more meaningful to consider the history of the Indians in the American West in terms of Indian-white confrontation than to treat this subject as a background study of one of the present-day minority groups in our country.

We have many ethnic minorities. But the Indians were and are different from any of the others. Not only is there a large and complex body of laws relating to Indians which spells out the responsibilities of all of us for them, but those laws also define certain rights and privileges of Indians which are shared by no other groups in this country—either majority or minority.[1]

Some years ago three Assiniboine Indians traveled from their homes in Montana to Washington to see their Great White Father. At Union Station they hailed a taxi to take them to their hotel. No sooner were they inside the cab than they began to drum and sing. The taxi driver's initial fright soon turned to curiosity, and he asked, "Say, where you all fellows from anyway?" One of his passengers stopped singing long enough to reply, "We ain't *from* nowhere. We're American Indians. We've always been here."

Well, perhaps not always. But surely the red men were here when the white and the black ones arrived, and their descendants will never let us forget that this land was their land. They can cite numerous decisions of the Indian Claims Commission within recent years to prove their point.

Even so, and despite the growing number of pan-Indian organizations since World War II seeking to find solutions to the persistent "Indian problem," we must recognize that the Indians of the Old West were not one big happy family. They had no common language, no political or cultural unity. They were divided into a host of independent tribes or villages, which distrusted one another as much or more than they distrusted the first white invaders. In fact, a sure way for whites to become enemies of some Indian tribes was for them to become known as close allies of other and neighboring Indian tribes.

It was common for the members of one tribe to refer to themselves as "the people." All others, regardless of their skin color, were foreigners. Some neighboring tribes were allied for their mutual protection against other and stronger tribes. Yet intertribal warfare among neighboring tribes, even those who spoke dialects of the same basic language, was both common and prolonged. Europe's Hundred Years War was not as long as many of the intertribal wars on the Great Plains. Take your choice—Chippewa versus Sioux, Sioux versus Crow, Crow versus Blackfoot, Blackfoot versus Cree, Osage versus Comanche, Comanche versus Apache—these are but a few examples of those perennial wars. Some of them were in progress when the first white men met members of these warring tribes, and they persisted until after the buffalo were gone and these Indians were settled on reservations. Less than twenty-five years ago I knew elderly Blackfoot veterans of the intertribal wars who had raided more than a half dozen neighboring tribes.

Save for a few cases in which autocratic chiefs managed to eliminate their rivals through the use of poison, tribal governments tended to be relatively democratic. The concept of Indian "kings," as well as "princesses," was a white man's fiction. Decisions effecting tribal policies were made by experienced and mature men in council by talking things out until they arrived at a consensus—a sort of prototype of (Lyndon) Johnsonian democracy. Yet numerous cases are known in which opposing factions could not reconcile their differences and permanent splits occurred: Assiniboine from Yanktonai, Crow from Hidatsa, River from Mountain Crow, and so on.

Furthermore, the mature leaders' decisions were not always respected by the younger men. Repeatedly, elderly chiefs complained that they wanted peace but could not control the warlike actions of their ambitious young men. Yes, there was a generation gap in the red man's West long before the first college was established west of the Mississippi River. But the warmongers in those days were the young men.

In the early West Indian-white differences were more than skin deep. One of my Blackfoot friends, Dick Sanderville, who used to entertain the tourists at the big hotel at East Glacier with songs, stories, dances, and demonstrations of the sign language, used to shock his audience by explaining the difference this way: "The Indian scalps his enemy. The white man skins his best friend."

Dick was thoroughly versed in the wiles and foibles of both races. He had served many years as official interpreter for the Blackfeet Agency, although the agents had to carry him on the rolls as a farmer, because no interpreter's position was authorized. Dick had farmed too, on the rich farms of the Quakers in eastern Pennsylvania, while he was a student at Carlisle Indian School. He had played for Pop Warner's famed Carlisle Indians against Harvard. He had met every Great White Father since the second Harrison, and he had adopted Franklin D. Roosevelt into his tribe, giving him the name "The Only Chief," that of the first Indian to sign the first Blackfoot treaty with the United States in 1855.

Dick loved to needle his white friends by saying, "I can't understand why you people want to get an Indian name, and be taken into our tribe. Ever since I was a small boy I've been told I ought to learn to act like a white man."

Certainly the red and white men's cultures had developed along different lines in the New and Old worlds during the millennia before red and white men met. The New World Indians had progressed most markedly in domesticating food plants and in using a great variety of plants for many medicinal purposes. Some tribes had sunburn preventatives, insect repellents, and even oral contraceptives. On the other hand, Europeans had made greater progress in the domestication of animals and the processing of minerals into deadly weapons as well as useful tools and utensils. They had developed such things as wheeled vehicles and such precision machinery as watches, which Indians had never heard of. As it turned out both races made substantial contributions to total world culture.[2] Perhaps the Indians' contribution of the "coffin nail" offsets the Europeans' gift of "fire water."

Surely whites introduced into America such Old World diseases as smallpox and measles which greatly reduced the Indian populations quite early during the period of contact between the races, because the red men had little resistance to them. Physical anthropologists, I am told, still argue the question of which race gave the other syphilis. They cannot be sure whether the lesions they find on pre-Columbian human bones in the Americas were caused by that dread disease.

Of course, too, during the fourteen centuries before Columbus, a relatively short span in human history, Europeans had accepted Christianity, and a majority of them had become nominal Christians while the Indians remained worshipers of the sun and the other powers of nature.

Perhaps the most important difference of all to the historian was that Europeans had developed written languages while the Indians remained illiterate—recording events as best they could by picture writings, by notching marks on sticks, and by transmitting knowledge of the past from one generation to the next by word of mouth.

Some of my historian friends have asked me in all seriousness, "How can you have a true history of Indian-white relations when you have only the white man's recorded version of it?" I can only answer that there was no North American Indian equivalent to the Rosetta stone. Only whites had a form of writing that enabled contemporary observers of and participants in Indian-white contacts to record what they saw or experienced at length and in detail. Fortunately, too, we have had attics, libraries, archives, and museums in which to preserve these records. The Indians' oral traditions tell us a great deal about their traditional beliefs and cultural values. But the origins and ages of most of these traditions are unknown, and their contents are susceptible to elaboration, contraction, or distortion with each mouth-to-ear transmission. They offer no reliable substitute for the written word. So we must learn to do the best we can with the sources we have.

I don't believe that all white men's writings about the Indians are so hopelessly prejudiced or lacking in understanding of the Indians' motives, as well as their actions and words, that they must be considered untrustworthy. Indeed, I find some of our earliest accounts of some tribes reveal remarkably keen observation and considerable sensitivity to the Indians' reactions to their initial contacts with white men and their strange ways.

At Beaver House in London last spring I was privileged to read a fascinating historic manuscript, Peter Fidler's account of his overland trek from Buckingham House on the Saskatchewan River to the Rocky Mountains during the winter of 1792 93. This Hudson's Bay Com pany trader-surveyor then saw from the northeast some of the very Rocky Mountains the members of the Lewis and Clark party first saw from farther south some thirteen years later.

On December 12, 1792, Fidler met a young Snake (Shoshoni) Indian who claimed that he had never before seen a European. And Fidler recorded his effort to smoke a pipe with this stranger.[3]

> I lighted the pipe with a Burning Glass that was fixed in the top of my Tobacco box—he eyed me all the time with the most circumspect attention, but when he saw the pipe smoke by means of the Glass he jumped up and wished to be farther from me—as he thought I was something more than common, to light a pipe without a fire—and the Indians we was with took good care not to let this good opportunity slip, to extol us in a very high manner to him—and they told the poor fellow such unaccountable stories relating to our conjurations that was very ridiculous.

Five weeks later, while in a large camp of Blackfoot Indians who

7

had never before seen a surveyor at work, Fidler observed,

> They have many whimsical notions concerning me and the instruments. They have such a dread of the sextant that none of them will touch it—had they been requested. They imagine that I could see all over the country with it, and know what and where other Indians was doing, as I generally had to look southerly on observing—in which direction is the Snake Indian country, I have frequently had the question put to me whether or not I saw these Inds—and what number of them.
>
> I have never filled their heads with any thing that I could tell more than what themselves knew—as had any accidents have happened to them, they would with very great probability have imagined that myself & instrument had been the sole occasion of such accidents—as they are full of superstition.

Of course, the Indians' reactions to Fidler and his burning glass and sextant can be explained in terms of something other than whimsical notions or mere superstition. These were the natural reactions of a people who believed that the land, the skies, and the waters were the abode of many supernatural spirits who took pity upon particular human beings and bestowed upon them some of their power. Any individual who possessed uncommon skills must, to their way of thinking, be the possessor of supernatural power, and any strange object must be imbued with that power. Power and medicine were to them synonymous, so that Fidler, the user of the burning glass and sextant, was regarded as a medicine man or conjurer, while his instruments themselves were medicine.

Time prevents my citing numerous other recorded examples of the wide range of wonders from the white man's world which Plains Indians once regarded as medicine; among them were horses, cattle, steamboats, the telegraph line, guns, metal tomahawks, blacksmith's bellows, peace medals, lucifer matches, watches, white artists' portraits of Indians, cameras, and any specimen of writing.[4]

Only 115 years ago Edwin T. Denig, the factor at Fort Union near the mouth of the Yellowstone, wrote that Indians in that neighborhood could "be made to believe almost any story, however absurd, if read in appearance from a book."[5]

During the period of the fur trade many of the objects from the white man's world became common Indian possessions and tended to lose their supernatural qualities in Indian estimation. The gun affords a good example of this changing attitude. White observers reported the Indians' terror at first hearing a gun discharged. If they heard guns fired at them by their enemies in battle, they ran away in panic, even though they were not hit. If the gun first was demonstrated to them by friends, they still believed there must be spirits within it—that white medicine men had harnessed thunder or lightning and placed it inside the strange metal tube. But after they conquered their fear of the noise and realized that they too could use these deadly weapons that discharged a small missile so fast that the eye could not follow its flight, they clamored for guns. Finally, as most warriors acquired guns, these weapons lost their uniqueness. They became secular necessities. Every Indian had to have one if he could afford it. At least five guns were reported to have been in Sitting Bull's cabin on the day he was killed.[6]

In that portion of the western Indian country best known to me, the northern Great Plains and Plateau, the fur traders comprised the first wave of whites to confront the Indians. Christian missionaries represent a second wave, establishing their mission stations at or near the trading posts. There Christianity confronted paganism. There the Indians' basic value system was seriously threatened—not by enemies who wanted to destroy them, but by representatives of the Prince of Peace, who sought only to save their souls.

Father Nicholas Point was the first Christian missionary among the warlike Blackfoot on the Missouri. He made his headquarters during the winter of 1846–47 at the American Fur Company's post of Fort Lewis, from which he extended his labors to the hunting camps of the nomadic Indians. Point's own testimony reveals that the Indians looked upon him and his new religion much as they had regarded their own medicine men and their magic powers. They called him Thunder Chief because they believed he could make the thunder roll when he was angry. They believed he had the power to cure sickness, and they implored him to treat them. They thought that baptism, like the native sweat lodge, would ensure bodily health. Furthermore, the most desperate warriors came to Father Point seeking baptism. But he refused them, stating, "I could not content myself with the persuasion generally existing among the savages, that when they had received baptism they can conquer any enemy whatsoever."[7]

Over that wide area of the American West first exploited by British and American fur traders, missionaries of different sects came to compete for the Indians' souls much as rival fur companies had struggled for their beaver pelts and buffalo robes. That was in the days when good Methodists believed they would be no more likely to find Presbyterians, Episcopalians, or Catholics in heaven than they would heathen Indians. Intelligent Indians saw more clearly than did the missionaries the irrationality of their rivalry.

During the winter of 1848 the artist Paul Kane visited the lodge of Chief Broken Arm, a Cree Indian on the Saskatchewan. Broken Arm said "Mr. Rundell had told him what he preached was the only true road to heaven, and Mr. Hunter told him the same thing, and so did Mr. Thebo, and as all three had said that the other two were wrong, and as he did not know which was right, he thought they ought to call a council among themselves, and then he would go with them all; but until they agreed he would wait."[8]

The common practice of polygamy among many tribes made it difficult for prominent Indian leaders to accept Christianity. When the missionaries told Sioux Chief American Horse that Christians had but one wife, he replied, "I took my wives according to the custom of my people. They have been with me in my joy and in my sorrow; they are the mothers of my children. They are now old and I cannot throw any of them away, but if the time ever comes when I have but one wife, I will join your church." That time did come. American Horse joined the Episcopal church, and was buried in its mission cemetery.[9]

Some Indians could see with clarity and tolerance the differences and similarities between their traditional religious practices and those of Christians. More than eighty years ago, Left Handed, a literate Sioux Indian, wrote, "The Catholics are strange; their religion is like the old Dakota religion. The priest has water in his rattle; our medicine men use beans or stones. They mumble something called Latin. Medicine men mumble and yell."[10]

It is sad to relate that in this country, founded upon the principle of freedom of religion, there was an extended period, when Church influence upon Indian affairs was very strong, when missionaries and government officials collaborated in trying to abolish Indian religion. Convinced that the Indian must be made over to think and to believe as well as to act like a white man, the government sought to abolish the sun dance and other Indian ceremonies, even to punish Indians who painted their faces or cut off their fingers in mourning for their dead relatives. But in spite of—or perhaps because of—this religious persecution, Indian religious beliefs and practices survived. The Indians outlived their persecutors. And so did the confusion in Indians' minds as to what was the true religion. I knew a number of fine old Indians twenty-five years ago who were so thoroughly confused that they accepted all religions—not because they thought they were basically the same, but because they didn't know which was right, and they said they were not going to take any chances. Only last year a friend told me he had paid his last respects to one of the elderly Blackfoot Indians whom we had both known. There were lighted candles at his head, a Methodist Bible in his hands, and his weather-worn old medicine bundle at his feet.

Fortunately there are signs that missionaries are reaching out to grasp the hands of Indians who are both confused and earnestly seeking to know what to believe. There are movements afoot to harmonize the basic elements of Christian and what used to be called pagan religion into a viable faith that has real meaning to Indians.

Father Paul Steinmetz, S.J., on the Rosebud Reservation has been seeking to reconcile both Christian and Sioux religion by incorporating such Indian symbols as the sacred pipe into his service and the architecture of his church. Father Peter J. Powell, an Episcopalian working among the Cheyenne, equates and reconciles the basic beliefs of their old-time religion with those of Christianity. Read his fascinating book, *Sweet Medicine*.[11]

Among Plains Indians no medicine was more sought by ambitious young men than war medicine. If they failed to acquire a personal medicine through their own dreams or visions, they appealed to older, successful warriors for some of their power. It was especially important that the medicine of a war party's leader should be of proven strength. His followers were volunteers. They would not join him if they doubted his ability to accomplish his party's mission and to bring his men home again.

Plains Indian warfare most commonly was prosecuted by numerous small war parties, which I have compared to the commando raiders of World War II.[12] Their purpose was not to destroy the enemy but to accomplish more limited objectives—to harry them, keep them off balance and at a distance, and weaken them by stealing their horses and depriving them of the means of effective, mobile retaliation. Analyses of these small raiding parties reveal that they were quite well organized, whereas camp defenses tended to be rather lax.

Some anthropologists used to believe that intertribal warfare was primarily a game in which Indians counted coups and accumulated war honors so that they could brag of their brave deeds for the rest of their lives. Most modern students have abandoned their interpretation in favor of economic motives for continued Indian intertribal warfare. Indians fought to defend or extend their hunting grounds, to capture women and children, to acquire loot in horses and other valuables, and to seek revenge on their traditional enemies. Because of the great number rather than the size of their war parties, and because of many small-scale skirmishes rather than larger battles, losses were considerable; during many years some tribes lost more than 1 percent of their total population from war casualties. Contemporary observers explained Indian polygamy as a practical adjustment to the fact that women greatly outnumbered men in the Indian camps, due to war losses. Even so, there is evidence that some women accompanied, and a few even led, war parties, and women took active parts in defensive actions.

During the long, bitter, intertribal wars these Indians learned to hunt men much as they hunted the larger animals, taking advantage of the terrain to conceal their approach, surprising their enemies by the suddenness and unexpectedness of their attack, or falling upon them when they were crossing streams or passing through deep valleys from which there was little chance to escape, and employing decoys to lure their enemies into ambushes. All these tactics Indians had used in hunting buffalo and antelope. In warfare they added the stratagems of the dawn attack and the quick getaway.[13]

At times Indians butchered their fallen foes almost as completely as they did the animals they killed. Firsthand accounts of intertribal actions repeatedly referred to mutilation of the dead or dying—the taking of arms as well as scalps as trophies, even the dismembering of the privates, and, particularly in Texas, cannibalism. Indian women who had lost relatives in previous actions with the same enemy were eager to participate in this bloody revenge. Make no mistake about it; the horrors of Indian warfare were not especially dreamed up for revenge on the whites. They were characteristic of intertribal warfare —the real training ground for the Indians who participated in the repeatedly described actions of the Plains Indian wars with the whites during the period 1851–90.

Many writers, however, have not bothered to point out how few tribes of the Great Plains were among the hostiles in these dramatic conflicts with white soldiers. There were more than thirty tribes of Plains Indians. You can count the hostile ones on your fingers and still have digits left over.

On the high plains the whites always could count on those smaller tribes, who had long suffered from the aggressions of the larger ones, as allies in their wars with the hostiles. These smaller tribes could neither forget nor forgive their traditional enemies. Not all historians of the Indian wars appear to be aware that many of the most dramatic battles with the Sioux were fought on lands which two or three decades

13

earlier had been the hunting grounds of the Pawnee, Crow, Assiniboine, or the small farming tribes of the Upper Missouri. Some of the best-known battles with the Sioux were fought on lands that had belonged to the Crow Indians less than twenty years earlier. Among the allies of the whites in these conflicts were Crow, Pawnee, Shoshoni, and some Arikara Indians.

Sitting Bull's efforts to form an alliance with the Blackfoot against the whites failed. Once the foremost military power on the northwestern plains, the Blackfoot had never been allies of the Sioux. They had been pacified in 1870, as much by the white man's smallpox and liquor as by the striking power of the army. They were not stupid. And they knew when they had had enough.[14]

No aspect of western history has appealed to the historically minded journalist more strongly than have the Plains Indian wars. They have appealed to his well-developed sense of the dramatic; in this last stand of the red plainsmen against the army of the United States there were conflicts, contrasts, and exciting action galore. There, locked in deadly combat, were the painted, feathered, and breechclouted red warriors and the more-or-less uniformed and civilized soldiers. The illiterate Indian chiefs matched wits with the West Point–trained generals; the wielders of lances, bows and arrows, and flintlocks fought those who manned repeating rifles and Gatling guns.

It has always been difficult for journalists to keep from taking sides in this conflict. Those who, in considerable numbers, followed the Indian wars for newspapers and magazines as far away as England and Germany, who lived with the army and never really got to know the "inscrutable savages," favored the boys in blue. Stories of the heroism of the soldiers abounded, while the bad guys wore the breechclouts. But since the smoke has cleared, the generals have published their memoirs, and their widows have passed away, the journalists have switched their allegiances. Belatedly they are rooting for Lo.[15] And they love to tell us in colorful detail of the savagery and selfishness of the Grattans, Chivingtons, Fettermans, and Custers, and of the nobility of the Red Clouds, Crazy Horses, and Sitting Bulls; and of how the illiterate Indians outwitted the inept generals until the red men were starved into submission or overwhelmed by superior technology and numbers.

Surely we cannot have it both ways. I believe the truth must lie somewhere between the two extremes. And I admire scholars like our past president Bob Utley who have painstakingly gone back to the archives and to the contemporary sources and tried to fit together and interpret what really did take place in those Indian wars. Their findings may not be melodramatic enough to appeal to Hollywood producers, but they are certainly much more accurate as history.

The journalists have tended to leave the impression that the opposing forces never understood each other, and never really tried because they hated each others' guts. They have loved to quote those eight words attributed to General Sheridan, "The only good Indian is a dead Indian," and that shorter quotation from Sitting Bull, "No Indian ever loved the white man."

These are journalists' oversimplifications. I think the Indian warriors had a great deal more admiration for some of the soldier-chiefs than they did for those easily frightened Indian agents who called for the soldiers to save their skins. And I believe that the generals who really won the Indian wars—the Crooks, Mileses, and MacKenzies—tried to understand the Indians and to earn their respect.

I have no desire to pose as an apologist for the army. I was a navy man during World War II, but I am still an unreconstructed civilian. Nevertheless, I must be impressed by the depth, the breadth, and the accuracy of the understanding of Indian life and cultures to be found in the writings of a number of army officers who served in the western Indian country before, during, and since the Indian wars. The army's record in this regard began with Captains Lewis and Clark, who were remarkably able amateur ethnologists. I shall not try to name all of their successors as officer-ethnologists or historians. But among them was Lt. James H. Bradley, writer on the Blackfoot and Crow, who was killed in action against the Nez Percé at the Battle of the Big Hole. Capt. John Bourke, Crook's aide at the Battle of the Rosebud, was an able recorder of both Plains and southwestern Indian customs. Some of

15

his best observations are still unpublished. Dr. Washington Matthews of the Army Medical Corps was a pioneer student of the Hidatsa on the Missouri, as well as of Navajo silverworking, weaving, sandpainting, and ceremonialism. All three of the classic studies of the Indian sign language were the work of army officers, Capts. Garrick Mallery and W. P. Clark and Gen. Hugh L. Scott. A goodly number of the monographs in the early annual reports of the Smithsonian's Bureau of American Ethnology were written by army officers. Most of them are still regarded as classics in their fields.[16] It is interesting to observe that some of this scholarly research on live Indians was actively encouraged by General Sheridan—he of that hackneyed "Only good Indian" quote.[17]

Doctors of the Army Medical Corps, stationed at isolated frontier posts, not only vaccinated Indians and cared for their wounds and illnesses but also made extensive collections of Indian artifacts for the Army Medical Museum in Washington. Some of these articles were weapons with which the Indian wars were fought by the red man. They were of practical interest to physicians who were studying the effects of arrow wounds and the best methods of treating them to preserve the lives of the wounded. But they also collected other artifacts indicative of the more peaceful pursuits of their Indian makers and of Indian artistic achievement.[18]

Some writers appear to think that we must find a scapegoat for the sad plight of the Indians in the American West. If it was not the fur trader who introduced new and fatal diseases among the Indians and encouraged them to destroy the very wildlife on which they depended for a livelihood; or the missionary, who sought to destroy the Indians' traditional religious beliefs, or the soldier, who pacified the Indians and broke their aggressive spirits, or the inept or dishonest Indian agent, who cheated the Indians or misled higher officials as to their progress toward civilization, then who was it?

Ah, surely, it was the settler, whether miner, cattleman, farmer, or town builder, who took from the Indian what little he had left—his land. I suppose that the settler has become the most popular candidate

16

for the scapegoat role. Was not he the fellow who, without regard for treaties, squatted on Indian land, then shouted for the army to protect him from the wrath of the aroused red men? Was not he the one whose insatiable land hunger could not be controlled by the central government? Was not he the epitome of greed and selfish interest? Even so, there is evidence that all settlers should not be branded "bad guys."

Let me illustrate my point with a short story.

Montana has been the scene of some of the most violent Indian-white conflicts. There, on the headwaters of the Marias in 1806, Meriwether Lewis killed two of the small party of Piegan Indians who tried to steal his guns and horses—the only time any members of the Lewis and Clark party fired their guns in anger at Indians. There John Colter and Jim Bridger fought many a desperate battle with the dreaded Blackfoot. There Custer was wiped out on the Little Big Horn. There the Nez Percé ended their long and masterful retreat when Chief Joseph surrendered at the Bear Paw Mountains.

Far less publicized, but equally dramatic, was a bloodless, fourteen-year battle which occurred in Montana during the early years of the present century, long after the Indian wars were supposed to have ended. I refer to the fight to find a home for Rocky Boy's Renegades. Rocky Boy was never a reservation Indian. He had entered Montana in 1885 along with Cree Indian refugees from the Riel Rebellion on the Saskatchewan in Canada. The buffalo were already gone. And for seventeen years these Indians scrounged a pitiful living by gathering and selling buffalo bones, hunting small game in the mountains, polishing horns and making beadwork to sell to travelers at the railroad stations, finding seasonal employment on ranches, and begging offal from slaughterhouses in the widely scattered Montana towns. Some of them starved to death in the subzero cold of Montana winters. During all this time Rocky Boy was not distinguished from the so-called British Cree who were not very welcome in Montana.

Then in 1902, with the assistance of an Anaconda attorney, Rocky Boy identified himself in a letter to the highest official in the land, President Theodore Roosevelt. He said that he was an American-born

17

Chippewa, the leader of a band of homeless Indians in Montana, and that he wanted a home for his people where they could make a living and send their children to school.

Rocky Boy wrote to the right man. For soon the first of a series of field investigators began to look into his claim for assistance. He was illiterate, and those who knew him best thought him more stubborn than brilliant. He was not consistent in identifying his followers, or in distinguishing them from the British Cree. Yet Rocky Boy became the symbol in a fourteen-year crusade to find a home for his people in Montana.

The brunt of the battle was fought for him by a few white settlers who championed his cause on humanitarian grounds. In addition to the Anaconda attorney, they came to include a U.S. senator from Great Falls, a congressman from Missoula, an insurance salesman from Helena, the crusading editor of the *Great Falls Tribune*, and an impractical, ex-cowboy artist named Charley Russell. Their weapon was persuasion, through conversation and liberal use of pen and ink, telegrams, and newsprint. Their opponents were both numerous and powerful. They were red men as well as white, including all of the reservation-based tribes in Montana, who objected to having Rocky Boy's people allotted on their reservations. They also included United States congressmen and some officials of the Indian Bureau, who thought it unwise to establish another Indian reservation; the Great Northern Railway tycoon, James J. Hill, who wanted the public lands served by his line to be settled by whites; and white citizens of Montana, ranchers, farmers, and townsfolk, many of whom would have agreed that Rocky Boy and his people should be given a home in Montana, so long as that home was not anywhere near theirs.

As the years passed three of the six white champions of Rocky Boy's cause remained active: the congressman, the insurance salesman, and the editor. Neither of the last two received one penny for their services. They gave freely of their time in meetings with the Indians and government officials, wrote numerous letters, and financed their own travels to Washington and elsewhere on the Indians' behalf.

18

Rocky Boy himself did not live to see the promised land. He died a year before the reservation which still bears his name was established on part of the abandoned Fort Assiniboine Military Reservation near Havre. This is only the bare outline of my story, of course. But I believe it shows clearly that Montana's white settlers were not all Indian-haters, or grabbers of Indian land.

Frankly, I believe there is enough blame for the sorry state of the Indians in the American West today so that we can all have a share of it—including those Indians who are most vocal in passing the buck for their plight to the white man. Certainly the historian is in no position to say, as did President Truman, "The buck stops here." He can trace the origins and intentions of past policies, and he can evaluate their effects. But the historian neither conceives nor implements new policies. If it is true, as the inscription on the National Archives building down the street from my office proclaims, "The Past Is Prologue," his findings, if they are known to policy makers and administrators, may be of practical value. They may help to prevent repetitions of past errors. They may even point to some aspects of past policies that have shown some promise. We have had so many Indian policies. Surely they cannot all have been 100 percent wrong.

At the Museum of the Americas in Madrid last June my wife and I saw a large photomural which the assistant director told us portrayed Queen Isabella on her deathbed dictating her last message to her subjects. She was saying that it was her dying wish that her people should always be kind to the Indians.

The good queen died in 1504. She did not live to hear of the ruthless actions of high-placed Spanish officials in the New World—of the ill treatment of Montezuma and his people by the conquering Cortés, of Pizarro's cruel conquest of the empire of the Inca, or of de Soto's bloody march through our own Southeast.

With our advantage of hindsight we know that the Spaniards were not the only whites who were not always kind to the Indians. We should know also that kindness is not enough. Some of the most kindly intentioned Indian policies failed in the long run to benefit the Indians

19

in the ways or to the extent they were intended to help them. Doubtless the missionaries and other "friends of the Indians" thought they were acting in the best interests of the Indians when they sought to remake them in the white man's image through such mechanisms as conversion, allotment of lands, and teaching of the three Rs.

We may become impatient because we still have an Indian problem in this country nearly a century after the buffalo were exterminated and the Indian wars ended. But we should have lived with it long enough to realize that there are no easy solutions to it. It cannot be solved overnight, nor is it going to fade away of its own accord. Older Indians tend to look upon new policies, offered as panaceas for the Indians' ills, with jaundiced eyes. Yet no solutions are possible without the active cooperation of the Indians.

Ninety-eight years ago, in the preface to the 1872 edition of his classic *Oregon Trail*, Francis Parkman predicted that "these plains would be grazing country, the buffalo give place to tame cattle, farmhouses be scattered along the watercourses, and wolves, bears, and Indians be numbered among the things that were." Part of this prophecy has come true. But the Indian—regarded as the vanishing American during the late decades of the nineteenth century—has not vanished. There are more Indians in the American West now than there were when Parkman's dour prophecy was written. On many reservations the population is growing at several times the rate of our national average. Lands and resources which appeared to be adequate for the support of a declining population when reservations were established are no longer anywhere near adequate for their many times more numerous descendants. The large-scale movement of Indians to the cities to find work since World War II has further complicated the "Indian problem." It has become urban as well as rural.

At the turn of the century people used to predict the assimilation of the Indians into the general population. Actually the reverse has been taking place. Non-Indians have contributed substantially to our present Indian population. Many persons now recognized as Indians are biologically more than half white. They have inherited Indian rights but none of what used to be called "the white man's burden."

Meanwhile, as historians, we should be able to sympathize with poor Lo. He has been living intimately with a white problem ever since the first pale-faced intruders appeared on the distant horizon of his hunting grounds. Over the generations since first white contacts, Indians have learned that white men are not the supermen they first thought them to be and that the wonders of the white man's world are not all good medicine for Indians. The modern Indian considers himself to be all-American. Yet he finds it difficult to identify with the people who landed on Plymouth Rock, who signed the Declaration of Independence, who crossed the plains in covered wagons. Only in very recent years have the last of the buffalo Indians passed away and the living links between the Plains Indians and their nomadic past been severed. Probably because that linkage is gone many younger Indians are looking backward, trying to establish their identity. They are, many of them, fearful of being lost in the crowd in the great urban centers. They are asking the historians and the anthropologists who they are in terms of their historical and cultural heritage.

I do not believe that Custer died for my sins. Nor do I believe that historians or anthropologists should try to expiate their sense of guilt by rewriting the history of the American West so as to portray all Indians as red knights in breechclouts, or all whites as pantalooned devils. Nor do I see the role of the historian of Indian-white relations to be that of being kind to either party in this historic confrontation. But I do think we should study this very complex theme in both breadth and depth, consulting and weighing all the sources we can find, so that we can be fair to both sides.

※≡※≡※

CHAPTER TWO

Indian Views of the White Man Prior to 1850

An Interpretation

I AM CALLING THIS PAPER "an interpretation," because I recognize the difficulties of trying to walk in the moccasins and to think the thoughts of people who lived more than one and one-quarter centuries ago. I have been studying the Indians of the northern Plains for more than forty years, but I have never talked to an Indian who was old enough to recall what *he* was thinking and other members of his tribe were saying before 1850. How then am I to know what Assiniboine, Cree, and Dakota Indians who met Frenchmen before 1700, Mandans who saw French traders in their villages in 1738, or even Crows who observed the first white explorers in their country in 1805, thought of those palefaces?

Paradoxical as it may seem, any interpretation of Indian views of whites prior to 1850 *must* rely heavily on the writings of some of the people who were the *objects* of the Indian's appraisals—white men. I believe, however, that a number of white writers reported objectively and with candor the views expressed by the Indians they met, and that some of those views are confirmed by evidence from Indian languages and by the Indians' own literature—picture writing. I believe also that Indian attitudes were reflected in their actions and that we do have a rich record of Indian behavior toward whites on the northern Great Plains before 1850.

It will simplify my problem some if I may confine my remarks to those tribes whose histories and cultures I have studied most intensively. These are the tribes who, in 1850, lived in the region my teacher, Clark Wissler, used to refer to as the Missouri-Saskatchewan area, which includes the valleys of the Saskatchewan River and its tributaries in present Canada and the valleys of the Upper Missouri and its tributaries in the United States. Many of the best-known tribes of the American West lived in that region. They included the Arikara, Hidatsa, and Mandan, who were sedentary farmers; and the nomadic, buffalo-hunting Plains Cree, Plains Ojibwa, Assiniboine, the three Blackfoot tribes, Gros Ventre (Atsina), Crow, and Teton Dakota (or Western Sioux).

Throughout the historic period prior to 1850, the tribes of this region prided themselves on their independence, their skill as hunters, their astuteness as traders, and their prowess as warriors. Archaeological evidence of strongly fortified prehistoric villages on the Missouri in the Dakotas indicates that intertribal warfare existed in this region centuries before the arrival of whites. It continued for more than three decades after 1850. For thousands of years, Indians hunted buffalo in this region, and this animal was still the staff of life for the nomadic tribes of this area in 1850. None of those tribes had ceded their hunting grounds to the whites in 1850. It was not until 1851 that the boundaries of many of those tribes were first defined by treaty, and the Blackfoot tribes did not negotiate their first treaty with the United States until 1855.

Present-day Indians, convinced of the need for pan-Indian organizations to protect Indian rights and to seek solutions to pressing Indian problems, may find it hard to conceive of a time when "Indianness" was not of prime importance to Indians. There was no basis, however, for such an ethnocentric concept *before* the whites arrived. Then all the Indians' friends and enemies were other Indians. Rather, Indians were then "tribocentric," if I may coin a term. They tended to remain so throughout the period of white contact well beyond 1850. The Indian owed his allegiance not to his race but to his family, his band or village, and his tribe. A warrior was proud to be a Crow, a Mandan, a Cree, or a Dakota. Each tribe spoke its own dialect and regarded its members as "the people." Members of other tribes were

23

outsiders. Whether they were friends or enemies depended on the extent to which their tribal interests were in harmony or conflict with one's own. Tribes in continual competition for hunting grounds became hereditary enemies—such as Cree versus Dakota, or Blackfoot versus Crow. Some tribes became allies of neighboring tribes for their mutual protection against strong, common enemies—such as Cree and Assiniboine, Blackfoot and Gros Ventre, Mandan and Hidatsa. Trading with the enemy was not unknown, however. The Mandan and Dakota negotiated temporary truces in order to exchange garden produce for products of the chase to their mutual advantage.

Inasmuch as the very great majority of whites known to Indians of this region prior to 1850 were traders, it is well to know that these Indians were experienced traders when they first met white men. Finds of marine shells from both the Pacific and Gulf coasts in prehistoric village sites on the Missouri indicate that extended trade routes led to and from these villages of farming tribes in prewhite times. Pre-eighteenth-century village sites also have yielded trade materials from less distant sources: obsidian, probably from present Yellowstone National Park in western Wyoming, and red pipestone, from the famed catlinite quarry in southwestern Minnesota.[1]

Through intertribal trade northward from the Southwest, the European horse reached the Crow and Blackfoot tribes in the western part of this area *before* those Indians met white men. By the time the first whites arrived in their country, members of those tribes were riding horses on the buffalo chase and to war and were using horses as burden-bearers in their camp movements. Horses had also become prized booty in warfare.

Through intertribal trade, also, limited quantities of European-made manufactured goods reached the tribes in the central and western portions of this area before they met whites. These items were brought by Indian intermediaries who traded directly with whites at distant trading posts. When Pierre Gaultier de Varennes, Sieur de la Vérendrye accompanied an Assiniboine trading party to the Mandan villages in 1738, he observed that the Mandans were "sharp traders and clean the

24

Assiniboine out of everything they have in the way of guns, powder, ball, knives, axes, and awls."[2]

The villages of the farming tribes were flourishing trading centers before the whites arrived. By the time the whites appeared, these and neighboring nomadic tribes had obtained enough articles of European manufacture to be sure of their usefulness as weapons, tools, or utensils, or their attractiveness as luxuries, and to whet their desire for more of these goods. The Indians were experienced barterers, knew something of values and markups, and were prepared to pay for what they wanted. These Indians had become literally "horse traders"—with all of the keen bargaining sense that term implies.[3]

Another very important aspect of Indian culture in this region at the time of first contact with whites conditioned Indian reactions to whites during the early years of interracial relations. I refer to the Indians' worldview—their belief in supernatural powers, or medicine in the religious sense. They envisioned the world around them—the sky, the land, and water—as the abode of powers which were stronger than their own and which could help or harm them. They sought to placate malevolent powers, such as thunder and serpentlike underwater monsters; they sought the aid of benevolent ones, such as sun, birds, and animals. Any object that was unique or strange to them was looked upon as medicine that inspired both awe and reverence. The individual who owned such an object, professed to know its origin and function, and used it to his own advantage was thought to be blessed with supernatural power.

Given this prevailing Indian worldview, or body of beliefs, it should not seem strange to us that the Indians of this region looked upon the white men's many technological inventions as awesome medicines; that they sought to obtain strange objects from the white man's culture for their own medicines; or that they regarded white men who appeared to be skillful users of these objects as possessors of very potent supernatural powers.

The literature of Indian-white contacts in this region is rich in white men's observations on these points. Among the many wonders of the white men's world which Indians once looked upon as medicine were the gun, ironpot, compass, telescope, burning glass, magnet, thermometer, sextant, music box, watch, steamboat, white artists' portraits of Indians, and any specimen of handwriting. Whites sometimes took advantage of the Indians' ignorance of some of these wonders, which remained incomprehensible to them, even after many years of contact. At the end of our period, Edwin T. Denig, the factor at Fort Union, wrote that Indians in that neighborhood could "be made to believe almost any story, however absurd, if read in appearance from a book."[4]

Ingenious Indians were eager to adopt strange objects from the white man's world as personal war medicines. François Larocque, the first white man known to have visited the Crow country, observed in 1805 that one Crow warrior had as his medicine a fragment of colored glass from a magic lantern; another wore the tail of a Spanish cow as a hair pendant.[5] Surely neither of these war medicines was more remarkable than was that of a Dakota chief to whom Father De Smet later gave a religious medal. That chief opened a box, unwrapped a buckskin covering, and unrolled a colored picture of General Diebitsch, a prominent Russian leader in the Napoleonic Wars, in full uniform and astride a beautiful horse. He explained to De Smet that for years this had been his war medicine. He offered his pipe to that general "before all his enterprises against his enemies, and attributed to him the many victories he had gained."[6]

Father Hennepin (in 1680) and the French trader Pierre-Charles Le Sueur (in 1700) knew the Dakota in Minnesota. Both claimed the Dakota called them "spirits."[7] James Kipp, regarded as the traders' best authority on the Mandan dialect of Siouan in 1833, translated their term for white man—*wasschi*—as "he who has everything, or everything good."[8]

Jean Baptiste Truteau, pioneer white trader among the Arikara, wrote of them in 1796: "They have a great respect and a great veneration for all white men in general, whom they put in the rank of divinity, and all that comes from them is regarded by these same people as miraculous. They do not know how to distinguish among civilized nations. English, French, Spanish, et cetera, whom they call indifferently white men or spirits."[9]

The persistence of the term Napikwan (old man person) for the white man among the Blackfoot shows that they likened him to an ambivalent worker in their own mythology. Napi was also a clever trickster with very human frailties. Likewise the Algonquian-speaking Gros Ventre, Arapaho, and Cheyenne named the white man after their trickster, Spider or "the wise one."

So much has been written in recent years about the Indians' contributions to world medicine that we may tend to forget that in this region during the early decades of white contact Indians regarded the white man's remedies for physical ailments as superior to their own. Lewis and Clark were repeatedly beseeched by Indians to treat their sick. Alexander Henry, a trader among the Blackfoot, wrote in 1811, "They are perpetually begging medicine from us, and place the greatest confidence in whatever we give them, imagining that everything medical which comes from the trader must be a sovereign remedy for all diseases."[10] In that same year, John Bradbury, an English botanist, made friends with an Arikara shaman while he was collecting plants near the villages of that tribe. The Indian looked upon Bradbury as a fellow practitioner and proudly revealed the contents of his deerskin medicine bag to him.[11]

Father Nicholas Point, the first Christian missionary among the Blackfoot on the Missouri in 1845–46, found that these Indians looked upon him much as they did their own medicine men. They thought he could cause disease or make the thunder roll if he became angry. They believed he possessed the power to cure sickness and implored him to treat them. They thought that baptism, like the traditional Indian sweatbath, would ensure bodily health.[12] We know, too, that for several decades, beginning at least as early as the early 1830s, the Blackfoot, who were fearful of handling their own dead, brought the bodies of prominent chiefs to Fort Benton where the white traders prepared them for burial.[13]

As Indians became better acquainted with whites, they became more impressed with their human qualities. Indeed, the Arikara appear to have removed Frenchmen from their pantheon of divinities by the year 1804. Pierre-Antoine Tabeau, who was trading with the Arikara when the Lewis and Clark Expedition reached their villages on their upriver journey that fall, observed: "It is only a little while since the Ricara deified the French, who, unhappily, have only too well disabused them by their conduct and their talk. Thus they have passed today from one extreme to the other and we are indeed nothing in their eyes."[14]

He noted that the only member of the Lewis and Clark party whom the Arikara regarded with great awe was "a large, fine man, black as a bear." He referred to York, Clark's Negro servant, the first black man the Indians of the Upper Missouri tribes had seen.[15] Because Negroes entered their country in the company of whites, they came to be known as "black white men" to those Indians.

The Mandan, near whom the Lewis and Clark party wintered in 1804–05, retained a higher regard for the supernatural powers of whites than did the Arikara. In their buffalo-calling ceremony, it was customary for younger married women to have sexual relations with older men of the tribe who were thought to possess very potent supernatural powers, so that the women in turn might transmit these powers to their husbands. They invited men of the Lewis and Clark party to play the roles of some of the older men in this religious ceremony.[16] Other writers on the Mandan around the turn of the century may have maligned their women by alluding to their easy virtue. These women also may have been interested in white men as sources of supernatural power.

As Indians became better acquainted with whites, they came to believe that some white men had stronger powers than did others. During the winter that the Lewis and Clark party resided near the Mandan and Hidatsa villages, their blacksmiths were kept busy making and repairing metal articles for the Indians in exchange for corn. Indians looked upon the smiths' bellows as medicine. A Hidatsa chief offered his frank opinion of the men of the American expedition to a British trader who was in his village: "There are only two sensible men amongst them, the worker in iron and the mender of guns."[17]

White artists were another occupational group whom Indians thought were gifted with exceptional powers. The Indians of this region had both religious and secular art traditions in which human figures were depicted. Successful warriors portrayed their coups in battle. Some Indians made crude representations of their personal enemies so that they might destroy them through witchcraft. Indian art could serve good or evil ends.

In their own art, as in their gesture language, they distinguished the white from the Indian by representing the former as a hat wearer. In their sign language, the white man was designated simply by passing the right hand across the brow, palm down, to convey the idea of a hat brim or visor. This was, of course, a purely descriptive gesture. Whether the white man was friend or enemy depended upon the larger context in which the gesture was used. In the winter counts of the Teton Dakota, white men were pictured as hat-wearers. Several winter counts picture the first white trader to establish a post in Dakota territory on the Missouri, and who supplied these Indians with guns. Known to the Dakotas as The Good White Man, he was probably Regis Loisel, a Frenchman from St. Louis, who built that trading post at the beginning of the nineteenth century.[18]

Indians had traditionally pictured humans with knoblike heads devoid of individual features. When white artists came among them who created lifelike portraits in two dimensions, some Indians refused to sit for their portraits, fearing that the reproduction of their likenesses would deprive them of their power. George Catlin wrote of his difficulties in convincing the Mandan that they would not be harmed if he painted their portraits. On the other hand, a Blackfoot warrior, the following summer (1833), bragged that he had survived a battle with the Assiniboine and Cree outside Fort McKenzie without a wound *because* "Mr. Bodmer had taken his portrait." At the Hidatsa villages the next fall, Bodmer painted birds and animals for Indians, which they thought "would make them proof against musket balls." These were probably the birds and animals that were those warriors' guardian spirits.[19]

29

In the British possessions in 1848, Paul Kane apparently convinced the Cree that by sketching their sacred pipestems he was enhancing their potency as war medicine.[20] Yet Rudolph Kurz encountered violent opposition from the Hidatsa when a cholera epidemic broke out among them as he was beginning to picture those Indians in 1851. They recalled that a disastrous smallpox epidemic had occurred in 1837, after both Catlin and Bodmer had painted members of their tribe, and they threatened to kill Kurz if he continued to draw them. The Swiss artist was forced to move upriver to Fort Union; he encountered no such resistance on the part of the Assiniboine, Cree, and Crow Indians who traded there.[21]

Whether Indians looked upon white artists' works as good or bad medicine appears to have depended on the circumstances under which they were made. In any case, a common interest in art seems to have afforded a basis for close rapport between some Indian and white artists, and the more detailed and more realistic renderings of humans and horses that began to appear in the works of Indian artists *after* they had opportunities to observe closely how the white artists worked, and after they gained access to smooth paper and precise drawing instruments (pencils and crayons), must have been in part due to white influence.[22]

It appears clear to me from an examination of the written record that white traders' penetration deeper and deeper into this region, in order to profit from direct trade with more and more tribes, threatened the interests of many tribes and roused both ill feelings and open hostilities toward the whites. Different tribes were affected in different ways and at different times as this movement progressed. This movement first threatened and then eliminated the profitable activities of the peripheral tribes in supplying manufactured goods to the more remote ones. It also upset the delicate balance of powers that had existed in the intertribal warfare of this region. Furthermore, the actions of these tribes indicate that they were fully aware of these threats to their interests.

In this region, the fur trade initially expanded from east to west. Those tribes on the eastern periphery of the region were the first to receive guns and other metal weapons. They were strengthened at the expense of their more remote Indian enemies who lacked those weapons. Surely the Assiniboine saw the advantage of gaining access to the flow of firearms from Hudson Bay when, even before 1700, they abandoned their Dakota allies and allied themselves with their former Cree enemies. By the early years of the eighteenth century, the Cree and Assiniboine also were receiving improved war materials from French traders operating from Montreal. As early as 1736, a Dakota war party wiped out a party of Frenchmen and mutilated their bodies. One of those Frenchmen was a son of La Vérendrye. Two years earlier he had joined a Cree campaign against the Dakota. The message of that Dakota action was clear: whites must not take sides in Indian warfare.[23]

There were early indications that the peripheral tribes were aware of the potential loss of profits to them if whites extended their trade to the more remote tribes. In 1797, the Assiniboine traders tried to dissuade David Thompson from visiting the important Mandan trading center by telling him of the danger of meeting Dakota war parties en route. In 1805, Mandan and Hidatsa traders, in turn, sought to prevent Larocque from going on to the Crow country by representing the Crows as thieves and liars and stressing the dangers of encountering hostile tribes. We know that the extension of the white man's trade did eliminate Assiniboine intermediaries from the trade with both the Mandan and the Blackfoot tribes, and the importance of the old Mandan trading center declined rapidly after whites opened direct trade with the still more remote tribes who had traded there.

Those tribes who had established direct trade with whites resented white traders' efforts to penetrate deeper into the Indian country to supply their enemies with war-making materials. Doubtless those Teton Dakota who sought to prevent the passage of Lewis and Clark's boats up the Missouri in 1804 looked upon those whites as traders who would supply their Mandan and Hidatsa enemies. The Blackfoot tribes tried to prevent British traders from carrying arms and ammunition to enemy tribes west of the Rockies, although the traders circumvented the Blackfoot blockade by crossing the mountains farther north and outside Blackfoot territory.[24]

I have quoted Tabeau's observation that the Arikara were disenchanted with the whites as early as 1804. By that time, his firm was already doing business with their enemies, the Teton, farther up the Missouri. Another factor helped to rouse the Arikara to open hostility. An Arikara chief died during a trip to Washington in 1805, and the Arikara thought the whites had killed him.

Arikara hostility toward whites continued until the smallpox epidemic of 1837 greatly reduced the population of that tribe. When Lieutenant Pryor tried to return the Mandan chief, Shahaka, who had been to Washington, to his people in 1807, the angry Arikara opened fire on his party and forced them to turn back to St. Louis. In 1823, William Ashley's large party of trappers who were bound upriver were stopped by the Arikara at their villages; in the ensuing battle, thirteen or fourteen of those whites were killed or mortally wounded. This action precipitated the only U.S. Army campaign against a tribe of this region prior to 1850. Col. Henry Leavenworth's soldiers, augmented by mountain men and a large contingent of Dakota Indian allies, moved against the Arikara villages. The Dakota warriors were eager to attack, but Leavenworth delayed, and the Arikara slipped away in the middle of the night. A lasting result of this inaction was the contempt for the courage of white soldiers that persisted in the minds of aggressive Dakota warriors. Arikara-Dakota warfare continued for three generations. By the 1860s, Arikara chiefs were pleading for white soldiers to help defend their people against repeated Dakota attacks.[25]

The Blackfoot tribes and their Gros Ventre allies, who hunted on both sides of the international boundary, had traded with the British in the Saskatchewan Valley for a half century before American mountain men roused their hostility—and with good reason. The Americans were supplying war materials to their Crow, Shoshoni, and Flathead enemies. The Blackfoot also profited by robbing the mountain men and taking their beaver pelts and other booty to friendly whites in the north to exchange for arms, ammunition, and other desirable goods. During the quarter century prior to 1831, numerous skirmishes took place between the Blackfoot (and Gros Ventre) and the trappers near the Missouri headwaters and in the mountains. Twice during that period (in 1811 and 1823) the Indians chased the trappers out of present-day Montana, leaving numbers of dead whites in the field. Not until 1831 were Americans able to open peaceful trade with the Blackfoot tribes. By then it was clear that a major cause of Blackfoot resentment had been the trappers' exploitation of the rich fur resources of their hunting grounds from which the Indians derived no share of the profits. As a Blackfoot chief confided to Indian Agent Sanford in 1834, "If you will send Traders into our Country we will protect them and treat them well; but for Trappers—Never."[26]

Much has been written about the profits whites made from the fur trade. It would be difficult to believe that Indians did not profit from that trade, also, before 1850. They offered furs, buffalo hides, and pemmican from animals which were abundant in their country in exchange for manufactured goods which they wanted. Standards of value were established by agreement between Indians and whites. The records of the trading companies contain many references to Indian refusals to accept articles they did not want, or ones of inferior quality. Firearms experts rate the popular Northwest trade gun as an efficient as well as a cheap weapon. The Crow and the Mandan (in the early 1830s) refused to accept liquor in their trade. Competition among white traders gave Indians a choice of markets, and it checked inflation of prices on manufactured goods. Indians employed metal tools and ornaments, cloth, twine, thread, beads, and other materials as replacements for aboriginal materials in ways that saved them labor and enriched their lives. At the same time, they became more and more dependent on whites for both luxuries and necessities other than food.[27]

The conduct of the trade brought some Indians into much closer relationships with whites than it did others. In the beginning, white traders visited Indian villages where they were protected and their actions regulated by members of the tribal Soldier Societies. After white traders built posts surrounded with palisades to protect them from attacks by hostile Indians, prominent Indian warriors continued to play important roles in regulating trade. I refer especially to the "Soldiers of the Fort," Indians who were recognized as tribal leaders but who also served the interests of the whites. Not only did they encourage members of their tribes to trade at particular posts, but they kept their white employers informed of tribal wants and activities, and they served as policemen who kept order and prevented thefts of white men's property while other Indians were at the forts.

Two of the best-known Indians of this region in the 1830s were Soldiers of the Fort for the American Fur Company. One was Four Bears, second chief of the Mandan, who claimed the best war record of any man in his tribe and who served as a director of his people's major annual religious ceremony, the Okipa. Another was The Light; he was the son of the prominent Assiniboine chief who selected the site for Fort Union, the principal trading post on the Upper Missouri for several decades after 1827. Both of these men were tragic figures. Four Bears died in the smallpox epidemic of 1837 that decimated his tribe. Shortly before his death, he cursed the whites as black-hearted dogs for repaying his long and faithful friendship with this fatal pestilence. The Light was the first member of his tribe to visit Washington and the cities of the East, in 1831–32. After his return, he was killed by a man of his own tribe who refused to believe his oft-repeated stories of the wonders of the white man's world.[28]

Many Indian women had even more intimate relations with whites that were longer lasting and ended more happily. I refer to the hundreds of Indian women of all of the tribes of this area who married white men. There is no complete record of the total number of these interracial marriages before 1850. Some of the brides were members of chiefly families whose marriages to prominent traders enhanced the positions of their relatives. Most of these Indian women married whites who held less important positions in the fur trade, clerks or laborers. White men were considered good catches because it was thought that their wives would not have to work so hard and that they would be better fed and dressed than were the wives of Indians.

Some of these interracial marriages did not last; others proved to be partnerships for life. In either case, we know that they were productive; there were a growing number of individuals of mixed Indian and white descent in the population of this region. Sons of the Indian women and white traders themselves became employees in the fur trade as factors, clerks, guides, interpreters, hunters, and laborers. Well before 1850, large communities of Métis or Red River Half Breeds were formed in the eastern portion of this region. They developed a way of life that was marginal to both Indian and white cultural traditions. They lived in log cabins, grew some crops, and took part in prolonged, semiannual buffalo hunting excursions, during which they killed large numbers of buffalo and carried tons of meat and hides homeward in their creaking, two-wheeled carts. Still other sons and daughters of mixed marriages became leaders in their mothers' tribes in later generations.[29]

It seems clear to me from my examination of the written record that Indian attitudes toward whites changed over the years prior to 1850. If indeed Indians of this region tended to view whites as divinities or supermen during the earliest years of contact between the races, Indians became increasingly aware of the white men's human qualities as they became better acquainted. It is also clear that different tribes and different individuals within those tribes held different opinions of whites. The Cree warrior who benefited from the white man's war materials during the early years must have held a more favorable view of whites than did the Dakota brave who believed the whites were helping his Indian enemies. The Blackfoot warrior of the 1820s certainly distinguished between the Hudson's Bay Company trader and the American trapper who exploited his hunting grounds without any advantage to him. The chief who was acknowledged by the trader with gifts of a medal, a handsome suit of clothes, and kegs of liquor must have had a friendlier feeling toward that white than did his younger rival for band or tribal leadership who had received no favors from the trader. The Indian woman married to a white man certainly understood white men's customs and values better than did her tribal agemate whose husband was an Indian. Indian attitudes toward whites probably varied as greatly as did white men's attitudes toward Indians prior to 1850.

This is not to say that misconceptions about Indians did not persist in the minds of white traders who lived in the Indian country. Even so, those traders had better opportunities to gain an understanding of Indians than Indian traders had of understanding either the larger culture of which white traders were a part or the many whites outside the Indian country who also had interests in the fur trade. The white trader in the Indian country could visit every camp or village of a tribe—to estimate their numbers, to reckon their potential for trade or war. He knew their leaders, and he observed their customs at firsthand. The Indian trader, on the other hand, met in the white trader only that tip of the white man's far-flung and complex civilization that protruded into the Indian country. He never met the English gunsmith, the Venetian bead-maker, the New England textile weaver, the Brazilian tobacco grower, the New Jersey maker of shell hairpipes, the Missouri lead miner, or the London, New York, or St. Louis investor—all of whom had stakes in the Indian trade. Before 1850, few Indians of this region had ever seen a white woman. Nor could the stay-at-home Indians of this region believe the seemingly fantastic stories told by the few Indians who had visited St. Louis, Philadelphia, New York, and Washington of the white men's teeming cities, his many-storied houses, his vast industrial and war potential.

A few Indians of this region learned of the white men's concepts of the universe, which differed markedly from their own, and these Indians reacted differently. At Fort Clark during the winter of 1833–34, the German scientist, Prince Maximilian of Wied-Neuwied, and his artist-companion, Karl Bodmer, exchanged ideas about the heavenly bodies and the origin of the universe with friendly Mandan Indians. The prince reported, "They laughed outright when we affirmed that the earth was round and revolved about the sun. Others, however, would not reject our views, and were of the opinion that, as Whites could do so much that was incomprehensible to them, it was possible they might be right on this point also."[30]

By the mid-nineteenth century, most of the tribes of this region had known whites for more than a hundred years. They knew that whites differed from Indians culturally as well as physically and that cultural differences went well beyond the fact that whites were hat wearers. In their conceptions of these differences, they revealed something of their attitudes toward whites. In 1854, a statement of an Indian viewpoint of these differences was written by Edwin T. Denig, who was probably the most knowledgeable white student of the tribes of the Upper Missouri at that time. The son of a Pennsylvania physician, he had traded with the tribes on the Missouri for more than two decades. He had married two Assiniboine women, and he fathered four children by them. Denig presented the Indian viewpoint in these words:

Now this Supernatural Unknown Cause or Mystery created all things in the beginning. After the earth a few men and women of different colors were made, from whom descended all people. Different races were created for different purposes. They say that the whites were allotted education, knowledge of the mechanical arts, of machinery, etc., and therefore the whites are in many ways Wah-con. They were also made rich and clothed, or have the means of getting clothing, and everything they want without hardship or exposure. The Indians, they say, were made naked and with such qualifications as to suit a hunter, knowledge enough to make his arms and use them at war or in the chase, a constitution to stand severe cold, long fasting, excessive fatigue, and watchfulness, and this was his portion. The position and pursuits of people were not defined by any laws, oral or otherwise delivered, but each with the powers granted to him was enabled to live.[31]

❌≡❌≡❌

CHAPTER THREE

The Influence
of the Fur Trade
upon the Indians
of the Northern Plains

SOME HISTORIANS of the American fur trade have treated the Indians as if they were mere bit players in this important wilderness drama. Concerned with the fur trade as a medium of geographical exploration, or as the pioneer white man's business enterprise beyond the frontier of settlement, they have tended to forget that the fur trade was *also* an Indian trade in which Indian traders were quite as active and involved as were the palefaces.

It would not be difficult to support a contention that the fur trade had a stronger and more lasting impact on the lives of the Indians, who lived in relatively small bands or villages within the area where the trading actually took place, than it did on the large and remote civilizations of France, England, eastern Canada, or the eastern United States, from which young men journeyed westward beyond Red River or the Mississippi to engage in the trade, and to which many of them returned after they had tired of or retired from this business. Generations of Indians—men, women, and children—who lived on the Canadian Plains or in the drainage basin of the Missouri below the 49th parallel, or in both, felt the influence of the fur trade on their lives from birth until death. And Indians were the major sufferers when the tail of the last buffalo disappeared from the plains and the era of the fur trade as an important factor in the history of this region came to an abrupt end.

We should recognize too that the Indians of this region were not inexperienced traders when the first whites appeared in their country. Through the medium of intertribal trade they had acquired considerable skill in disposing of things they could accumulate in quantity through their own labors for desirable articles their Indian neighbors possessed in some quantity but which they did not have. Archaeologists in recent years have become increasingly aware of both the existence and the significance of an aboriginal trade among the Indians of this region. The presence of marine shells from both the Pacific and Gulf coasts in prehistoric village sites beside the Missouri River in the Dakotas is evidence of extended trade routes leading to the horticultural tribes in prewhite times. And other materials from less distant locations, such as obsidian, probably from present Yellowstone National Park, and red pipestone from the quarry in present Pipestone National Monument in southwestern Minnesota, also have been found in pre-eighteenth-century village sites on the Missouri. Surely the Indian traders were interested in luxuries as well as necessities before they met white men.[1]

Archaeologists with whom I have talked about prehistoric trade in this area seem to recognize that the full range of materials traded cannot be determined from the limited range of trade objects preserved in these sites and that probably most of the articles traded were perishables which are rarely preserved in archaeological contexts.

There can be no doubt that the semipermanent, earth lodge villages of the Mandan, Hidatsa, and Arikara on the Missouri were flourishing trading centers before the first white men visited them. But we only begin to learn of the Indians with whom villagers traded and the range and quantities of materials these farming Indians traded with their nomadic red-skinned neighbors when we read the historic records written by the early white explorers who visited those centers of trade.

As early as January 1734, Pierre Gaultier de Varennes, Sieur de la Vérendrye, learned that the Assiniboine were accustomed to visit the Mandan and Hidatsa villages to trade for corn. This may be the earliest historical reference to the aboriginal trade of garden produce by the village tribes to the nomadic tribes in exchange for products of the chase.

In Lewis and Clark's time (1804) we know that the farming tribes also offered beans, squash, and tobacco as well as both dried and cooked corn in exchange for the nomads' offerings of dried buffalo meat, dressed buffalo and deer skins, buffalo skin lodge covers, and articles of dress clothing, such as skin shirts, leggings, and moccasins. This surely was more than a fur trade, and it may well have been a kind of trade that had been carried on on the northern plains for centuries before the coming of the whites.[2]

As early as La Vérendrye's time another type of trade was also under way at those horticultural villages, in which Indian intermediaries, who themselves had direct contact with whites, were supplying some materials of European manufacture to the Mandan, who as yet had no direct trade with whites. At the Mandan villages in 1738, La Vérendrye observed that the Mandan Indians "are sharp traders and clean the Assiniboine out of everything they have in the way of guns, powder, ball, knives, axes, and awls."[3]

By Lewis and Clark's time articles of European origin employed in the trade between Indians at the Mandan villages included horses, mules, riding gear, weapons, tools, household utensils, and some articles of clothing and adornment. Of major importance was the exchange of horses, supplied by Indians from the south and west, for guns obtained from tribes living north and east of the village tribes.

So it was that many tribes of the northern plains became familiar with the white man's guns and metal tools, as well as with horses, some years before they met white men. Hundreds of horses and guns were exchanged at the Mandan and Hidatsa villages in the years 1804–5. It was common practice for the Indians trading there to exact a markup of 100 percent on the goods they offered. Thus the Crow sold horses to the Mandan at double the price they paid for them in their distant commerce with the Shoshoni, and the Mandan again doubled the price of these horses in trading them to the Assiniboine or Cree northeast of the Missouri.[4]

I have dwelled on these practices in Indian intertribal trade in this region at some length in order to dispel any romantic ideas any reader may have had that these Indians were unsophisticated children of nature who became easy dupes of cunning white traders. In reality these Indians were *horse traders*, both literally and figuratively—and possessed all of the keen bargaining sense that term has come to imply. They knew a great deal about values, and something of markups. Furthermore, they knew what they wanted and would pay the price, if they could.

The extension of the white man's fur trade to distant tribes was made at the expense of those Indians who had been active intermediaries between whites and other Indians who had not yet bargained directly with the palefaces. There are a number of references in the literature to the Indian intermediaries' efforts to dissuade whites from extending trade to their own customers. Thus in 1797 the Assiniboine tried to dissuade David Thompson from going to the Mandan villages by telling him of the great danger from hostile Sioux, who resented white men's supplying their Mandan enemies with ammunition. In 1805 the Hidatsa sought to prevent François Larocque from opening trade directly with the Crow Indians on the Yellowstone by pointing out the dangers he would face from hostile Assiniboine, Cheyenne, and Arikara—and by representing the Crow as thieves and liars.[5]

Self-interest also caused Indian tribes to discourage whites from extending their direct trading contacts to the more distant tribes with whom *they* were at war—to prevent firearms and ammunition from getting into the hands of their enemies. During the early years of the nineteenth century the Blackfoot sought to prevent the whites from trading with the small tribes west of the Rockies who had not yet been armed. Both white traders and distant Indians sought to circumvent the Blackfoot blockade. It is likely that the few guns Lewis and Clark saw among the Shoshoni in 1805 reached those Indians by a long and circuitous route—passing from Hudson's Bay Company or North West Company whites to the Assiniboine or Cree, who transported them in late fall or early winter to the Mandan or Hidatsa in present North Dakota, who, in turn, traded them to Crow Indian visitors to their villages the following summer. Next spring these Crow traders may have taken the weapons to their trading rendezvous with the Shoshoni and

Flathead west of the Continental Divide in present Wyoming, where the eager Shoshoni acquired them. Fully a year and a half may have been consumed in this passage of guns from a trading post on a tributary of the Red River to the Shoshoni Indians on the upper tributaries of the Columbia. If the price of a gun doubled each time it changed hands en route, the Shoshoni must have paid eight times the value received by the white trader who first bartered this weapon to an Indian.[6]

So it is easy to see why distant tribes would have wanted to do business directly with the white traders. Nevertheless, due to the white men's efforts to trap the lands of the powerful Blackfoot in the headwaters of the Missouri, the extension of peaceful trade into that region was delayed until 1831. Only when the Blackfoot were assured that by trading with whites they too could profit from this enterprise did these Indians become active participants in the fur trade of the Upper Missouri.[7]

By that time, six years before the remarkable Mandan tribe was decimated by smallpox, the importance of the Mandan villages as a trading center had waned. The Mandan had little to offer white traders in terms of valuable furs. The major centers of trade on the Missouri became the white men's posts in the territories of those tribes most able to contribute substantially to the white traders' profits—Fort Pierre at the mouth of the Teton in Sioux country; Fort Union at the mouth of the Yellowstone in Assiniboine territory; and at successive posts near the mouth of the Marias in the land of the Blackfoot and on the Middle Yellowstone in Crow country. More than three decades earlier white traders north of the 49th parallel had established posts as far west as the headwaters of the Saskatchewan in the shadow of the Rockies.

These stockaded posts, or "many houses" as the Blackfoot Indians called them, came to serve a variety of functions for the Indians. Not only did they visit them in fall to obtain supplies for their winter hunts and in spring to bring in their winter's catch, but the local records indicate that Indians frequented the posts in large or small numbers throughout the year. They were more than wilderness general stores stocked with a dazzling variety of useful and ornamental articles.

42

The trading post also became, in a sense, an Indian recreation center—his bar, if you will, where liquid buffalo-hunters' delight was thought to flow freely. Begging for liquor seems to have been almost as common as trading for it. And post managers soon learned that it was not good business to let begging chiefs of hunting bands go away thirsty.

The trading post also came to serve as the Indian's bank, where he could receive credit for his winter's hunt in advance of making it. I do not know how much earlier Indians began to place some of their valuable belongings in pawn at the fur posts, but certainly Henry A. Boller referred to that custom at his post among the Mandan-Hidatsa in the fall of 1858, when he wrote, "A few of known probity were trusted with goods to the value of several robes, while others of doubtful standing were obliged to deposit dresses, ornaments, and bonnets of eagle-feathers as security." He also noted, "Many deposited their valuables in our store for safekeeping, and we soon had a motley array of medicine-bags, drums, rattles, lances, saddles, and other articles useful and ornamental."[8]

These services of the Indian trader to the Indian have long survived the era of the fur trade in this region. During my residence on the Blackfeet Reservation in Montana a quarter century ago some older Indians pawned their dress clothing and other traditional articles at the traders' stores; while a few favored ones used the traders' premises as safe deposit vaults where they left their infrequently used fine clothing or medicine bundles for safekeeping.

Again, the trading post served as a health and welfare center. I have mentioned the frequency of begging visits. Post records also tell of Indians coming in for treatment of wounds or illnesses. I know that it was customary for the Piegan, who were notoriously fearful of the spirits of the dead, to bring the bodies of their dead leaders to Fort Benton so that the traders would attend to their burial.[9]

Finally, the trading post served as an Indian news and social center. At all of the major posts Indians of many scattered hunting bands of the same tribe as well as Indians of different tribes met. To Fort Union in the 1830s came not only the nearby Assiniboine but also the more distant Cree, Ojibwa, Crow, and Blackfoot. Some of these tribes were normally hostile, and sometimes mortal conflicts took place at or near the posts. But the posts also served as neutral ground where Indians, who would have been at each others' throats had they met elsewhere, managed for a time to get along together.

At the posts, also, Indians met some of their own folk, Indian girls married to post factors or engagés, and they participated in Christmas or New Year's parties that sometimes lasted several days and nights. Here too they met white travelers who were eager to see and to learn about Indians, and artists who had traveled far to draw or paint the Indians and the wilderness.[10]

It would be idle to contend that only *things* were transmitted from whites to Indians at these trading posts. Ideas must also have been passed along. Through observation and conversations with mixed-bloods, or whites who spoke their languages, Indians must have learned a great deal about the strange customs of the whites.

Basic to the interests of both parties to the fur trade was the establishment of a standard of values by which most articles offered in trade could be measured. Where standards of value were lacking or poorly defined, troubles arose. Thus Jean Baptiste Truteau, pioneer white trader among the Omaha near the present-day city of that name, encountered resistance when he asked a price for trade cloth in 1794. He offered the material by the "brasse," the distance covered by his outstretched arms. The Indians protested, not that his arms were so short, but that "it was too much to pay two beaver or otter hides and two or three deer hides for a brasse of cloth."[11]

By the 1830s the dressed buffalo hide had become the standard of value at all the Missouri River trading posts. Much earlier, in the British possessions and on the Missouri, the made beaver pelt (a prime skin in good condition) served as the standard of value. At Hudson House on the Saskatchewan in 1795 a made beaver would bring an Indian 12 iron arrowheads, or a pound and a half of gunpowder, or two bayonets that would serve as lance heads. But a tomahawk pipe would cost him 2 beavers, and a flintlock gun 9 to 12 beavers, depending on the length of the barrel. For a made beaver his wife could acquire 24 awl blades, or 24 needles, or 3/4 pound of common beads. Brass kettles were traded by weight—a one-pound kettle for one beaver pelt. A yard of cloth cost 2 made beavers, a greatcoat 5, and so on.[12]

Undoubtedly, one of the most inspired innovations of the Hudson's Bay Company was the famous point blanket. Indians had little difficulty understanding what the point marks meant—for a one-point blanket would cost them one made beaver, a 1½ point blanket 1½ beavers, and so on. So popular was this item that at least as early as 1805 the United States government distributed point blankets in payment of annuities to Choctaw and Chickasaw Indians far to the southeast in Mississippi.[13] Law may have required that these blankets were woven in the United States. If so, they were almost certainly inferior in quality to the original Hudson's Bay Company product. As late as 1829 John Jacob Astor complained to Sen. Thomas H. Benton that "none of the woolen goods fit for the Indian trade, such as Indian blankets, strouds, and cloths, . . . are as yet manufactured in this country."[14]

What did he mean by "goods fit for the Indian trade"? Simply that the red traders expected quality merchandise in exchange for their furs and robes and that they would not be inclined to accept sleazy goods from traders if they could get better from those traders' competitors. At the time Astor wrote (1829) the American Fur Company was vigorously expanding its operations up the Missouri where it came into strong competition with the Hudson's Bay Company for the trade of the border tribes. Blankets served other purposes than as mere bed covering. The warriors made from them the hooded coats and leggings worn on cold-weather war and hunting excursions. They preferred blankets with white backgrounds, which provided effective camouflage against snow-covered hills and plains.[15]

White traders carefully observed the kinds and qualities of merchandise offered to Indians by their competitors. As early as the 1760s Hudson's Bay Company officials made it their business to examine goods in the possession of Indians obtained from the peddlers from Montreal. They were happy to report that the Canadians' guns were much heavier in the barrel and bent in the stock, "which the natives dislike."[16] Nevertheless, it was on the recommendation of a former Canadian trader, Germain Maugenest, that the Hudson's Bay Company in 1781 began to furnish copper kettles with covers, which became very popular among the red men.[17]

When whites extended their trade to new tribes they tried to find out—early in the game and in detail—what kinds of objects the Indians wanted. In his instructions to Jean Baptiste Truteau, charged with pushing the trade from St. Louis up the Missouri toward the Mandan villages in 1794, the director of the newly formed Company of Explorers of the Upper Missouri wrote,

> When he has the opportunity he shall take note of the articles most desired by each nation, this is, bagatelles and things of little value, since it is not desirable to cause them to wish for goods that are dear, and which transportation a long distance will make still more dear.
>
> If he suspects that his information is insufficient to give us a good idea of the cheap materials most salable, he shall send us patterns or samples so that we shall make no mistakes. He shall also instruct us in regard to the favorite colors of each nation, as well as those that are disagreeable to them, and he shall not fail to inform us if neighboring nations have the same tastes.[18]

Traders' correspondence, both north and south of the 49th parallel, tells of the Indians' color preferences in beads and cloth, and of their refusal to accept faulty merchandise. The Manchester House journal for 1786 tells of burning sixty pounds of tobacco that had been damaged by flood, and of guns with springs "so weak that the Indians refuse to take them, as they will not give fire in cold weather."[19]

In the American Fur Company correspondence are references to Indian refusals of guns with faulty stocks, of beads of sizes or colors they did not like, and of long shell hairpipes in which the central holes had not been bored completely through. No doubt high officials of that company in St. Louis took notice when the trader from distant Fort Union wrote in 1832 that the round and square-headed axes "are for Indian women and if they have any but *good* axes their whole time is consumed in getting wood and consequently very few robes are pressed."[20]

Again in 1849 the Fort Union trader reported that the white beads ordered arrived *all* blue. He added, "This is a serious mistake as to its effect upon the trade."[21]

These may seem like very small matters. But the white trader in the field did not want to take chances on losing Indian trade to his competitors for want of the proverbial horseshoe nail.

When nonstandardized items were bartered, considerable dickering was involved. Inasmuch as horses varied greatly in quality and usefulness, they also varied in price—a fast racer or trained buffalo-hunting horse being worth several ordinary packhorses.

On 11 December 1792 an Indian tied an old horse to the door of Peter Fidler's tent. Fidler gave the Indian "7 fathoms of Brazil tobacco, a 2 Gallon Kettle, 1 Bayonet, 1/2 lb. Powder, 2½ lbs. Shott, 1/4 ounce vermillion, 1 gun worm, and 2 flints," but commented wryly in his journal, "such was the price of that generous Indian's gift."[22] We can be sure that Peter Fidler was neither the first nor the last white trader to pay dearly for a Plains Indian's gift, or to realize that he had been taken by a red-skinned horse trader.

Indian acquisition of new materials from white traders precipitated marked changes in men's and women's handicrafts. Not only were some of the ready-made articles they obtained more efficient than ones they had made themselves to serve the same or similar purposes, but available new materials also encouraged the development of new crafts. On the one hand, metal arrow- and lance heads, tomahawks, axes, files, awls, scissors, and ornaments rendered obsolete former weapons, tools, and ornaments of stone, bone, horn, and other materials. Metal kettles, introduced in quantity into Indian homes, led to the decadence and later the disappearance of pottery making, even among the more sedentary tribes. On the other hand, even though metal

47

arrowheads first reached them ready-formed, Indians learned to fashion their own arrowheads from hoop iron and with metal hammers, chisels, and files obtained in trade. They learned to make pipe-drilling and other handy tools from scrap metal. The Crow Indians were reputed to have been ingenious makers of metal tools as early as 1805.[23]

There is some evidence that the parfleche, the common "Indian suitcase" made from cut and folded, tough rawhide, decorated with geometric painted designs, was developed after Indians acquired sharp metal knives and that stone, if not wood carving as well, became more common among the Indians of this region after metal knives and files became available through the fur trade.[24]

Long before they began to obtain chemical dyestuffs in the trade Indian women began to dye some of their porcupine quills by boiling them in water with pieces of colored trade cloth.[25]

If the acquisition of glass beads led to the gradual decline of the older, more sacred woman's craft of quillwork, it stimulated the new craft of bead embroidery. Commercial paints obtained from white traders broadened the palette of the Indian painters of buffalo robes, tipi covers and linings, shields, and a variety of rawhide containers.[26]

But as long as Indians continued to make articles for their own use these things continued to bear a stamp of Indian taste and ingenuity—regardless of the facts that the textiles they used were woven in England, the beads were manufactured in Venice, or the shell hairpipes were columns of Bahama conch shells shaped and drilled by whites in New Jersey.[27]

In the revival of Indian handicrafts on the Blackfeet Reservation in Montana during the depression years of the 1930s and early 1940s, under the sponsorship of the U.S. Department of the Interior, Indian beadworkers were encouraged to return to the geometric designs and colors their grandmothers had learned to employ during the late years of the fur trade. To this extent, at least, Indian art of the fur trade era still persists.

Even though Indians could not make guns—the most sought-after items in the white traders' inventory—they did determine how these new weapons best could be used as well as the variety of roles firearms would play in their culture. They wanted a light, cheap, serviceable gun that could be used at all seasons of the year. Consequently it was furnished with a large trigger guard so the trigger could be pulled by a mittened finger. To decrease the weight they sometimes filed several inches off the end of the barrel and reused the rejected portion to make other tools. Portions of barrels of old guns, no longer useful as weapons, were made into skin-dressing tools, or even smoking pipes.[28]

Before repeating rifles were introduced in the late 1860s Indians of the northern plains rarely used guns for hunting. The old muzzle-loading, smoothbore flintlock, the so-called Northwest gun, made too much noise and was too difficult to reload while running buffalo on horseback. Nor could a hunter identify a buffalo he had killed with a ball from a musket as he could one that had been dispatched with his marked arrow.

So the Indians employed guns primarily in warfare. In action the Indian warrior held his fire until his enemy was in close range, but he learned to reload rapidly by carrying the balls in his mouth and spitting them down the gun barrel.

The taking of an enemy's gun came to rank as a war honor, or coup; among the Blackfoot this was the highest war honor. Men who had taken guns from the enemy symbolized this deed by painting guns on their dress shirts or the buffalo robes they wore as outer clothing.

To protect their guns from rusting and keep them in working order Indians greased them with animal fat. They also made buckskin gun cases, some of which were handsomely fringed and beaded. Sometimes they went into battle with these cases wrapped around their heads. Crow and Assiniboine women were especially proud of the beautiful gun cases they made for their menfolk.[29]

Some peculiarly Indian gun usages were reported by white observers. The Cheyenne and Arapaho regarded thunder as a malevolent killer. They fired their guns to drive off thunder and lightning. Prince Maximilian, in 1834, witnessed a Mandan ceremony for consecrating a gun in which the ritual closely resembled that of some of their presumably much older religious ceremonies. Among the Blackfoot a method of treating a horse suffering from an unknown illness was to load a gun with powder only and fire it at the horse's side. As a result of this shock treatment, so my elderly informants told me, "the horse *might* get well."[30]

It became customary for Indians approaching a trading post, or another party of Indians whom they did not wish to fight, to discharge their guns in the air. A meeting with empty guns was a sign of friendship and mutual trust.

The need for replenishing supplies of ammunition induced Indians to make frequent visits to trading posts, and it was important that each post have a gunsmith to repair Indian weapons. It was also customary for traders to confiscate the Indians' guns before they furnished them liberal quantities of liquor as a prelude to trade. This was one way of minimizing the harm they might do one another when they were in their cups. Even so, several cases are known in which hostile tribes attacked parties of Indians outside trading posts when the latter were both intoxicated and deprived of their firearms. It was the practice of Kenneth McKenzie at Fort Union to confiscate the guns of the members of both parties when Indians of two traditionally hostile tribes came to his post to trade at the same time.[31]

So the gun became more than just another, or even a better, weapon to the Indian. As a trophy it symbolized the highest warlike accomplishment. It found a place in Indian etiquette, in medicinal practice, and even in Indian religion. As Indians came to regard the gun as a necessity, it provided a closer link between the red and the white trader.

Some of the articles that came to be most desired by the Indians in their trade with whites were not really novelties to them. We all know that the nasty habit of smoking tobacco was one of the American Indians' many contributions to world civilization. It might seem like carrying coals to Newcastle for white traders to furnish tobacco and pipes to the Indians of the northern plains, who had been pipe smokers from prehistoric times. But they did.

Anthony Henday, the first white trader to leave an account of his meeting with Indians on the Upper Saskatchewan, in 1754, observed, "They think nothing of my tobacco, & I set little value on theirs; which is dryed Horse-dung." I'm sure the latter comment was the trader's frank opinion of the quality of the native tobacco, not an identification of its substance. These Indians did mix dung with tobacco seeds for planting, but the crop was the real thing—nicotiana. It was strong, and well cured. Indians soon came to prefer the white man's milder weed for their own pleasure smoking. In 1775 the elder Henry reported that one foot of Spencer's twist fetched a beaver pelt at Fort des Prairies. When Peter Fidler left Buckingham House during the fall of 1792 on his historic overland exploration to the Rocky Mountains he took along Brazil tobacco for presents to the Indians he might meet, and 131 pounds of tobacco roll to trade with the Piegan.[32]

Tobacco continued to serve as a very acceptable present to Indians as a prelude to trade with whites. Indians also purchased it, either in the form of a cigar-shaped plug, which the Blackfoot called "big tobacco," or in a long, thin but wide roll, which they termed "gut tobacco." David Thompson noted that by 1800 the Piegan had become so fond of trade tobacco that they stopped raising their own. The Blood Indians were said to have last planted tobacco in 1871. Only the North Blackfoot, of the three Blackfoot tribes, continued to raise small plots of ceremonial tobacco until World War II.[33]

Whether the clay pipes unearthed in some numbers at early trading post sites were smoked by Indians as well as traders we may not be sure. But certainly some Indians on the Missouri and Saskatchewan were smoking clay pipes by the mid-nineteenth century. Kurz mentioned "clay pipes from Cologne" in the traders' stock at Fort Union in 1851. Other trade pipes were made in England, and some in Virginia. I bought one of the Virginia-made clay pipes in a trader's store on Fort Peck Reservation as recently as 1953. By the mid-1860s the Northwestern Fur Company was turning out red catlinite pipes on lathes by the hundreds, and trading them to Indians on the Upper Missouri.[34]

Through trial and error traders learned that it was not novelty or practicality but Indian acceptance that should be the measure of what goods they should carry in stock. The law of supply and demand operated in the remote Indian country as well as elsewhere. At one time the American Fur Company tried to introduce metal shields among the Upper Missouri tribes. This may have seemed logical enough. The rawhide shields Indian warriors carried into battle would not stop a well-aimed musket ball. But the traders failed to reckon with the Indians who placed their faith in the supernatural rather than the physical properties of their shields—the protective designs painted on them or the medicines attached to them. Metal shields they did not want.[35]

Apparently Nicholas Garry, a director and later deputy governor of the Hudson's Bay Company, also failed to recognize what Indians demanded of their shields. After his 1821 tour of the Indian country he noted, "Copper Shields or of Tin with paintings of a frightful Animal, red color, will please the Plains Indians." He did not seem to understand that the "frightful animals" he saw on the Indians' shields were the likenesses of supernatural beings who had bestowed some of their power on them in their own sought visions or dreams.[36]

Throughout the greater part of the history of the fur trade on the northern plains the Indians profited from the competition that prevailed among rival companies for their business. Even though the Hudson's Bay Company remained supreme north of the 49th parallel after 1821, their monopoly of the trade of the borderland tribes was effectively challenged after Fort Union was established at the mouth of the Yellowstone in 1828 and American posts were built in the Blackfoot country in the early 1830s. Such border tribes as the Blackfoot, Gros Ventre, Assiniboine, Plains Cree, and Ojibwa soon learned that it was to their advantage to play both sides of the imaginary line. Indians frequently traveled long distances either north or south of that line to trade or to beg at the posts.

These Indians were sharp enough to take advantage of white men's rivalries, from which they obtained better prices for their furs as well as certain fringe benefits, in the form of gifts to induce them to trade with particular companies.

Well before 1800 the Hudson's Bay and North West companies were competing with one another in "dressing" Indian chiefs. Duncan McGillivray of the latter company, at Fort George on the Saskatchewan, noted in his journal for 24 April 1795 that he had clothed 22 Sarsi, Cree, Piegan, and Blood Indians before midnight, "a greater number than ever was cloathed in one day at any settlement in the North West." At Fort MacKenzie in the Blackfoot country, during the late summer of 1833, Prince Maximilian witnessed a solemn ceremony in which American Fur Company officials replaced the scarlet chiefs' coats that the Hudson's Bay Company had given Blackfoot chiefs with their own half-red and half-green coats which the German Prince likened to "the dress of some of our prisoners in Bridewell."[37]

At scattered posts throughout the northern plains many a chief's daughter became the bride of a prominent trader in a marriage which brought her security and her father special consideration from the trader, who believed he was luring the trade of that chief and his followers away from his white competitors.[38]

A few Indian men also gained status and favors for themselves by serving as soldiers at particular forts—encouraging fellow tribesmen to trade there, as well as keeping order among them and minimizing Indian thefts from whites when they came to the post to trade. These were the first Indian policemen in white employ—the forerunners of the blue-coated reservation policemen in the Upper Missouri country in later years.[39]

Competition also has been blamed for that seamiest aspect of the fur trade in this region—the liquor trade. Before the advent of white traders, these Indians had known no intoxicating beverage. Yet it was not long before the traders' rum or brandy, diluted with branch water, became the Indian buffalo hunter's delight. Its liberal dispersal, coupled with the Indians' low resistance to it, caused qualms of conscience among some of the traders. Their standard excuse for its continued use in the trade seems to have been, our competitors use it excessively, so we must use some.

As early as 1787 the trader at the Hudson's Bay Company post, Manchester House, was trying to woo the trade of the Piegan, who prior to that time had had little experience with liquor. Of them he wrote: "They are the quietest Nation in this country, except the Blood Indians, and I make no doubt will continue so till the Canadians gets among them, which is the ruin of every Nation by debauching their women and destroying themselves with poisonous rum." The previous day's entry of this righteous trader recorded his gift of a large keg of brandy to each of four Piegan leaders who visited his post.[40]

By 1810 the younger Henry found that the Piegan had become "fully as addicted to liquor as the Crees, though unlike the latter, they will not purchase it. They cannot be made to comprehend that anything of value should be paid for what they term 'water.' "[41] Blackfoot-speaking Indians still call liquor by a name that can be literally translated "white man's water."

American traders claimed they had to use liquor in their trade with the borderland tribes because their Hudson's Bay Company competitors dispensed it freely. After Congress prohibited the introduction of liquor into the Indian country for trade to red men in 1834, the clever Upper Missouri traders managed to conceal their upriver shipments from cargo inspectors.[42] Four decades later both of the licensed Indian traders in the wide-open town of Fort Benton complained to the government that unlicensed traders were supplying liquor to the Blackfoot. Yet investigators found that the licensed traders were in fact the suppliers of the unlicensed ones.[43]

In the matter of liquor, too, the law of supply and demand operated effectively, once Indians were introduced to the fiery fluid. As early as 1800 the drunken frolics of the Cree and Ojibwa on Red River frequently ended in the murders of fellow tribesmen. All of the tribes of this region seemed to want it during the early years of their contacts with white traders—save one. The Crow Indians on the Yellowstone had an aversion to what they termed "white man's crazy water." Their trade was in solid stuff, and they were widely known as the wealthiest as well as the soberest tribe of the entire Upper Missouri region. They had the most and the finest horses, the largest and best-furnished tipis, the handsomest and most expensive clothing. But by the 1860s they

54

were driven off their easternmost lands by the more numerous Sioux, and were caught between the Sioux and the Blackfoot. Some of the River Crow began to drink, and the heyday of their prosperity began to wane.[44]

In both the United States and Canada the sale or prohibition of liquor on Indian lands is now a matter of local option. Bars have replaced bootleggers on a number of reservations, but the Indian liquor problem persists. Other factors are involved in this problem. But we may consider it as part of our heritage from the fur trade era—when Indians learned to drink it, but not necessarily to carry it well.

It is apparent that generations of experience in the fur trade failed to prepare the Indians for a money economy. If they had learned nothing of the value of money, it was because they had had no need for it in bartering with whites. The story has been told of the Piegan chief Little Dog who prior to 1850 had led an attack on a wagon train along the Oregon Trail far to the south of his homeland. The Indians massacred the men and plundered the wagons. Only years later did Little Dog learn of his folly in failing to bring home a large box filled with what he thought were useless "buttons without eyes"—silver and gold coins.[15]

In 1868 the English collector William Bragge traveled west to end-of-track on the Union Pacific Railroad. From a Sioux Indian he purchased a stone pipe for an agreed price of fifteen dollars. But Bragge found that by the time he had counted fifteen half-dollars into the Indian's hand, the seller was completely satisfied.[46]

Again, in 1877, after the Blackfoot Indians received their first per capita payments from Treaty No. 7 with the Canadian government, sharp white scoundrels tried to fleece them by exchanging fruit jar labels for their money—until the Mounted Police discovered the fraud.[47]

These examples tell of the Indians' innocence of money matters at the time—not their stupidity. I recall talking with storekeepers who had traded with the Blackfoot Indians as early as the 1890s. Like the fur traders before them, they extended credit over the winter months.

They told me that the illiterate Indians' memories of these transactions were often as reliable as the written records. In some cases the Indians, when they came in to settle their accounts, caught careless mistakes in the storekeepers' accounts.

Again the fur trade taught the Indian little of the value of their most valuable resource—their land. Fur traders were not real estate men. And during the period of the fur trade the Indians still owned their land in common. Not until reservations were established and their lands allotted during the early years of this century in the United States did most of the Indians of this region know what it was to own private property in land. Then the whites who managed to purchase numerous tracts of Indian land at small fractions of their true values moved in. They were not fur traders.

The Indians of this region suffered the devastating effects of the epidemics of white men's diseases during the era of the fur trade. I believe these epidemics were more numerous and wreaked more havoc with Indian population and culture than scholars have demonstrated to date. My list of known epidemics among the Blackfoot tribes includes smallpox in 1781, 1837–38, 1849–50, and 1869–70, scarlet fever in 1837, and measles in 1864–65. I am not sure this list is complete. The cumulative effect of these repeated visitations of mass destruction should be studied in terms of their influence on the beliefs and customs of the Indians who survived, as well as on the downward trend of tribal populations. We ought to consider their effects on the numbers and compositions of bands, tribal movements, and the factor of Indian alliances and delicate balances of power in intertribal wars. Might not persistent losses from these introduced diseases have been influential in the lifting of taboos against marriage within bands? Was not the growing concern with health magic stimulated by Indian fears for the uncertainty of life in the face of recurrent epidemics which Indian medicine men could neither prevent nor alleviate by their primitive medicinal practices? Such questions, however, may be ones with which the anthropologist rather than the historian should wrestle.

In any case, we cannot blame these epidemics on the fur trade *per se*. They occurred with equal virulence and frequency in other parts of the New World where the fur trade was not a factor. They were one of the disastrous by-products of Indian and white contact—the fatal result of the introduction of new diseases to which the red men had little resistance. They could have been avoided only if Columbus and other European explorers had stayed home until medical science had developed effective inoculations for the most common European diseases.

The modern Indian—blessed with the luxury of hindsight—can make one very serious indictment of the fur trade: its lack of concern for the future. Intent on reaping immediate profits, white traders encouraged Indians to kill many more buffalo than they needed for their own subsistence. For the Indians this practice proved self-destructive. As the buffalo range contracted, traditionally hostile tribes of nomadic hunters moved closer and closer together, and intertribal wars were intensified. When the buffalo were exterminated these Indians could no longer even feed themselves.

There is evidence that far-sighted white men foresaw this extermination at least six decades before the last of the wandering herds were destroyed. Edwin James, chronicler of the Long Expedition and himself a naturalist, wrote in 1823: "It would be highly desirable that some law for the preservation of game might be extended to, and rigidly enforced in the country where the bison is still met with."[48] Influential citizens, even government officials, had financial interests in the Upper Missouri fur trade. The fur trade was a factor of importance to the American economy. Regulation was limited largely to the licensing of traders who went into the Indian country. It did not extend to the limiting of the number of furs or robes they brought out of that country.

In 1841 an impractical artist, George Catlin, in a widely read book, advocated that the entire plains region be set aside as a national park to preserve both the buffalo and the Indians who depended on it for their livelihood. He was too far ahead of his time to be taken seriously. None of his readers had heard of a "national park," or of the conservation of western wilderness resources for the future.[49]

57

Five years later Father De Smet accurately predicted that the plains from the Saskatchewan to the Yellowstone would be the "last resort" of the buffalo. But his gloomy prediction that the many tribes of the region would themselves become extinct fighting over "the last buffalo steak" did not come to pass. The people of Canada and the United States did not permit the vanishing red men to disappear.[50]

From the 1850s on, treaty commissioners and Indian agents repeatedly warned the Indians of the coming extermination of their staff of life—the buffalo. But as long as there were buffalo to be hunted their efforts to induce nomadic hunters to become sedentary farmers met with very little success. The Indians were too thoroughly committed by both experience and inclination to the roving life and a hunting-trading economy to abandon them as long as they had any choice in the matter.

So rapid was the final extermination that many Indians died of starvation before the Canadian and United States governments could provide adequate rations to feed the survivors. Yet these survivors were unprepared to make a living in a gameless land. Over the nearly nine decades since buffalo days many Indians have become self-supporting as farmers, stockmen, or wage workers. But the poverty that still exists on many reservations of the northern plains is stark proof of the persistence of Indian inability to adjust to the changed conditions which followed the sudden death of the fur trade in this region. And the horrible example of the effect on human lives of the extermination of the buffalo must continue to haunt those who are concerned about the future of man's relationship to his environment in North America.[51]

Wherever the historic fur trade flourished in North America unions between white traders and Indian women occurred. Perhaps Andrew Garcia, a free trader in the Musselshell Valley, justified this close relationship most frankly when he wrote: "About the only way you could learn the grunts and twists that go with most Indian talk is from a sleeping dictionary."[52] Whether or not the white fur traders' interests in Indian women could be entirely justified as a business expense, the fact is certain that these relationships were common, that many of them became partnerships for life, and that they were productive. On the northern plains there emerged a hybrid population who played a very important role in regional history. Even before the fur trade era ended, the mixcd-bloods far outnumbered the white traders and were more numerous than the full-blood members of any single Indian tribe. Although commonly referred to as Métis, I believe the term "mixed-bloods" is more accurate. Even though Frenchmen of the fur trade contributed substantially to the early growth of this population, men of many other nationalities also fathered mixed-blood children.

Not a few part-Indian sons of fur traders themselves became fur trade employees, serving as factors, guides, interpreters, hunters, or laborers at many wilderness posts. Others followed their mother's side of the family and lived among her people. Still others, most notably the Métis or so-called Red River Half Breeds of French and Indian descent, formed their own communities and developed a way of life that was neither white nor Indian. Their women were expert crafts workers and have commonly been credited with introducing floral designs into the quill- and beadwork of the Indian tribes of the region. Residing in log cabins and raising crops, these people also took part in long, well-organized, semiannual buffalo hunting excursions, during which they traveled westward far from home, made temporary camps of tipis, killed buffalo in great numbers with firearms, and carted tons of meat and hides homeward in their creaking, two-wheeled carts. Catholic priests accompanied them on these hunting excursions, as did parties of Ojibwa or Cree Indians. Sometimes they met, fought, and bested Sioux war parties on the Dakota plains.[53]

As the buffalo range contracted westward they extended their hunting operations farther and farther in that direction, to and beyond the Cypress Hills in present southern Alberta and southward into Montana. There, along with Indians of many tribes and white hide hunters, they helped to exterminate the last of the great northern buffalo herd during the early 1880s.

Before and after the buffalo were gone government officials on both sides of the 49th parallel were plagued by the problem of what to do about these people who were both Indian and white. In the United States some of them applied for citizenship, received it, and homesteaded on the public domain as did non-Indians. Others became enrolled members of tribes recognized by treaty, remained on reservations, and were allotted land along with the Indians. But there are still descendants of the earlier mixed-bloods among the so-called landless Indians in Montana.[54]

In Canada mixed-bloods enrolled in tribes recognized by treaty have also shared Indian rights. But the many who lived in mixed-blood communities did not. Their dissatisfaction with the central government's delays in providing for them precipitated armed uprisings in Manitoba in 1869 and on the Saskatchewan in 1885. Both were led by a brilliant, but unstable, one-eighth Indian named Louis Riel who, ironically enough, obtained United States citizenship in Montana less than three years before he was hanged in Canada.[55]

Since buffalo days the mixed-blood element in the populations of many U. S. reservations on the northern plains has grown rapidly. A high proportion of the Indian and Métis leaders of the northern plains in recent decades have been men and women of this mixed-blood population who can trace their ancestry back to one or more of the white fur traders.

Today—three hundred years after the Hudson's Bay Company was founded—there are thousands of descendants of the fur traders living on the northern plains. Many of them are mixed-bloods who can claim descent from both the red and the white participants in that historic enterprise.

The Use of Artifacts and Pictures in the Study of Plains Indian History, Art, and Religion

I HAVE BEEN PRIVILEGED to devote almost a half century to the study of Plains Indian artifacts and artworks in more than one hundred public and private museums from West Germany to the coast of California and from the Prairie Provinces of Canada to the Florida Keys and Mexico City.

I actually began the serious study of Plains Indian art and material culture right here in New York City during the summer of 1933—some forty-eight years ago—initiating research for a master's thesis in ethnology at Yale. I had spent a year after college studying at the Art Students League of New York and had gone on to Yale hoping to learn more about what was then commonly called "primitive art." My interest in Plains Indians went back to a boyhood fascination with the artifacts and pictures of Sioux and Cheyenne Indians of Buffalo Bill's Wild West Show that I had seen in the den of my maternal uncle, Henry B. Cody, a cousin of the great showman. But it was my faculty adviser at Yale, Clark Wissler, who rekindled my boyhood interest in Plains Indians when he convinced me that there was a real need for a study of Plains Indian painting by someone who was interested in *both* art and ethnology.

At that time Clark Wissler was widely recognized as the leading authority on the Plains Indians. He was also head of the Department of Anthropology at the American Museum of Natural History. So my museum studies began there. It was in the depths of the Great Depression, and few students were working with the American Museum's collections that summer. Dr. Wissler assigned me one of those spacious, well-lighted, turretlike rooms on the top floor, where I could spread out that intriguing series of buffalo robes and other Indian-painted objects from the museum's large collections. Many of those pieces had been obtained in the field by one or another of three of America's most eminent ethnologists of the early twentieth century—Robert Lowie, Alfred Kroeber, and Wissler.

For nearly a month I sketched and made extensive notes on those Indian paintings on animal hides—the colorful geometric patterns painted by women and the religious symbols and human and animal figures executed by Indian men. Almost every afternoon Dr. Wissler climbed the steps to the museum attic from his administrative and curatorial offices on the floor below, to visit with me and to generously share his vast knowledge of the Plains Indians who had created the works I was studying. He suggested books I should read and works by white artist-observers of those Indians I should consult. He whetted my interest in the works of such pictorial interpreters of Indian life as George Catlin and Karl Bodmer three decades before I wrote *Artists of the Old West*. I shall always be grateful to Clark Wissler for his patience in guiding me during my days as a greenhorn.

With an introduction from Wissler I moved uptown to meet George Heye in his fabulous Museum of the American Indian on Audubon Terrace at Broadway and 155th Street. Heye graciously provided space for me to examine his even larger collection of painted works. Perhaps if I had not gained some ability to recognize the more common geometric patterns and representational styles before I visited Heye's establishment, the sheer size of his collection might have been discouraging.

I am glad that Dr. Wissler encouraged me to extend my studies to encompass the holdings of as many of the larger museums in the eastern United States and Canada as my limited financial resources would permit. Thus I learned early in my career that studies of Indian art and material culture tend to become both broader and deeper through examination of the holdings of a goodly number of museums. As I look back on those pioneer studies of Plains Indian art and artifacts conducted by Clark Wissler and his colleagues and published in the *Anthropological Papers of the American Museum of Natural History* during the first quarter of this century, I can see that their greatest limitations are the result of too exclusive reliance on the collections of that one museum.

Before my master's thesis was published I was able to include additional data from other museums, several of them on the West Coast. The world was still deep into a financial depression, and book publishers had to be very careful of their budgets. I felt lucky to find one who would take a chance with me—an unknown author of a book that required many illustrations. I was grateful that Stanford University Press would allow me *one* color plate. Even so *Plains Indian Painting* was beautifully designed, and the American Institute of Graphic Arts selected it as one of the Fifty Books of the Year 1940. I was happy when Eric Douglas reviewed the book very favorably in the *American Anthropologist*, and L. Adam did likewise in *Man*. But I was proudest when Clark Wissler reviewed it approvingly in *Natural History*. I had dedicated that book to him.

That is how my career as a published student of Indian art was launched. The book was researched and written without any grant support. Its publication brought me no royalties. Yet it paid off royally by encouraging me to continue in the field of Plains Indian studies.

I had offered that first book as a historical as well as a descriptive study, and historical curiosity has motivated many of my later investigations of Plains Indian art and artifacts. I have been curious about the prehistoric background as well as historic trends in Plains Indian art and crafts. I have been interested in the survival of certain basic concepts over long time spans; in the ingenuity of Plains Indians in adapting new materials obtained in trade to their own uses and in ways European manufacturers would not have dreamed of; and in both the introduction of new and the disappearance of old art styles and crafts techniques. I am as interested in the accurate dating of artifacts and works of Indian art as I am in determining their tribal provenience.

Over the years since 1940 I have sought to combine information from the verbal testimony of older informants with data gleaned from published and archival writings and pictorial sources and from the study of museum specimens in tracing the history of such Plains Indian crafts as the making of quillwork, beadwork, moccasins, clothing, horse gear, and pipes I have also illustrated various ways in which Plains Indian artists portrayed white men during the nineteenth century. And I have indicated the ways in which Plains Indian artists symbolized Indian beliefs in the supernatural powers of animals by creating painted, carved, or cut rawhide images of buffalo, horse, elk, bear, weasel, and even the longhorn cattle of the Spaniards.

Of recent years I have become interested in studying the history of collecting historic Plains Indian art and artifacts in the hope that the identification of groups of well-documented examples will be helpful in the closer dating and tribal identification of the great many unidentified or erroneously identified specimens from the plains in museum collections. That hope stems from a conviction that it is a waste of both time and money to put inadequately and/or inaccurately documented specimens on computers in the hope that they may someday be of value in research. Working alone, progress on this study has been rather slow. I have found it desirable to limit the study to collections made before 1900. Even so, there seems to be no way an investigator can cast his net wide enough to catch all collectors. I am repeatedly learning from unlikely sources the names of collectors previously unknown to me. I have become rather certain that all traces of some nineteenth-century collectors have disappeared, so that it will never be possible to identify many of them. A few years ago I estimated that I might eventually be able to identify as many as 500 collectors of Plains Indian objects of the pre-1900 period. But I now have some data on more than 600 of them, and I am learning of others every month. I may have a tiger by the tail!

Perhaps the time is approaching when I can offer at least some preliminary findings. Those 600+ collectors may comprise more than a fair sample for they must include virtually all the major collectors prior to 1900, as well as many less important collectors whose names may be unfamiliar to most curators in charge of Plains Indian collections.

By and large the number of collectors increased rather steadily as the nineteenth century progressed. Even so, collecting of Plains Indian materials began with Coronado in 1541, and I have found written references to the collecting activities of a number of Spaniards, Frenchmen, and Englishmen before 1800, including a French king, Louis XV, who received presents from a small delegation of Indians as early as 1725.[1]

We know that Toussaint Charbonneau, interpreter to Lewis and Clark on their overland journey from the Mandan villages to the Pacific Ocean and return in 1805–1806, became himself a collector of Indian pipes, and that he seems to have had a preference for effigy pipes that realistically portrayed humans in erotic situations. Perhaps Indian sculptors carved those pipes to please their French patron?[2]

I am finding evidence that Indians were actively engaged in making artifacts for sale to whites and that Indian traders were collecting artifacts in some quantities for resale to other whites decades before the buffalo were exterminated and the nomadic tribes of the plains were settled on reservations.

Suggestions are strong that following the establishment of military posts in the western Indian country artists and artisans of nearby tribes created objects for exchange with officers (and perhaps enlisted men as well) stationed at those posts. Fort Snelling, built at the site of the present Twin Cities, near the Falls of St. Anthony, at the head of navigation on the Mississippi in 1818 and the years following, was probably one of the first of those unofficial field centers for trade in Indian artifacts and works of art. One of them appears to have been this elaborately carved effigy pipe in the Old War Department Collection at the Smithsonian. This pipe is also an interesting Indian comment on the liquor trade. At that time (1830s) it was illegal to introduce liquor into the Indian country upriver from Fort Snelling, but Indian leaders managed to obtain it, and the possession of a keg of liquor became something of a chiefly status symbol among the upriver Sioux. Here a highly talented Santee carver portrays a chief, recognizable by the

Fig. 4.1. Effigy pipe of catlinite portraying chief offering liquor to one of his followers, Santee Sioux, ca. 1830. (Cat. no. 2622, Smithsonian Institution)

medal hanging from a ribbon around his neck, doling out a drink to one of his followers (see fig. 4.1).[3]

As early as December 10, 1840, a St. Louis merchant advertised Plains Indian artifacts for sale in the *Missouri Republican* of that city as follows:

Indian Curiosities

REC'D from the Rocky Mountains, a splendid lot of Indian curiosities, consisting of Indian war coats, worked with porcupine quills; saddles, ornamented with the porcupine quills and made by the Blackfeet Indians for going to war; also, shields used in battle for fending off the arrows; shot pouches, knife scabbards; arrow cases; leggings; sashes; kinakneck bags; also the scalp of one of the most celebrated warriors who roved the mountains, and was a terror to the several tribes that was at war with his tribe, the Blackfeet Indians; also 2 pipes that is equal to any curiosity that ever was made by an Indian; . . . also, a large lot of beautiful moccasins, worked with the porcupine quill together with many other curiosities, for sale at the Emporium of Fashions.

L. Deaver

Deaver's word "curiosities" as a general term for Indian arts and artifacts seems to have been accepted in both trade and museum circles until after the mid-nineteenth century when the Smithsonian Institution sought to introduce the more awkward and pedantic word "ethnologica."

It is remarkable how many kinds of Plains Indian artifacts were desirable collectibles over an extended time period. Moccasins seem to have been the most popular, for they were both inexpensive and useful as carpet slippers. I have found a number of references to enlisted men returning from frontier duty buying moccasins as souvenirs shortly before they left the Indian country. There are more moccasins than any other Plains Indian artifacts in museums in this country and abroad. Perhaps their very commonness explains why no adequate historical and descriptive study of Plains Indian moccasins has been published.

On the other hand, another once very common and inexpensive Plains Indian artifact is exceedingly rare in museum collections. That is the simple digging stick commonly used by Indian women in collecting prairie turnips in early summer. It generally had a fire-hardened tip and a rounded handle. The latter was sometimes used to induce abortions.

During the nineteenth century several collectors in this country and abroad specialized in collecting artifacts illustrating the uses of tobacco in all parts of the world. These people included numerous Plains Indian tobacco pipes and pouches in their sizable collections. These collectors generally were men of some wealth who obtained their specimens indirectly from field collectors and/or dealers. But William Bragge, a major English collector, did make one collecting trip to the plains before the buffalo were exterminated. These private collections tended to wind up in public museums.

I suppose one might think that the tipi, the typical residence of the nomadic tribesmen, would have been too large and bulky to have been regarded as a collectible prior to 1900. But I have found references to a number of them having been collected, even though few have survived. As early as 1599 the Spanish explorer Oñate's sergeant major collected a finely dressed, painted tipi weighing as little as fifty pounds during an exploratory journey on the southern plains.[4] We know that George Catlin collected a Crow painted tipi that he pictured as it appeared as the centerpiece of the exhibition he installed in the Louvre in Paris in 1845 for the edification of King Louis Philippe of France and his court.[5]

Probably the best-preserved buffalo hide tipi dating back to buffalo days is now exhibited in the Plains Indian section of the Smithsonian Institution. It was field-collected by Vincent Colyer, artist and Secretary of the Board of Indian Commissioners, from the Arapaho in 1874, for exhibition in the Centennial Exposition at Philadelphia in 1876. Indians formerly sized their tipis according to the number of buffalo cow skins needed to make them. This drawing of the layout of skins in the Arapaho tipi in the Smithsonian collections shows that fourteen skins probably were required to make it (see fig. 4.2). It is slightly larger than the average tipi among the nomadic tribes in the early 1870s. Dr. Loretta Fowler, a modern student of the Arapaho, tells me that the porcupine-quilled thunderbird motif at the top of the back may indicate that this served as a ceremonial tipi for one of the Arapaho military societies (fig. 4.3).

Warbonnets were much-coveted war trophies in the estimation of both Indian and white enemies of the Plains Indians. As early as 1779 the Spanish governor of New Mexico proudly told of his acquisition of the one-horned bonnet worn by the most famous Comanche war chief of that time, Cuerna Verde (Green Horn), when that Indian leader was killed in a battle with the Spanish.[6]

During a visit to Washington in the later 1870s the noted Cheyenne warrior and medicine man, Crazy Mule, presented his warbonnet to Secretary of the Interior Carl Schurz, saying that the Indian wars were over, so he had no further need for a warbonnet. A drawing portraying this historic presentation was published in *Frank Leslie's Illustrated Newspaper* for November 1, 1879 (fig. 4.4).

Another Plains Indian chief, Plenty Coups, the last Crow war chief, placed a traditional Crow warbonnet upon the casket of the Unknown Soldier of World War I as a tribute from all American Indians at the

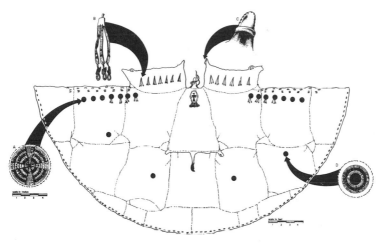

Fig. 4.2. Drawing of Arapaho tipi cover collected by Vincent Colyer in 1874 showing construction of fourteen buffalo cow skins and details of ornamentation. (Cat. no. 18,900, Smithsonian Institution)

solemn ceremonies in Arlington Cemetery on November 11, 1921. This bonnet may be seen on exhibition in the Trophy Room overlooking the monuments to our Unknown Soldiers of both world wars in Arlington.[7]

I was privileged to accession for the Smithsonian collections another significant symbol in the history of Indian-white relations. It was the Model 1866 Winchester rifle the famous Sioux chief Sitting Bull turned over to Major David H. Brotherton of the U.S. Army at Fort Buford in the summer of 1881, when that chief returned from his extended exile in Canada. On that occasion Sitting Bull was alleged to have told the major, "I want it to be known that I was the last man of my tribe to surrender my gun."[8]

In studying the history of collecting I have tried to determine the occupation of each collector. Army officers lead all other occupational groups numerically. I now have names of more than two hundred army officers who collected Plains Indian artifacts during the nineteenth

Fig. 4.3. Porcupine-quilled thunderbird motif at upper back of Arapaho buffalo-skin tipi cover. (Cat. no. 18,900, Smithsonian Institution)

Fig. 4.4. Crazy Mule, prominent Cheyenne Indian war leader, presenting his warbonnet to Secretary of the Interior Carl Schurz after the Indian wars ended. (*Frank Leslie's Illustrated Newspaper*, November 1, 1879)

century, beginning with Captains Lewis and Clark and Lt. Zebulon Pike, the pioneer explorers of the trans-Mississippi West after the Louisiana Purchase of 1803. Of special interest are the weapons with which the hostile tribes fought the army during the 1860s and 1870s. Many of them were collected by army doctors at frontier posts and on battlefield sites. Some of them were of practical value in the Army

Medical Corps' ongoing studies of the effects of arrow and lance wounds on civilian and military personnel.

Most army officers did not restrict their collecting to weapons. Their collections reveal a broad range of Indian manufactures that illustrate the technological knowledge, the handicraft skills, and artistic talents of Plains Indians in the years before, during, and after the Indian wars (fig. 4.5).

Many army officers had opportunities to closely observe Indian life, and many of them reported their observations in writing. Among them were Col. Richard I. Dodge, author of the classic *Our Wild Indians* (1881); Dr. Washington Matthews, who wrote an important mono-

72

Fig. 4.5. Interior of army officer's quarters at Fort Keogh, Montana, 1891. Shows a portion of that officer's Indian collection including painted muslin war history on far wall and ghost dance shirt at left. (Courtesy National Anthropological Archives, Smithsonian Institution)

graph on the Hidatsa before he became a pioneer authority on the Navaho; Capt. John Bourke, who was Gen. George Crook's adjutant in his campaigns against the Sioux and the Apache; and Col. Garrick Mallery, who first became interested in Indian picture writing while he was a communications officer at Fort Rice in the Sioux country and later became the Smithsonian's leading authority on the subject. Surely the sincere appreciation of Indian accomplishments and abilities revealed in the writings of these and other officer-collectors refutes the contentions of more sensational writers to the effect that all army officers hated the Indians.

Traders may be very inadequately represented in my lists of

collectors, because they were the important intermediaries for many collectors of other occupations. We know that they obtained artifacts directly from Indians in trade or in pawn, and they also acquired them as gifts from their Indian friends. One of my favorite western photographs depicts Henry A. Boller, who dropped out of the University of Pennsylvania to find adventure as a clerk at the trading post near Like-a-Fishook Village where the remnants of the once-important Mandan, Hidatsa, and Arikara tribes lived. Young Boller wears a buckskin coat and trousers (probably made for him by an Indian woman) and a beaded cloth shoulder pouch made for him by the Indian wife of his boss and given him as a Christmas present in 1858 (fig. 4.6).[9]

Other occupational groups represented in some numbers among the pre-1900 collectors were artists, Indian agents, naturalists, missionaries, sportsmen, journalists, and museum proprietors. William Clark founded the first museum west of the Mississippi when he added a large room to his residence in St. Louis in 1816 which served as both a council chamber for meeting delegations of visiting Indians and as an Indian museum.[10] Some of these collectors of various occupations wrote objectively about Indians, but very few professional anthropologists began collecting among the tribes of the Great Plains before 1900.

I have been interested to determine whether or not collectors of certain occupations were partial to particular kinds of artifacts. I think there are suggestions that artists exhibited considerable taste in selecting well-made and aesthetically pleasing pieces. Witness the beautiful, delicately quilled Santee Sioux cradle collected by George Catlin in the mid-1830s, now in the Smithsonian collections (fig. 4.7). There are a number of well-painted buffalo robes and attractive ledger book drawings known to have been collected by white artists.

We should not be surprised to learn that some missionaries collected medicine bundles and traditional religious effigies as evidence of the superstitious beliefs of the heathens they were trying to save. There is evidence that both Catholic and Protestant missionaries took some of those objective symbols of traditional Indian religious beliefs

74

Fig. 4.6. Henry A. Boller, young clerk at trading post on the Upper Missouri, wearing a beaded shoulder pouch made for him by his employer's Indian wife as a Christmas present in 1858. (Courtesy State Historical Society of North Dakota)

back to New England and other eastern settlements when they sought financial support for their labors among the Indians. Many of the Indians who supplied missionary-collectors with traditional religious objects during the nineteenth century must have been recent converts to Christianity. Other converts burned or otherwise destroyed individually owned bundles and other objects associated with their former religious beliefs.

Surely students of Plains Indian religion can gain insights into traditional values and beliefs by studying the artifacts in museum collections that had religious associations. We should recognize, however,

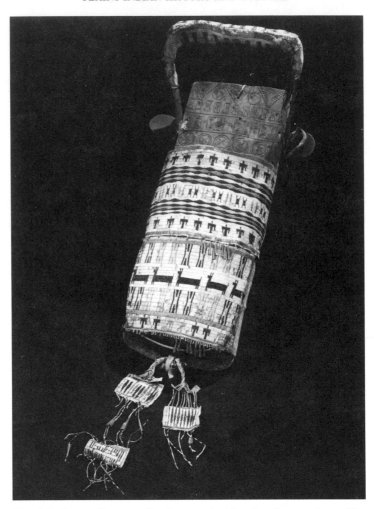

Fig. 4.7. Santee Sioux cradle, decorated with colored porcupine quills. Collected by the artist, George Catlin, in the mid-1830s. (Cat. no. 73,311, Smithsonian Institution)

that a number of the objective expressions of Indian religious beliefs are not and will not be represented in museum collections. Some of these symbols are as ephemeral as Navaho sand paintings—and for the same reason. They were painstakingly created in sacred rituals only to be deliberately destroyed as those ceremonies drew to a close. Yet these uncollectible material symbols were as much a part of Plains Indian religious life as were medicine pipes or beaded navel cord amulets. I refer to such creations as the images of enemies drawn in the earth with a finger or stick and gradually rubbed out in the course of witchcraft rituals, and to those colorful altars carefully constructed of colored earths and destroyed soon thereafter in the sun dance, the medicine pipe, and horse medicine cult ceremonies of the Blackfoot.[11]

We should be aware, too, that some traditional religious symbols that may have been of great age among a few tribes of Plains Indians never have been offered for sale or exchange precisely because their retention was thought to be essential to the welfare and survival of those tribes. I refer to those unique sacred objects which James Mooney termed "tribal palladia"— tribal medicines which continue to be so closely guarded by their selected keepers that few whites and members of other tribes have ever seen them. I refer to such tribal treasures as the Taime of the Kiowa, the Sacred Arrows of the Cheyenne, the Buffalo Maiden Pipe of the Dakota, the Medicine Wheel of the Southern Arapaho, and the sacred Flat Pipes of the Northern Arapaho and their relatives the Gros Ventres.

Cared for and guarded by selected holy men or women, exposed to view only briefly in proper ceremonial contexts, the very secrecy surrounding these tribal medicines may have enhanced the curiosity of non-Indian students of Plains Indian religion. These sacred objects have been held in so much awe by tribal members that they have only rarely dared to attempt to picture them. The Kiowa Taime was last displayed in 1887, at the last performance of that tribe's sun dance. To the best of my knowledge only one Kiowa artist has attempted to picture the Taime. He was Silverhorn, a member of the prominent Kiowa family long headed by Tohausen, the tribal head chief for three decades prior to 1864. Silverhorn was himself a religious traditionalist. But he became an enlisted man in Lt. Hugh L. Scott's renowned Company L of the 7th Cavalry stationed at Fort Sill during the 1890s, and the close friend of Lt. Scott. He illustrated Scott's detailed account of the Kiowa sun dance, which was published in the *American Anthropologist* in 1911. One of Silverhorn's original sketches for those illustrations, drawn in an old Army Target Record Book and preserved in the National Anthropological Archives, portrays the Taime as a carved image of a man's head, colored blue, and mounted on a short pole while displayed in the Kiowa medicine lodge during the tribal sun dance (fig. 4.8).[12]

During the late nineteenth century and the early years of the present one, other Indian artists served as picture-making informants on the details of Plains Indian religious ceremonies and ceremonial regalia for anthropological field-workers. They pictured aspects of tribal ceremonies which they and/or their tribal agemates had witnessed but which had ceased to be performed by the time inquisitive anthropologists appeared. Such artists were George Bushotter, who pictured the torture in the Teton Sioux sun dance for James O. Dorsey, and Charles Davis, who illustrated the costume and accessories of participants in the Cheyenne sun dance for George Dorsey. Clark Wissler employed Oglala and Blackfoot artists to portray sacred objects of those tribes that he had not seen or could not collect for his museum—shields, tipis, bonnets, medicine pipes, and so forth.

Although the most sacred medicines of the Plains Indians never were offered for sale, there is evidence that Plains Indian conceptions of rights to supernatural powers also permitted the remaking and sale of duplicates of individually owned sacred objects.

While I was curator of the Museum of the Plains Indian on the Blackfoot Reservation during the early 1940s I purchased for the collections of that museum one of the shirts that I had seen worn during the performance of the Crazy Dog Society from the wearer of that shirt. A few years later I learned that he had remade that shirt and sold the new version to a collector. When I returned to the reservation a year

Fig. 4.8. Watercolor sketch of the Taime, the Kiowa tribal medicine, drawn from memory for Lt. Hugh L. Scott by the Kiowa artist Silverhorn, at Fort Sill during the 1890s. (Courtesy National Anthropological Archives, Smithsonian Institution)

or so after that as associate curator of ethnology at the Smithsonian Institution, the same man offered me yet a third version of his Crazy Dog shirt for the Smithsonian collection.

Was this maker and remaker of a Crazy Dog Society shirt a scalawag? Not really, by Indian standards. I learned that traditional Blackfoot Indians believed that unless the supernatural power that a religious object symbolized was ceremonially transferred to a new owner the previous owner retained the right to remake that object for

79

his own use or transfer to another. My informants cited numerous cases of shields, sacred bonnets, and other religious articles that had been stolen by the enemies of the Blackfoot Indians, and were remade by their Blackfoot owners because they had never relinquished possession of the powers of those sacred objects. Ownership was vested in the supernatural power, not in the symbolic physical object. When a religious symbol was sold or given to someone else, Indian or white man, without formal transfer of its associated power, that object became powerless. Apparently many museum curators who have qualms about the handling of Plains Indian objects in museum collections are not aware of the Indian concepts of power transfer and power loss.

My most unforgettable experience in collecting Plains Indian artifacts involved one I failed to collect.

During the years I served as the curator of the Museum of the Plains Indian on the Blackfoot Reservation, the Indians gathered each summer on the large flat behind the museum to perform their major tribal religious ceremony, the sun dance. My wife and I tried to visit the Indian encampment as often and for as long as we could, to observe and to photograph the religious and varied secular activities that took place.

One evening as I entered the encampment an hour or so before sunset a teenaged Indian boy approached me and said that his grandmother had something to show me that I might want to buy for the museum collections. I followed him to the entrance of one of the tipis in the camp circle and he invited me in. Within the dimly lighted lodge I became aware of a single person sitting on a blanket to my left. She was a bent-over, deeply wrinkled woman who looked older than any other Indian I ever had met. The teenager introduced me to his grandmother, and then rather gruffly, I thought, asked her to show me the article that he believed I might purchase. Slowly she withdrew a small packet from the bosom of her dress. Her frail hand quivered as she held it out for me to examine. It proved to be the most handsomely beaded navel cord amulet that I had ever seen.

She told me this packet contained her own navel cord; that it had always been carried close to her body; and that I could see it had ensured her a very long life. She had thought it ought to be buried with her, but her grandson was suggesting that it might be sold to the museum.

As the grandson pressed me to make the old lady an offer, her eyes filled with tears. She reached out her hand for the amulet and gathered it in both arms to her breast. Clearly that lady needed that amulet much more than did the museum. I thanked her as graciously as I could for permitting me to see her beautiful treasure—and left the tipi. Some months later she died. Presumably, her navel cord was buried with her.

CHAPTER FIVE

The Influence of Epidemics
on the Indian Populations and Cultures
of Texas

THAT EUROPEANS INTRODUCED epidemic diseases into the Americas which drastically reduced the numbers of Indians during the historic period is a fact well known to both historians and anthropologists. But the long-range effects of successive epidemics on the populations of particular tribes have not been sufficiently studied, and the effects of these epidemics on the beliefs and customs of the Indians who survived them have been little considered by scholars.

Texas provides a fertile field for studying the influences of epidemics on neighboring tribes of different cultures over an extended period. Nowhere else in the American West did tribes of so many cultures live in such close proximity in the historic period. In Texas alone, buffalo-hunting nomads of the plains met not only horticultural tribes of the plains and woodlands but also hunter-gatherers of the southwestern deserts and fishermen of the Gulf Coast.

Furthermore, there is a rich and lengthy record of Indian-white contacts in Texas dating back to Cabeza de Vaca's first meeting with Indians on the Gulf Coast in 1528. Most Indian tribes were removed from Texas during the 1850s, but we can follow them to their new homes in present Oklahoma and New Mexico and continue to study epidemics among them and the possible effects of epidemics on their numbers and lifeways to the end of the frontier period in 1890.

Texas was also a region of extensive tribal movements during the historic period. There were movements into this region from both north and east before 1820, and out of it before 1860. For purposes of

Map 5.1. Indian tribes of Texas considered in this chapter.

this study let us consider as Indians of Texas those tribes who resided wholly or partially within the area of the present state prior to 1820—with the exception of those portions of woodland tribes who entered East Texas from the east before 1820 (all of whom, save the Alabama-Coushatta, moved on to present Oklahoma or Mexico before 1860) and the Tigua of the El Paso area, who were Puebloan in culture.

The tribes with whom we shall be concerned, and their relative locations prior to 1820, are shown on map 5.1.

Any attempt to determine the effects of epidemics on the populations of these tribes must face the difficult problem of estimating their

83

populations at a relatively early date. This is a fascinating numbers game in which a high degree of certainty is impossible because of the general lack of precise contemporary population figures. No actual census of the Indian tribes of the Indian Territory (Oklahoma) was undertaken until 1875, at which time a count of all the men, women, and children of each tribe was needed as a basis for establishing ration rolls. Before that time tribal populations were estimated. James Mooney has reminded us that the first Kiowa census of 1875 yielded a figure almost 50 percent *less* than an *estimate* of that tribe's population made only two years earlier.[1]

Before 1875, estimates usually were calculated by formulas—by counting or estimating the number of warriors, or the number of lodges, or the number of families in a tribe, and then multiplying by certain arbitrary factors to arrive at a total tribal population. Not only were the numbers of warriors, lodges, or families usually set down in round numbers, but different estimators employed different factors in their multiplication. Obviously, the man who multiplied the number of warriors by five obtained a tribal total 25 percent greater than the one who used four for his factor.

Mooney estimated that the Kiowa averaged "6 or 7 souls to a tipi," but he recognized that this ratio "varied greatly with different tribes."[2] It also must have varied in the same tribes at different periods, say, before and after a serious and fatal epidemic. On the other hand, Newcomb and Field recently estimated only 10 to 11 occupants in a two-family grass lodge among the horticultural Wichita.[3] Whether one estimates 5 or 7 individuals to a family can make a difference of nearly 40 percent in one's total population for a tribe.

In view of the difficulties in evaluating early estimates of Indian populations, it is not surprising that most anthropologists have relied on the figures cited in James Mooney's posthumously published study, *The Aboriginal Population of America North of Mexico* (1928).[4] Because Mooney's industry was enormous, his knowledge of Indians and of the literature was great, and his integrity was beyond question, this study of Indian population became the classic work in its field. Nevertheless, A. L. Kroeber, who carefully reviewed Mooney's estimates for the entire North American continent, concluded that "the best of Mooney's estimates can hardly pretend to be nearer than 10 per cent or more from it."[5]

Mooney's earliest population figures for the Indian tribes of Texas with whom we are concerned in this study are cited in table 5.1—not because they are accurate in any absolute sense, but because they comprise the best single set of figures now available. Mooney's estimates, of course, are *not truly aboriginal*. He did not deem it possible to estimate the populations of the tribes of south and east Texas before 1690, or of the tribes farther north (who were not even known to whites in 1690) until 1780. Making allowance for the fact that Mooney did not try to distinguish the Coahuiltecan tribes of Texas from those south of the Rio Grande, and he made no separate estimates for the northern and southern divisions of the Cheyenne and Arapaho, of whom only the southern ones lived on the Texas frontier, Mooney's estimates yield a relatively early population for the tribes of Texas (as I have designated them) of about 42,000, a little less than the 1960 population of the town of Brownsville, Texas.

Some of Mooney's tribal estimates now appear too high, and others too low. Kroeber considered Mooney's estimate of Coahuiltecan population far too high;[6] Swanton reduced Mooney's estimate for the Caddoan tribes of East Texas by 500, and he thought Mooney's estimate for the Karankawan tribes "decidedly too high."[7]

On the other hand, Newcomb and Field's study of the population of the tribes of the Wichita group suggests that Mooney may have greatly underestimated their numbers in 1690.[8] Mooney's figure for the Lipan Apache is also far below the missionaries' estimates of Lipan population in the mid-eighteenth century.[9] I believe Mooney's estimate of 7,000 for the Comanche in 1780 should be increased by at least 50 percent.[10] On the whole, Mooney's estimates for the Indian tribes of Texas appear to be conservative. He may have erred more grievously in underestimating some of the more populous tribes than in overestimating some of the smaller ones. A total population for the tribes

85

Table 5.1. Depopulation of the Indian Tribes of Texas, 1690–1890

Tribe or Group of Related Tribes	Linguistic Stock	Mooney Estimate for 1690	Mooney Estimate for 1780	Census for 1890	Percent Reduction
Karankawan tribes	Karankawan	2,800		Extinct	100
Akokisa	Atakapan	500		Extinct	100
Bidai	Atakapan	500		Extinct	100
Coahuiltecan tribes	Coahuiltecan	7,500*		Extinct	100
Tonkawan tribes	Tonkawan	1,600		56	97
Caddoan tribes of East Texas	Caddoan	8,500		536	94
Wichita group of tribes	Caddoan	3,200		358	89
Kichai	Caddoan	500		66	87
Lipan Apache	Athapascan	500		60**	88
Mescalero Apache	Athapascan	700		473	32
Kiowa-Apache	Athapascan		300+	326	9
Comanche	Shoshonean	7,000		1,598	77
Kiowa	Kiowa-Tanoan		2,000	1,140	43
Arapaho‡	Algonquian		3,000 }	5,630	13
Cheyenne‡	Algonquian		3,500 }		

* Coahuiltecan tribes in Texas estimated at one-half Mooney's total for these tribes in Mexico and Texas.

** Includes 20 Lipan among Tonkawa and 40 among Mescalero Apache in 1890.

+ Yet Mooney (1898: 253) states: "They have probably never numbered much over three hundred and fifty."

‡ All figures for Cheyenne and Arapaho include both northern and southern divisions, although only the Southern ones lived on the frontiers of Texas.

considered of at least 50,000 might not be excessive.

By 1890 census figures for these same tribes indicate that their total populations had declined to 12,243, or less than 25 percent of Mooney's "aboriginal" total for these tribes (table 5.1, cols. 5–6). Before 1890 the Karankawan, Atakapan, and Coahuiltecan tribes had become extinct. The Caddoan and Tonkawan tribes, as well as the Lipan Apache and Comanche, appear to have suffered reductions of more than 75 percent. Only the Kiowa, Kiowa-Apache, Mescalero Apache, Arapaho, and Cheyenne appear to have been reduced by less than 50 percent.[11] It is noteworthy that, with the exception of the Mescalero Apache, all of the last group of tribes had limited contacts with whites prior to 1790, and none of them were missionized during the Spanish period (see map 5 1).

Epidemics certainly were not the sole cause of this radical reduction of more than 75 percent in the population of these tribes during the period prior to 1890. Intertribal warfare and wars with Spaniards, Mexicans, Texans, and citizens of the United States also took their toll. Overindulgence in liquor on the part of the Indians living near white settlements also contributed to this decrease, as did venereal disease, malnutrition, and starvation. Nevertheless, Mooney's contention that epidemics were the major cause of marked population decrease among the tribes of North America prior to 1900 appears to have been true of the Indians of Texas.

Mooney listed but five "great epidemics" in Plains Indian history which decimated some or all of the tribes of Texas: an unidentified disease reported to have killed 3,000 Caddoans in East Texas in 1691; widespread smallpox epidemics in 1778, 1801, and during the late 1830s; and a widespread cholera epidemic in 1849.[12] Yet I found references to no less than *thirty* epidemics which appeared among one or more of the tribes of Texas (as I define them) between 1528 and 1890. There was still another one in 1892 (table 5.2). Even this may not be a complete record. The absence of references to any epidemic among these Indians during the 146-year period 1528–1674 may reflect our paucity of information more accurately than it does their state

Table 5.2. Chronology of Known Epidemics among the Indians of Texas, 1528–1892

Date	Disease	Tribes Infected	Mortality	References
1528	Cholera?	Karankawan tribes	One-half local band, possibly much more widespread	Cabeza de Vaca, in Bandelier 1964: 63–64; Nixon 1946: 32
1674–75	Smallpox	Coahuiltecan tribes	Widespread north and south of Rio Grande	Bosque, in Bolton 1916: 298; Castañeda 1936, 1: 225; Nixon 1946: 53
1688–89	Smallpox	La Salle's Fort, St. Louis	French definitely, Karankawans?	Massanet and De León, in Bolton 1916: 395, 403; Nixon 1946: 54
1691	?	Caddoan tribes of East Texas	Estimated 3,000	Father Casañas 1927: 294, 303; Mooney 1928: 12; Swanton 1942: 17
1706	Smallpox	Coahuiltecan tribes in the Rio Grande missions	Mission Indians almost wiped out	Tunnell and Newcomb 1969: 147
1718	?	Caddean tribes of East Texas	Nearly 100 baptisms *in articulo mortis*	Father Espinosa in Nixon 1946: 46

Date	Disease	Location/Tribes	Effect	Source
1739	Smallpox and measles	The five San Antonio missions	Missions almost depopulated by death and desertion	Castañeda 1936, 3: 71; Nixon 1946: 10, 54
Pre-1746	Smallpox and measles	Tonkawan and Atakapan tribes	Epidemics prevented any population increase, 1734–46	Bustillo in Bolton 1914b: 334; Nixon 1946: 54
1750	Smallpox	San Xavier missions, Tonkawan and Atakapan tribes	40 at mission	Bolton 1915: 223; Nixon 1946: 54; Tunnell and Newcomb 1969: 151
1751	?	San Antonio missions	Epidemic "ravaged" the mission Indians	Father Dolores, in Bolton 1915: 303
1753	Malaria or dysentery?	San Xavier missions, Tonkawan and Atakapan tribes	"a mortal sickness"	Nixon 1946: 44–45
1759	Smallpox	At Nacogdoches (East Texas)	?	Nixon 1946: 54
1759	Measles	Caddoan tribes of East Texas	"took its toll of lives"	Nixon 1946: 11
1763	?	The San Antonio missions	"half the population died"	Bolton 1908: 304; Nixon 1946: 10–11

Table 5.2. (*Continued*)

Date	Disease	Tribes Infected	Mortality	References
1763–64	Smallpox	San Lorenzo de la Santa Cruz Mission, Lipan Apache	"devastating scourge"	Castañeda 1936, 4: 179; Nixon 1946: 11,54; Tunnell and Newcomb 1969: 171
1766	Smallpox and/or measles	Karankawan tribes	"devastating scourge"	Castañeda 1936, 4: 200; Nixon 1946: 11, 54
1777–78	Cholera or bubonic plague?	Widespread among East Texas Caddoans, Wichita, Tonkawan, and Atakapan tribes	mortality very high	De Mézières in Bolton 1914, 2: 189, 231–32, 250, 257, 274, 311, 313; Nixon 1946: 11
1778	Smallpox	Widespread in Texas and beyond its borders	mortality high	Stearn and Stearn 1945: 46–48; Mooney 1928: 12; Nixon 1946: 44, 46, 54
1801–2	Smallpox	Widespread among Texas tribes, especially on Red River	high among the Caddoan tribes	Sibley 1832: 721–22; Mooney 1898: 168; Mooney 1928: 12; Stearn and Stearn 1945: 75
1803	Measles	Caddoan tribes of East Texas	Considerable	Sibley 1832: 721–22

Year	Disease	Tribes	Impact	Sources
1816	Smallpox	Caddo, Wichita, Comanche, Kiowa, Kiowa-Apache	Including estimated "4,000 Comanche"	Trimble, in Morse 1822: 259; Mooney 1898: 168; Stearn and Stearn 1945: 86
1839–40	Smallpox	Kiowa, Kiowa-Apache, Comanche	killed "great number in each tribe"	Mooney 1898: 172, 274; Mooney 1928: 12; Stearn and Stearn 1945: 86
1849	Cholera	Widespread in Southern Plains, Kiowa, Kiowa-Apache, Cheyenne, Comanche	killed "half the Cheyenne"; less than half Kiowa; possibly more Comanche	Mooney 1898: 173, 290–91; Mooney 1928: 12; Grinnell 1962, 2: 164–65; Wallace and Hoebel 1952: 298; Fitzpatrick, in An. Rept. Com. Ind. Aff. 1850: 52
1861–62	Smallpox	Kiowa, Kiowa-Apache, Comanche, Cheyenne, Arapaho	"terrible ravages especially among the Arapaho"	An. Rept. Com. Ind. Aff. 1862: 131; Mooney 1898: 176, 311
1864	Smallpox	Wichita, Caddo	"fatal in many cases"	An. Rept. Com. Ind. Aff. 1864: 319
1867	Cholera	Wichita, Caddo	"18 deaths in 5 days among Wichita," "47 Caddo victims"	An. Rept. Comm. Ind. Aff. 1867: 322

Note: Tribes of the present Oklahoma region were vaccinated against smallpox in 1865

Table 5.2. (*Continued*)

Date	Disease	Tribes Infected	Mortality	References
1877	Smallpox	Mescalero Apache	carried off "a considerable number"	An. Rept. Com. Ind. Aff. 1877: 157
1877	Measles and fever	Kiowa, Kiowa-Apache Cheyenne, Arapaho	Killed 136 Cheyenne and 83 Arapaho children; Kiowa losses heavy but not enumerated	An. Rept. Com. Ind. Aff. 1877: 85; Mooney 1898: 218, 341–42
1882	Whooping cough and malarial fever	Kiowa, Kiowa-Apache, Comanche, Wichita	"malarial fever fatal in number of cases"	An. Rept. Com. Ind. Aff. 1883: 70; Mooney 1898: 219
1889–90	Influenza	Cheyenne, Arapaho	"fatal in large number of cases"	An. Rept. Com. Ind. Aff. 1890: 177, 182; Rept. of Indians Taxed and Not Taxed 1894: 543
1892	Measles, influenza and whooping cough	Kiowa, Kiowa-Apache, Comanche, Wichita, Caddo	"deaths chiefly among infants and children; Kiowa loss nearly 15% of pop.; Cheyenne and Arapaho "mortality very light"	An. Rept. Com. Ind. Aff. 1892: 374, 377, 386, 388; Mooney 1898: 223, 235, 362–63

of health, or freedom from epidemics.

Contemporary writers did not identify the diseases involved in a number of the epidemics of the pre-1800 period. However, Dr. Pat Nixon, a San Antonio physician who reviewed the literature on these early epidemics, suggested the diseases on the basis of the symptoms described.[13] Throughout the entire period, smallpox was the most common cause of epidemics.

There were smallpox epidemics in 1674–75, 1688–89, 1739, about 1746, 1750, 1759, 1763, 1766, 1778, 1801–2, 1816, 1839–40, 1861–62, and 1864. Although the Indians of present Oklahoma were vaccinated against smallpox in 1865, an epidemic of this disease occurred among the Mescalero Apache in New Mexico in 1877. Yet another smallpox epidemic was averted among the Mescalero during the winter of 1882–83, when timely vaccination enabled these Indians to escape "without a single case of smallpox."[14]

Next to smallpox, measles and cholera appear to have been the most deadly, although epidemics of malaria, whooping cough, and influenza also took their tolls of Indian lives.

The frequency of epidemics within a tribe must be regarded as a very important factor in the progressive decline of Indian population, for it inhibited the recovery and growth of tribal populations. The French biologist Jean Louis Berlandier, who explored Texas in 1828 and subsequent years, reported that smallpox occurred among the Indian tribes "every sixteen years, making great ravages for a year at a time."[15] He was not precisely accurate in defining the interval between epidemics, but the record is clear that there was a smallpox epidemic among one or more of the tribes of Texas at least once each generation from 1739 to 1877. Losses in these epidemics must have been high among children and teenagers who never lived to reproduce. Older people (including women beyond childbearing age), who gained immunity by exposure to previous epidemics, presumably survived.

Data on mortality from epidemics are fragmentary, and some of the most precise figures may be exaggerations. Mooney discounted the Kiowa tradition that they had lost half their number in the cholera epidemic of 1849.[16] Yet the Cheyenne told of a similar loss, and Comanche mortality must also have been high in the 1849 epidemic.[17] Comanche mortality in the 1816 smallpox epidemic was estimated at 4,000.[18] There appears to be no record of any tribe in Texas having suffered as severe a population loss from a single epidemic as did the Mandan of the Upper Missouri River during the smallpox epidemic of 1837, which reduced that tribe from about 1,600 to less than 140—a loss of more than 90 percent.[19] Nor were epidemics the sole cause of the extinction of any of the Texas tribes who became extinct before 1860. Warfare, liquor, malnutrition, and perhaps the absorption of the last remnants into other Indian or Mexican populations also played parts in the disappearance of those tribes.

How small a tribe could survive and maintain its political and social identity under the conditions of competition with other Indians and whites which prevailed in Texas prior to 1860? There may have been a few cases among the Caddoan tribes of East Texas of remnants of less than 150 persons who managed to maintain their tribal identity for a short time before they combined with one or more related tribes to ensure their biological survival—just as the Mandan combined with the Hidatsa and Arikara on the Upper Missouri River following their disastrous losses in the smallpox epidemic of 1837.

The influence epidemics may have had on the beliefs and customs of those who survived should be of particular interest to the ethnologist.

To what extent could Indians distinguish between the most common epidemic diseases? Nixon was of the opinion that even the Spaniards, who observed and reported epidemics among the Indians of Texas prior to 1800, tended to confuse smallpox and measles.[20] Keepers of the nineteenth-century Kiowa pictorial calendars designated epidemics of smallpox and measles by the same graphic symbol—the figure of a standing man, clothed only in a breechclout, his head, body, arms, and legs covered with small dots (fig. 5.1a-b). However, the Kiowa verbally distinguished "hole sickness" (smallpox) from "pimple sickness" (measles). They called the cholera "cramp sickness," and identified the years of cholera epidemics on their calendars by the figure of a man

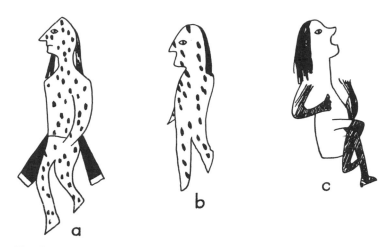

Fig. 5.1. Pictographic representations of epidemics among the Kiowa: a) smallpox (winter 1839–40), b) measles (summer 1877), c) cholera (summer 1849).

with his legs drawn up in pain (fig. 5.1).[21]

Indian beliefs regarding the causes of epidemics varied. Interestingly enough, the fragmentary records of two of the earliest epidemics indicate that the afflicted Indians initially, and probably correctly, blamed the whites for these plagues. Cabeza de Vaca wrote that the Karankawa *at first* blamed his Spanish party for communicating the epidemic of 1528 to them, "believing we had killed them and holding it to be certain, they agreed among themselves to kill those of us who survived." But one Indian saved the Spaniards' lives by pointing out that if the white men had "so much power" they would not have suffered so many of their own men to perish.[22]

Caddoan survivors of the disastrous epidemic of 1691 among the Indians of the East Texas missions at first blamed the high mortality on the priests' practice of baptizing the stricken Indians during their death throes. But Father Casañas believed that he convinced even the most hostile Indian medicine men that the priests' attentions had not

95

caused the Indian deaths.[23]

Other and later Indians attributed epidemics to the angry forces of nature. Morris Opler's conservative Chiricahua Apache informants of the 1920s believed that offenses against the Mountain Spirits caused epidemics and that earthquakes and eclipses of the sun or moon were warnings of approaching epidemics. Once warned by these signs, the Apache sought to ward off epidemics by performing masked ceremonial dances. One informant told Opler that as recently as 1903, when these Apache lived near Fort Sill, the neighboring Comanche suffered deaths from smallpox. The Apache masked dancers performed for four nights. "And you know," said the Indian, "we never got the smallpox."[24]

The common practice among the nomadic tribes of scattering once an epidemic struck one of their camps, as well as their avoidance of the locality of the initial outbreak for a considerable time thereafter, must have helped to minimize losses among them. The desertion of the missions by some of the missionized Indians during the epidemics of the eighteenth century must have had a similar effect. The loyal neophytes who remained with their priests perished, while many of the dispersed apostates survived.

Significantly, the greatest population losses during the eighteenth century and the early years of the nineteenth century were suffered by the least mobile tribes. These were the mission Indians and the Caddoan farming tribes. The latter—the Wichita and the tribes of East Texas—lived in compact, semipermanent villages of multifamily lodges, where conditions were as favorable for the rapid communication of diseases as they were in the mission compounds.

The succession of epidemics must have encouraged a trend in religion toward a greater emphasis on prayers and ceremonies for protection against sickness and death. This is not to say that they ceased to seek supernatural aid to bring them success in hunting, protection from their enemies, and an abundance of crops (among those who farmed). But their most destructive enemies came to be those unseen ones— epidemics which struck down and killed their women and children, and against which their warriors had no defense. Health magic must not only have grown in importance, but it survived into the reservation period after the buffalo were gone and the Indian wars had ended.

At the turn of the century George A. Dorsey was told by an aged Caddo that as a boy he was taught to pray each morning when he returned from his bath, and cast a stick into the family fire, "Grandfather, help me to live and become a good man, and help others to live."[25] One must wonder whether Caddo boys uttered this ardent prayer for life itself in the days before the dread epidemics began to materially lower the life expectancy of children?

Even though traditional curing practices proved ineffective in saving lives of victims of epidemic diseases, Indians persisted in employing them. They may unwittingly have alleviated the patients' sufferings by hastening their deaths. David Burnett described the Comanche treatment of smallpox during the epidemic of 1816.

> The patients were strictly confined to their lodges, excluded from the air, and almost suffocated with heat. In many instances while under the maddening influence of the disease, exasperated by a severe paroxysm of symptomatic fever, they would rush to the water and plunge beneath it. The remedy was invariably fatal.[26]

Even as late as 1892 the agent for the Cheyenne and Arapaho reported that they treated measles

> by subjecting the patient to a severe sweating process, following it with a plunge in the river. . . . In cases of measles this treatment usually proves fatal.[27]

Early accounts of the Karankawan and Caddoan tribes of East Texas refer to the common practice of infanticide. It was also the custom of the Caddo to bury a live, nursing infant with its dead mother, and of the Comanche to kill a warrior's wife at his grave.[28] These customs do not appear to have survived among these tribes beyond the middle of the nineteenth century. Why? Did not the continued decline in tribal populations encourage the abandonment of customs so wasteful of human life?

The population decline also may have brought about significant changes in Indian war practices during the nineteenth century. Eighteenth-century accounts indicate that the eating of prisoners, the hideous torture of captives, and the trade of captives as slaves were common among the Indian tribes of Texas. As the nineteenth century progressed only the Tonkawa continued to practice cannibalism to any extent, and both the torture and sale of captives became less common. Captives became more valuable as adopted members of a family—to replace children, wives, and husbands who had been lost in epidemics—than as human sacrifices or human trade goods.

In 1853 the experienced mountain man and Indian agent Thomas Fitzpatrick observed that Comanche and Apache raids south into Chihuahua and Durango were made to capture Mexican prisoners as well as to "sharpen their appetite for pillage and rapine," and that these raids "tend [ed] to keep up the numbers of the tribe." Fitzpatrick found that Mexican captives were "so intermingled amongst these tribes that it is somewhat difficult to distinguish them." At that time the Comanche refused to make any treaty with the United States that would require them to give up any captives. "They stated briefly that they had become a part of the tribe; and that they were identified with them in all their modes of life; and they were the husbands of their daughters and the mothers of their children."[29] Mooney estimated that during the 1890s "at least one-fourth of the Kiowa had captive blood."[30]

Even so, the Comanche and Kiowa practice of inducting prisoners into the tribe failed to reverse the continued downward trend in tribal populations during the nineteenth century. It did, however, result in marked biological changes in the composition of the tribes. In 1931, Marcus Goldstein, a physical anthropologist studying the Comanche, doubted that more than 10 percent of the members of that tribe were full-bloods.[31]

Surely the nineteenth-century Comanche and Kiowa were well aware of their dwindling populations, and they became reluctant to have their true numbers known to whites. The Comanche did not want their numbers counted in 1837.[32] As late as 1890 the Kiowa were "strangely averse to being counted."[33] In the light of history this aversion to being counted cannot be interpreted as mere superstition: the Comanche and Kiowa were proud peoples who had been much more numerous, and they had no desire to advertise their weakness in numbers.

On the other hand, the declining numbers of tribesmen among the southern plains tribes hostile to the United States during the third quarter of the nineteenth century must have made the army task of Indian fighting much less difficult than it would have been had they fought these Indians when they were as numerous as they were in 1780, or even before the cholera epidemic of 1849.

Epidemics strongly affected Indian tribal organization—or more properly, disorganization and reorganization. Certainly the Karankawan, Atakapan, and Coahuiltecan tribes, all of whom were repeated victims of epidemics, suffered the ultimate in social disorganization—extinction. The Lipan Apache lost their political and social autonomy and survived only as minority groups of a few individuals living among friendly Apache tribes in Oklahoma and New Mexico. Remnants of the Tonkawa were preserved from extinction under the protection of the United States Army at Fort Griffin during the waning years of the intertribal wars. The horticultural Caddoans, who numbered nearly thirty tribes before the epidemic of 1691, were reduced to three small tribes, identified as Caddo, Kichai, and Wichita, by the end of the frontier period.

There is need for a thorough study of the processes by which the Caddoans managed to survive, through repeated combinations and reorganizations into fewer and fewer units as their numbers declined. In this process the names of many of the earlier tribes became almost forgotten. But they survived (to a degree) biologically long after they lost their political identity. There are indications of tribal combinations following the deaths of important chiefs and many of their followers during the eighteenth-century epidemics. Why the names of some of these tribes, such as Anadarko, survived, while those of

99

other once equally numerous and prominent tribes disappeared, needs explanation.

Significant changes in social organization also took place among some of the nomadic tribes of the southern plains during the nineteenth century. Grinnell found evidence that the Cheyenne relaxed their tribal taboo against marriage within one's own band *after* the cholera epidemic of 1849 had decimated some of their camps.[34] During his fieldwork among the Comanche in the 1930s Hoebel found that most Comanche marriages "took place within the band."[35] Might not a shift from band exogamy to permissive endogamy have taken place among both Comanche and Cheyenne *after* destructive epidemics, when they needed to strengthen weakened bands by any practical means?

Finally, we may consider briefly the effect the succession of epidemics may have had on Indian attitudes toward death itself. An observer among the tribes of western Oklahoma in 1890 noted that "with characteristic stoicism an Indian accepts sickness as inevitable, evinces no interest in its cause, and expects no relief."[36] But by 1890 conditions had changed. Acute smallpox had been brought under control through vaccination, and chronic tuberculosis had become the slower-acting killer of reservation-bound Indians. Might not this passive acceptance of sickness and death also have been historically conditioned?

One finds no indication of this passive acceptance of sickness in the dramatic account of the death of a Cheyenne warrior during the cholera epidemic of 1849, as told by George Bird Grinnell.

> Little Old Man . . . donned his war-dress, mounted his war horse, and rode through the camp with a lance in his hand, shouting, "If I could see this thing, if I knew where it came from, I would go there and fight it." As he was doing this he was seized with the cramps, fell from his horse, and died in his wife's arms.[37]

CONCLUSION

The cumulative effect of thirty or more epidemics among the Indians of Texas played a major role in the marked decline in population among these tribes during the historic period prior to 1890. Even though our best available set of early population estimates for these tribes, those of James Mooney, cannot be considered exact, comparison of them with 1890 census figures for the surviving tribes clearly indicates both a general population decline and a differential rate of decline among the different tribes. The sedentary, missionized and horticultural tribes suffered the most severe losses. Some of them became extinct; others sacrificed their tribal independence as their numbers decreased but ensured their biological survival by combining with other linguistically and culturally related tribes. This practice was most common among the Caddoan tribes of East Texas. The nomadic tribes of the northern periphery appear to have suffered least, due to a combination of factors such as their relative remoteness from whites until the early years of the nineteenth century, their common practice of scattering once they learned of the presence of disease among their people, and their very positive efforts to recruit additional tribal members through raiding for captives—both Indian and non-Indian. Yet even these tribes could not maintain their numbers, and as their total populations decreased the non-Indian blood quantum increased among them.

Obviously, they were aware of their decreasing numbers and revealed that awareness in a reluctance to be counted. Obviously, too, they tried to prevent further losses as best they could. Their traditional methods of treating the sick proved futile in the cure of infectious diseases such as smallpox and measles. Frequent and fervid appeals for supernatural protection from illness and death proved little more effective in preventing the occurrence of epidemics. They also appear to have taken positive steps to ensure survival by abandoning earlier practices that were wasteful of human life. Instead of killing and eating prisoners, or trading them to other tribes outside the area, they adopted them to take the place of their own dead relatives. Infanticide, the burial of a nursing infant with its dead mother, and the sacrifice of a wife on the death of her husband became obsolete. New political groupings emerged through the merging of remnant tribes. Even among the larger tribes who continued to retain their tribal identity, endogamous taboos may have been relaxed in the extensive band reorganizations necessitated by severe losses in the most disastrous epidemics.

Smallpox, the most destructive of the epidemic diseases, was only brought under control through vaccination shortly before the opening of the reservation period, and before 1890 tuberculosis had replaced the earlier epidemics as a slower-acting killer.

I hope this paper may serve to encourage further studies in a too-long-neglected field. Such studies should not stop with efforts to determine the effects of epidemics on tribal populations: they should encompass efforts to find the influence of epidemics on the lifeways of those Indians who survived those epidemics.

CHAPTER SIX

Symbols of Chiefly Authority
in Spanish Louisiana

THE PROBLEMS of establishing and maintaining friendly relations with Indian tribes were ones which confronted all those European powers which sought to gain footholds in the New World. Indian alliances were never won by force or by promises alone. They had to be purchased with trade goods and presents. This paper is concerned with the roles of a few extraordinary presents bestowed on prominent Indian chiefs by Spanish officials in Louisiana in the Indian diplomacy and culture of the times.

When Spain acquired Louisiana the major tribes south of the Platte River—Pawnee, Osage, Wichita, and Comanche—were already known to Spanish officials in New Mexico and Texas, although primarily as enemies. Before Spain ceded Louisiana four decades later she extended her diplomatic and trade relations to those and to more than a score of other tribes who inhabited the vast drainage basin of the Mississippi west of that great river—tribes as far north as the Mandan in present North Dakota. This in itself was no small accomplishment.

To ease the transition from French to Spanish rule in Louisiana Spanish officials took pains to assure the Indians, who had had relations with the French, that there would be no fundamental change in the white man's relations with them. Not only would trade be encouraged, but the Indians would continue to receive the presents to which they had been accustomed. Indeed, the Spanish went so far as to try to impress upon those tribes who had been loyal to France that the Spanish and French were really the same people.

In his instructions to Captain Don Francisco Riú, leader of the first official Spanish expedition up the Mississippi from New Orleans, dated March 14, 1767, Governor Antonio de Ulloa wrote,

> Since it may happen that one must honor the chiefs of certain tribes who come to the fort, as has always been practiced, by giving them the medal of the king, a report will be given to the government of the tribes which come there, with information of the names and relations of the principal and secondary chiefs, in order that these medals may be sent. This is to be understood in regard to the tribes which can come anew to offer their friendship, since the old tribes have them from the time of the French government. And so far as they are concerned it is the same as though the medals were those of our king, for the Indians have been told so, in order that they might understand that no innovation is being made in anything.[1]

In October 1769, Ulloa's successor, General Don Alexandro O'Reilly, summoned nine chiefs of tribes living within sixty leagues of New Orleans to his home. He assured them that the Spanish king "did not wish to demand of them any other gratitude than their constant fidelity." Then, impressively, he "arose from his chair to place about the neck of each one of the chiefs the medal which hung from a silk ribbon of deep scarlet color. He first had them kiss the royal effigy, and then with his bare sword he touched them on both shoulders and chest and made over their heads the sign of the Cross, and finally gave each an embrace and his hand, whereupon they again showed such admiration that it was evident how pleasing to them was the ceremony and that it was the first time they had seen it."[2]

The Spaniards, like the French, were keenly aware that the ritual and pageantry of formal ceremonies made deep and lasting impressions on Indians who witnessed or participated in them. Written instructions were given to men who were to serve as the king's representatives in presenting symbols of chiefly allegiance and authority to newly contacted tribes, carefully detailing the ceremonies to be conducted and even the words to be spoken on those occasions.

Jacques Clamorgan's June 30, 1794, instructions to Jean Baptiste

Truteau, commander of the first expedition up the Missouri of the newly formed Commercial Exploration Company of St. Louis, were very specific: not only must Truteau present the chief of the distant Mandan Indians "a medal which the governor sends him in order that he may make strenuous efforts to establish peace with all neighboring nations and to live in friendship with us," but Truteau must give the Mandan chief the "most beautiful" of the three Spanish flags he was to carry upriver to present to chiefs of different tribes.

Truteau also was instructed:

On his arrival among the Mandanas, he shall proceed to convoke a council among the chiefs, which he shall hold in the name of the Chief of the Spaniards, announcing to them that the latter sends them a flag of his nation, and a medal which bears the likeness of his Majesty, the great Chief of the Spaniards, protector and friend of all red men, who loves the beautiful lands, free roads, and a serene sky; he shall tell them that the flag which they receive is the symbol of an alliance and of most sincere friendship which he is able to give to the Mandanas nation, and that the medal ought to be the symbol of an eternal memory, that the Chief of the Mandanas ought to believe in the sincerity of the Chief of the Spaniards; finally that the sons of the Mandana chiefs are also the sons of the Chief of the Spaniards, that he will ever protect them from all those who may wish to harm or injure him.[3]

Actually it was the Welshman John Evans who gave the first and probably the only flags and medals to the Mandan in the name of "their Great Father the Spaniard" two years later. But Spain failed to exploit her brief foothold in the Mandan villages, and both the trade and allegiance of those Indians reverted to the British.[4]

Spain's greatest success in Indian diplomacy during her four decades of rule in Louisiana resulted from subtler maneuvering than the cases previously cited. For nearly two decades officials in New Orleans, Natchitoches, San Antonio, and Santa Fe sought to make peace with the warlike Comanche. Divided into several strong, autonomous divisions, those nomadic, mobile warriors had long been a thorn in the side of the Spanish in both New Mexico and Texas. It was not until 1786 that Don Juan Bautista de Anza, governor of New Mexico, made peace with them. Painstakingly he elevated the status of Ecueracapa (Leather Coat or Iron Shirt) to that of head chief of all the Comanche, promising him both a medal and a staff of office to be displayed in all the Comanche camps as symbols of his chiefly supremacy. On July 15, 1786, Governor Anza formally "decorated Captain Ecueracapa with his Majesty's medal." And "in order that this insignia might be displayed with the greatest propriety and luster, he presented him with a complete uniform and another suit of color."[5]

These examples indicate that the important symbols of chiefly authority bestowed on tribal leaders in Spanish Louisiana were not one but several. In addition to those mentioned in the foregoing accounts—medals, flags, uniforms, and staffs of office—they also included *patentes*, or commissions. Let us consider each of these in a little more detail.

MEDALS. These were symbols of allegiance and authority bestowed on Indian chiefs by the French and English in North America long before Spain acquired Louisiana. Spanish officials in Louisiana presented large medals only to the principal chief of each tribe, and smaller ones to chiefs of second rank. The medals were silver, and bore on one face the likeness of the reigning Spanish monarch. The Spanish also made a point of furnishing red silk ribbon for the suspension of the medals from their wearers' necks. By the year 1787, if not earlier, the Spanish also recognized a third grade of chiefs by presenting gorgets to them. I have found no detailed description of these Spanish gorgets.[6]

I have found a single reference to a gold or gilt Spanish medal given to an Indian of Louisiana, the notorious Omaha chief Black Bird, who was probably the only true despot among the tribes of Louisiana during the Spanish period. Black Bird achieved dominance of his tribe by administering poison (said to have been a crude arsenic obtained from traders) to his rivals, effectively eliminating all would-be contestants for Omaha tribal leadership. He regarded himself as the greatest of all Indian chiefs, and demanded a gold medal of the Spaniards. Because his tribe was strong and strategically located astride the Missouri above the mouth of the Platte, where it could easily prevent St. Louis traders from proceeding upriver to trade with more distant tribes, and because the English were also actively wooing the allegiance and trade of Black Bird and his tribe, Governor Carondelet provided a gilt medal for "the great Maha chief, in order to flatter him most."[7]

FLAGS (*pabellones*). Some at least of the flags given to prominent chiefs by the Spaniards in Louisiana bore the cross of Burgundy, perhaps in red on a white field. They were large enough to be flown from a staff in front of a chief's lodge. Some may have been of silk, but obviously not all of them were, because Black Bird complained to Spanish traders that their English rivals gave "only silk flags, which would cause them to despise ours."[8]

Flags, of course, were less substantial than medals, but the Spanish do not appear to have replaced them with any regularity. On February 5, 1779, Fernando de Leyba wrote Governor Gálvez from St. Louis that the chiefs were "very urgently asking me for flags." He reminded the governor that flags had been distributed "only once since our establishment in this colony. . . . As it is their custom to have the flag always flying above the cabin of the head chief, there are tribes which have only a flag pole and on it usually some rags full of holes and patches."[9]

COMMISSIONS (*patentes*). This was a printed or hand-lettered certificate of an individual Indian's chiefly status (see fig. 6.1). Sometimes, if not commonly, these commissions were supplied by the governor to his field officers with the name of the Indian recipient omitted so that they could fill in the names of the Indians to whom they were presented. That the illiterate Indians prized these documents even if they couldn't read them is remarkable only to the scholar who fails to understand the veneration in which they were held among the Indians. In 1787 the Caddo head chief requested that his old *patente*

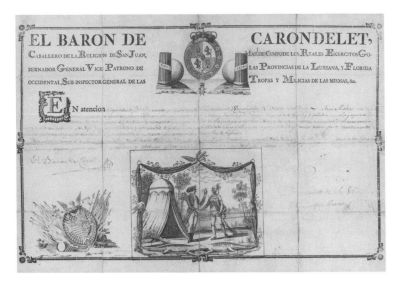

Fig. 6.1. Spanish certificate presented to the Omaha chief L'oseau Noir (Black Bird) in 1796. It bears the signature of the Baron de Carondelet, governor of Louisiana. (Courtesy Nebraska State Historical Society)

be replaced by a new one, because it had been damaged by water and torn.[10]

UNIFORMS. These were colorful coats and hats of military or semimilitary design. The coats may have been of different colors, and quite likely the facings were of contrasting colors (see fig. 6.2). There were repeated references to their decoration with (metal) lace embroidery (i.e., galloons). Don Pedro Bautista Pino tells us that the coats given to the Comanche by the Spaniards in New Mexico were "made of blue Querétaro, with red lapels for the big chiefs." Apparently they were fashioned from fabrics woven in Querétaro, Mexico. He also stated that three-cornered hats were given the Comanche to be worn with these coats. Earlier references simply mention hats with feather plumes.[11]

Fig. 6.2. Payouska (White Hair), chief of the Great Osage, by Charles B. J. F. de Saint-Memin. The chief wears the large medal and handsome officer's coat presented to him by the United States when he visited Washington in 1804. (Courtesy Collection of The New-York Historical Society)

109

When Great Sun, head chief of the Tawehash, was on his deathbed in 1784 or 1785, he "asked to be buried in his Chief's headdress and coat with the Spanish Royal flag." I suspect this was the final disposition of many chief's uniforms given to Indians by the Spanish in Louisiana: they continued to be worn by their chiefly recipients even after death. Perhaps historical archaeologists, if they are aware of this Indian custom, may recover at least the buttons and metal lace ornaments from the graves of some of these chiefs, provided of course these Indians were buried in the ground rather than exposed to the elements on elevated scaffolds or in the trees.[12]

STAFFS OF OFFICE (*bastones*). These were canes with ornamented gold or silver heads. The *baston* must have been both an old and a peculiarly Spanish symbol of chiefly authority. It was employed in Spanish-Indian relations in East Texas as early as 1690. On May 25 of that year General Alonso de León presented to the head chief of the Nebedache village "a staff with a cross, giving him the title of governor of all his people." The chief "accepted the staff with much pleasure, promising to do all that was desired of him, and the company fired three salutes."[13]

In the course of reestablishing Spanish rule in East Texas in 1721, the Marqués de Aguayo gave silver-headed canes, as well as suits of clothes, to those chiefs whom he recognized as captains in a number of villages of Caddoan-speaking Indians.[14]

After the governor of Louisiana, through his lieutenant in Natchitoches, Athanase de Mézières, assumed responsibility for diplomatic relations with the southern Plains tribes north of the Red River, he followed the precedent of the Internal Provinces of Mexico in presenting staffs of office to those Indians whom he recognized as *capitanes* or *gobernadores* of their tribes or villages. Those chiefs appeared to prize their *bastones* as highly as they did their medals.[15] Nevertheless, the Spanish governors of Louisiana do not appear to have furnished staffs of office to the chiefs they recognized among the tribes farther north, who had had no diplomatic relations with the Spaniards of Mexico prior to 1763.

Throughout the period of Spanish rule in Louisiana the medal, flag, and commission appear to have been the three symbols of chiefly authority most widely distributed among Indian tribes from the Red River northward as far as Spanish explorations were carried up the Missouri—that is, to the Mandan villages.

The governor in New Orleans assumed responsibility for providing these symbols and for their discriminate and limited distribution among the Indian tribes by his regional representatives in Natchitoches, Arkansas Post, and St. Louis, as well as by licensed trader-explorers of the Upper Missouri. Correspondence between regional officials and successive governors indicates that the former had to justify to their superiors their requests for medals, flags, commissions, uniforms, and/or staffs of office, and that sometimes their requests had to be repeated before favorable action was taken on them in New Orleans. A full year might transpire between the regional official's request for and the actual presentation of these symbols to the chiefs for whom they were requested.

As an anthropologist, I am particularly interested in the effects the distributions of these symbols of chiefly authority and allegiance may have had on the beliefs and actions of the Indians—both those few individuals who received them and the many members of their tribes who did not. Granted that the illiterate Indians left no records testifying to their regard or disregard for these symbols. Nevertheless, some of the writings of the whites who presented these objects to chiefs in the field provide revealing insights into the Indians' attitudes toward them.

Especially revealing are some observations by Jean Baptiste Truteau, the St. Louis fur trader, who first presented Spanish medals, flags, and commissions to the Arikara and Cheyenne chiefs far up the Missouri in present South Dakota, in the middle years of the last decade of the eighteenth century.

When Truteau attended an important council in the earth lodge of Crazy Bear, chief of the first village of the Arikara, on July 7, 1795,

111

he observed that this chief had placed his flag before the door of his lodge and his medal around his neck.

"At the furtherest end of the hut, exposed on a mat, [was] the letter patent which his Spanish Father had sent him by me, having placed before it some live coals on which was burned a certain kind of dried grass the smoke of which produces a very strong odor, and which they use as we use incense."

Truteau went on to explain: "They hold such things as medals, flags, and letters in such deep veneration that whenever these are taken from their wrappings, they are smoked and hold the most important place at their feasts."[16]

In other words these Indians accepted these gifts not merely as secular symbols of allegiance and authority, but as sacred objects to be preserved in wrappings, ritually unveiled, and displayed with the same reverence they had employed in the care and manipulation of their most cherished traditional medicine bundles. Doubtless the incense Truteau smelled was the odor of burning sweetgrass, which was employed by the tribes of the Upper Missouri "in any ceremony or ritual to induce the presence of good influences or benevolent powers."[17]

That the Indians regarded these objects as personal medicines possessing powers to bring good or bad fortune to their recipients is also attested in Truteau's field observations of that summer of 1795.

The previous spring Truteau had formally presented a medal, flag, and commission to La Lance, a young man among the Cheyenne, whom the most important men of that tribe had chosen as "most worthy to wear the medal and to be made the great Chief of their Nation." Upon his acceptance of these symbols La Lance had promised to "do all the good which had been recommended to him, in the letter which his Father, the Chief of the White Men, had sent him." But La Lance failed to carry out the Spanish admonition to keep the peace with neighboring tribes. Not only had he stolen horses from the Mandan and Hidatsa, but he had murdered a family of Sioux who were living at peace among the Cheyenne.

The Indians believed, Truteau observed, that "the medal, the flag and the letter, who were great spirits, had become angry" with La Lance, for three of his children had died and lightning had struck the lodge of his brother and reduced it, the brother, his wives, children, dogs, and horses tied before the door to ashes.

Truteau continued: "This accident happening to befall this man, above all others, known to have broken his promise to the White Men, and not having behaved in the manner imposed upon him, in the presence of all the esteemed ones of his Nation, had a terrible effect on the minds of all these Nations and confirmed anew their belief that the White Men were great spirits and all powerful."[18]

Nearly two decades earlier (November 21, 1776) Francisco Cruzat informed Governor Unzaga that the Sioux of the Mississippi were "very angry because of the death of five chiefs who had come down to see us and ask for the medal which had been granted them."[19] Might not this misfortune have been *one* reason why the English were more successful than the Spanish in winning the allegiance of the powerful Sioux?

Nevertheless, the great majority of Indian leaders in Louisiana appear to have coveted these visible symbols of Spanish recognition of their status as tribal leaders of distinction. These symbols not only distinguished them from their own warriors but also caused them to be respected by strangers—both members of other tribes and white traders and settlers.

How then did the introduction of these symbols affect the Indian political system? We know that the traditional Indian polity among the Plains tribes tended to be both democratic and highly competitive. Men rose to the chieftaincy through their deeds, and retained their leadership only as long as they could maintain it in competition with other vigorous achievers. Chiefs did not enjoy life tenure, and their positions were not hereditary. Furthermore, the number of chiefs recognized by the tribe was not limited. Generally, among those tribes who were divided into bands, each band had at least one chief.

The introduction of the white colonial policy of recognizing only a few chiefs in each tribe resulted in the elevation of some chiefs at the expense of others. Once these few chiefs were recognized they tended to remain in office for many years, in many cases for life. The hierarchy of chiefs of the large medal, the small medal, and the gorget tended to crystallize the system. Ambitious young men found little opportunity for advancement. Consequently, young men who found their way to power within their tribes blocked by intrenched incumbents had reason to become both frustrated and jealous of the chiefs as well as resentful of chiefly authority. Yes, the generation gap was *not* invented in this country during the 1960s!

The new system imposed by the whites also engendered jealousy within the chiefly hierarchy—of the wearers of the small medal or gorget toward the wearers of the large medal, while the latter looked to the whites to help them maintain their positions. Undoubtedly there must have been factionalism within the tribes of the Great Plains before the 1760s, but the system of external recognition of and discrimination among chiefs must have intensified rather than alleviated intratribal discord.

The best-documented cases of chiefly jealousy in the records of the Spanish period in Louisiana refer to the Great and Little Osage, who comprised the largest and most aggressive Indian confederation between the Arkansas and the Platte, and whose combined force numbered some 1,200 warriors.

On March 18, 1776, Francisco Cruzat in St. Louis wrote Governor Unzaga seeking his help in solving a problem of the relative recognition to be given two jealous Osage chiefs, both of whom coveted a medal. Traders had told Cruzat that the man previously regarded as second in rank actually had a larger following than the first chief. Cruzat's predecessor had given the second chief a coat and hat, and the Spanish official feared that if he was denied a medal he would show his displeasure by stealing horses from neighboring towns and insulting the traders. Eventually the first chief was given a large medal and the second a small one—more than three years later. Doubtless this Spanish solution to the second chief's problem did not satisfy him.[20]

Nine years later, during the spring of 1785, Governor Esteban Miró,

114

desirous of ending the prolonged intertribal warfare between the Osage and the Caddo, brought Tenihuan, great chief of the Caddo, and two Osage chiefs to New Orleans. There he publicly decorated both Osage chiefs with the small medal and obtained the promise of the older one, Brucaiguais, to make peace with the Caddo.

Later that year Miró sent a small medal, suit, and hat to another Osage leader, whom he wanted to bring to New Orleans to impress with the marvels of the city. Brucaiguais was so jealous that another man of his tribe should have that privilege that he renewed open warfare upon the Caddo and effectively prevented his rival from going down the Arkansas to New Orleans.

Governor Miró then ordered Brucaiguais to be brought to New Orleans as a hostage for the good behavior of the Osage Indians. When the governor's order reached Arkansas Post it was found that Brucaiguais was near death. Nevertheless, he was degraded from his rank, and his medal, commission, and flag were sent to the governor in New Orleans.[21]

This stripping of an uncooperative chief of his symbols of authority must have been an exceedingly rare case. I have found no other example of it in the records of Spanish Louisiana.

Intertribal jealousies also became intensified when the members of some tribes were led to believe that other tribes were receiving preferential treatment from the Spaniards.

In 1780 Antonio Gil Ybarvo reported from Natchitoches that the Tawehash were so irritated when they saw loads of Spanish goods transported to the Tonkawa and Tawakoni while their trade was virtually cut off that they "are destroying at every step my flags, staff of command, and medals, saying they cannot live on the luster of these." Ybarvo feared that these angry Indians would also show their displeasure by attacking Natchitoches.[22]

Some fifteen years later Jacques d'Eglise made the mistake of showing members of the small Ponca tribe the five medals and five flags he was taking up the Missouri for the Mandan chiefs. This "sight brought about a great jealousy between these two nations," and it also occasioned "bad words" against the Spanish.[23]

As a means of establishing and maintaining intertribal peace the bestowal of symbols of authority along with verbal admonitions to the recipients to make friends with other tribes were of relatively little avail. Intertribal warfare against traditional enemies was too much a part of Indian life to be ended so quickly or easily. Repeatedly— in 1773, 1786, and 1792—the Spaniards had to resort to the stronger measure of prohibiting trade with the Osage, thus cutting off their ammunition and other supplies, to try to stop them from raiding other and less powerful tribes. But this measure too was of little avail. When the Spanish officials prohibited their own traders from doing business with the Osage, English and later American traders were only too happy to take their places.[24]

If the bestowal of these symbols of chiefly authority upon the Indians disrupted tribal political organizations, encouraged both individual and tribal jealousies, and failed to end intertribal warfare, why did the colonial powers, and later both the United States and Canada, continue to make use of this means of diplomatic negotiation with the Indians? Perhaps the best answer may be that this was both an economical and a rather effective means of eliciting Indian allegiance.

Some twenty-six years after Governor Anza made peace with the Comanche in 1786, Pino wrote of the advantages to New Mexico of the practice of giving presents to that very warlike tribe on the Louisiana-Texas-New Mexico frontiers.

We would never have believed the benefit that has accrued to the province from this practice if we had not seen it. A continued state of peace and friendship of the greatest importance in checking other tribes has been the result of the small number of presents given them. At first the Comanches thought they had to reciprocate. They brought all the fine pelts they could collect in order to exceed the munificence of our presents. When they were informed that favors given them in the name of our king should not be returned, they were greatly astonished. Thus they were placed under obligation to us; their gratefulness continued to increase, and their esteem for the King of Spain, whom they call the general chief [*capitan grande*],

116

has likewise increased. In order to get an idea of the esteem in which they hold the king, one needs only to note that any appointments they receive from their government are ignored unless they are confirmed for our officers in the name of the general chief.[25]

This diplomacy must have inspired among the Indians of many tribes strong feelings of attachment to and regard for the individual head of state—whether this was the *capitan grande* in far-off Spain or in later years the Great White Father in Washington or, for Canadian Indians, the Great Mother (Queen Victoria).

We know that shortly after the flag of the United States was first raised in St. Louis, Lewis and Clark embarked on their long overland journey to the shores of the Pacific Ocean. Their baggage included both large and small medals bearing the likeness of President Jefferson, commissions, and uniforms, which they presented to Indian chiefs of different tribes on the Missouri in very solemn ceremonies in which the chiefs were informed of their new father in Washington and his interest in their welfare. Even before these famed explorers began their historic trek, Pierre Chouteau was on his way to Washington with a delegation of Osage chiefs to meet and talk to that new White Father.

The United States continued until 1889 to give so-called Indian peace medals, bearing the likenesses of successive presidents, to tribal chiefs. By that time the western Indians were confined to reservations and the United States was coming to regard white Indian agents rather than red chiefs as the persons primarily responsible for the management of the Indians.

It was different north of the 49th parallel. There Indian chiefs continued to receive medals bearing the likeness of the British monarch, as well as uniforms. I recall that as recently as World War II young Blood Indians in Alberta volunteered for military service, not because their country was in danger, but because, as they said, "their king needed them."

There may be a moral to this little study—one which has some relevance to the solution of our current Indian problem. Over the past

117

eighty years our Indians' feelings of close personal relationship with our head of state may have become weakened by the interposition of a large and impersonal Bureau of Indian Affairs, which in turn is but a small part of a huge Department of the Interior which is more concerned with land and resource conservation and management than it is with Indian problems.

As recently as February 11, 1969, a task force established to study the Indian and the Bureau of Indian Affairs submitted its findings to the White House. Its first and major recommendation reads: "A meaningful and determined reorganization of the administration of Indian affairs, together with the providing of an effective Administration thrust to go forward to the opportunities of tomorrow and not simply solve the problems of yesterday, can only be accomplished by moving the Bureau of Indian Affairs to the Executive Office of the Presidency, for the objectives of Indian affairs in 1969 require nothing less than the priority, the mandate and visibility which the President himself can give them."[26]

In the light of history this recommendation may appear much less novel than its wording in the future tense would suggest. Is it not an attempt to recapture through governmental reorganization that intimate association between the Indian and his head of state which existed in the very heart of our country two hundred years ago, when Indian chiefs wore the likeness of their *capitan grande*, "protector and friend of all red men," over their chests, suspended from scarlet silk ribbons?

118

❌▬❌▬❌

CHAPTER SEVEN

Climate,
Acculturation, and Costume

A History of Women's Clothing
among the Indians of the Southern Plains

DURING THE FIRST QUARTER of the present century the Department of Anthropology of the American Museum of Natural History conducted an intensive program of ethnological field research among the Plains Indians. Three of America's leading anthropologists of that period—Alfred L. Kroeber, Robert H. Lowie, and Clark Wissler—were major participants in that program. Ethnological theorists may be most aware of their findings on military societies and the sun dance. But the entire program was in considerable part justified by that museum's need for sizable collections of Plains Indian artifacts for exhibition and study. Among the more than fifty scholarly papers resulting from that research were several devoted to art and material culture, based primarily on laboratory studies of the many specimens collected.

In 1915 Clark Wissler published *Costumes of the Plains Indians*, a portion of which was devoted to a comparative study of the women's dresses in the museum's collections at that time. From this study he concluded that the typical body garment of Plains Indian women was a long, sleeveless, skin dress, which hung from the wearer's shoulders and extended well below her knees, made from two whole animal skins—one forming the front, the other the back of the garment. Wissler found this structural pattern in dresses from seventeen tribes—ranging from the Plains Cree, Assiniboine, Blackfoot, and Sarsi southward to the Apache, Comanche, and Kiowa and westward to the Ute, Nez Percé, and Yakima beyond the Rockies. He interpreted variations in the outline of these dresses as indications of tribal preferences in the styling of this basic, two-piece pattern.[1]

Wissler plotted these so-called tribal dress outlines on a map, here reproduced as Map 7.1. He also cited descriptions of women's body garments from the published reports of field observers of Plains and Woodland tribes during the prereservation years. In seeking to determine the origin of this garment, which he termed the "Plains type of woman's dress," he eliminated from consideration all those tribes for whom he had found references to a different style of woman's dress in earlier years. Thus he eliminated all but six of the seventeen tribes represented in his sample—leaving only the Nez Percé, Crow, Mandan, Hidatsa, Arapaho, and Kiowa as possible originators of the "Plains Indian woman's dress."

Observe that Wissler was *not* content to try to determine the origin of this dress *solely* on the basis of tribal distribution of the trait. More than "age-area" was involved in his thinking. He also employed historical sources in this study, and he strongly advocated their use in studies of the origin of other perishable artifacts, stating, "For perishable objects, such as costume, real historic data is usually available."[2]

Those of us who knew Clark Wissler as a stimulating teacher in the Yale Graduate School during his later years are well aware of the high value he placed on what we now refer to as "ethnohistorical sources." As I look back on his pioneer study of the history of Plains Indian women's clothing from the vantage point of the passage of sixty-four years it appears to me that the deficiencies in that study lie less in "age-area theory" than in Wissler's limited use of then available specimens and historic references. One cannot honestly fault Wissler for not having consulted significant references to women's clothing in the writings of prereservation period observers that were not published until *after* 1915. But his use of historic sources was more limited than was the range of pertinent references then available, and his specimen sample was limited to a relatively small and relatively late series of artifacts, nearly all of which were in the collections of the American Museum of Natural History. Had he examined older, documented examples of Plains Indian women's garments in other museums, and

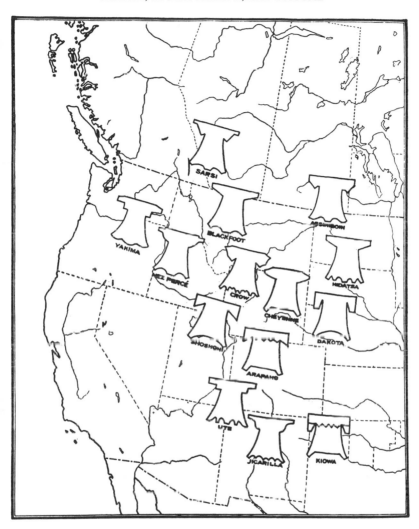

Map 7.1. "Distribution of the Plains type of Woman's Dress" as plotted by Clark Wissler (From Wissler, 1915: Fig. 27).

had he consulted all of the earlier observations in the literature to his time, he probably would have found that the "Plains Indian woman's dress," as he defined it, was not an aboriginal form of garment among *any* tribe of Plains Indians and that a very different type of woman's costume persisted among the tribes of the southern plains well into the nineteenth century.

Wissler's sample was weakest for the tribes of the southern plains because the American Museum of Natural History staff did relatively little fieldwork and artifact collecting among those tribes. Remember that ethnologists were few in those days. And Wissler and his American Museum colleagues knew that James Mooney of the Smithsonian's Bureau of American Ethnology and George A. Dorsey of the Field Museum in Chicago were already involved in intensive fieldwork among the Plains Indians of western Oklahoma. Both of these men were known as highly competent ethnologists and collectors so that there appeared to be little justification for seeking to duplicate their work.

My research on the history of the women's body garments of the southern Plains tribes has revealed three distinct styles—none of which answers the description of Wissler's "Plains type of woman's dress."

THE SKIRT AND PONCHO

In the historical section of Wissler's 1915 paper he cited a single reference to the women's costume of the southern plains in prereservation days, and for some reason he inferred that it referred only to the Cheyenne. In reality this was a description of the clothing worn by the women in a large, combined encampment of Arapaho, Cheyenne, Kiowa, and Kaskia (Kiowa-Apache) Indians visited by one of the two divisions of Major Stephan H. Long's Exploring Expedition on the Arkansas river, July 26–28, 1820.

The observer was Thomas Say, the very able naturalist of that party, who wrote of the women he saw in that camp:

Their costume is very simple, that of the female consisting of a leathern petticoat, reaching the calf of the leg, destitute of a seam, and often exposing a well-formed thigh, as the casualties of wind, or position influence the artless folds of the skirt. . . . [A] kind of sleeveless short gown, composed of a single piece of the same material, loosely clothes the body, hanging down the shoulders, readily thrown off, without any sense of indelicacy, when suckling their children, or under the influence of heated atmosphere, displaying loose and pendant mammae.[3]

Obviously Say was describing a woman's costume that bore no resemblance to Wissler's "Plains Indian woman's dress." It *was* composed of two pieces of skin. But each skin was a *separate* garment—one a skirt, the other "a sleeveless short gown . . . hanging down the shoulders."

My experience leads me to believe that mere men may have considerable difficulty in describing women's clothes. Fortunately, I have received much valuable assistance in this study from my wife, Margaret. Yet Say in 1820 may have given us a better than average man's description of the clothing of those southern Plains Indian women. Even so, he did not tell us how that upper garment was constructed.

It was not until I found in the collections of the U.S. National Museum a specimen of a Comanche woman's upper garment that I could appreciate how "very simple" (to use Say's words) that short gown probably was. This specimen had been in the Smithsonian collections since 1853. It was collected by the French naturalist, Jean Louis Berlandier, some time between his first meeting with the Comanche in 1828 and his death in 1851. As the accompanying illustrations reveal (figs. 7.1, 7.2) this garment was made from a single deer or antelope skin (including the leg extensions) with a transverse slit near the center for insertion of the wearer's head. Its handsome painted decoration and added long skin fringes should not distract our attention from this garment's basic structural simplicity—for it is as primitive a pattern as one can imagine—one complete animal skin.

A second example of this Comanche woman's upper garment, also collected by Berlandier, passed from the Smithsonian to the National

Fig. 7.1. Comanche woman's skin poncho, period 1828–51, worn by Vivian Poolaw, a Kiowa-Comanche. (Cat. no. 1480, Department of Anthropology, U.S. National Museum, Smithsonian Institution)

Museum in Copenhagen more than one hundred years ago. In 1914 Gudmund Hatt published a line drawing and a description of this specimen. Because Hatt's monograph was written in Danish and dealt primarily with Arctic skin clothing, it received little attention from students of Plains Indian culture. Fortunately, it is now available in English. Of this specimen Hatt wrote: "Such a garment is only capable of covering the upper part of the body. Two deerskins are required for a dress that covers the entire body." He termed this garment "a very simple poncho" and defined poncho as "a piece of cloth or skin

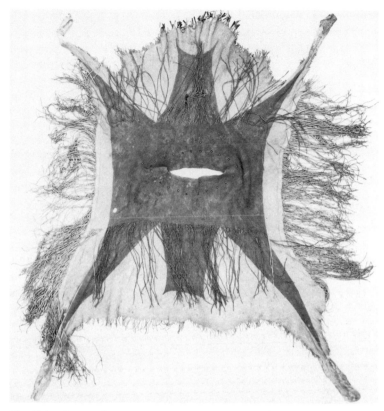

Fig. 7.2. Comanche woman's poncho of period 1828–51 showing construction of a single deer or antelope skin, with transverse slit in center. (Cat. no. 1480, Department of Anthropology, U.S. National Museum, Smithsonian Institution)

with a hole in the middle for the head, the poncho resting upon both shoulders and covering the breast and back."[4]

As we shall see, contemporary observers referred to this upper garment by a variety of terms, but I shall follow Hatt in calling it a poncho. Berlandier himself termed it a "camisole." And curiously enough his own illustrator, a Lino Sánchez y Tapia, pictured a Comanche woman of the 1830s wearing a more closely fitted upper garment with a V-neck and short sleeves, rather than the loose poncho of the type he himself collected.[5] Perhaps this was a somewhat more sophisticated upper garment known to the Comanche at that time, but not a common one. Observe, however, that this garment was worn in conjunction with a short skirt—no more than knee length—and skin moccasins (fig. 7.3a).

During the 1790s a Spanish priest, Vicente Santa Maria, writing of the Comanche, mentioned only a skirt in his two-sentence description of the women's clothing: "Their women wear knee-length skirts made of well-tanned buffalo hides. The hems of skirts are adorned with fringes, shells or pieces of bone."[6] Probably the priest was referring to the women's warm weather attire, when the poncho was omitted. Even so, I would doubt if the skirt was commonly made of as heavy a skin as buffalo. However, there is some evidence that skins of animals other than deer or antelope were used for the ponchos. Don Pedro Bautista Pino in 1812 observed that Comanche women made "tunics" of mountain sheep skin and that "experienced Comanche women execute beautiful designs on these chamois."[7] Presumably those "designs" were painted on the skins.

Victor Tixier, a French traveler among the Osage in 1840, did not see the Comanche, but he obtained a description of them from Edward Chouteau, who had traded with them in their own country. Tixier learned that Comanche "women wear skirts and blouses of white skin, which are also decorated with paintings."[8] Likely Tixier's "blouses" were actually "ponchos." This description certainly provides further evidence for the idea that Comanche women, prior to 1850, wore two separate garments of skin—a skirt and an upper garment—and

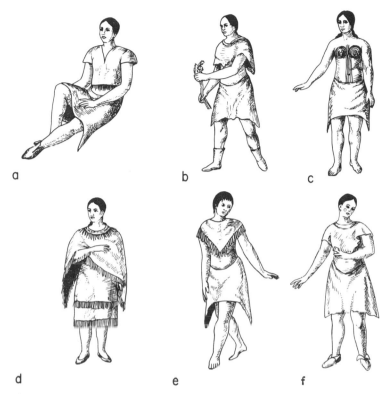

Fig. 7.3. Women's clothing of period 1830: a) Comanche, b) Tawakoni, c) Tonkawa, d) Lipan Apache, e) Karankawa, and f) Cocos. (Redrawn from Lino Sánchez y Tapia's watercolors in Berlandier, 1969)

substantiates their custom of decorating their skin clothing with paint.

The series of watercolor illustrations of costumed Indians of seventeen Indian tribes of Texas which accompanies Berlandier's manuscript in the Thomas Gilcrease Institute of American History and Art in Tulsa provides the earliest known pictorial evidence of the clothing worn by women among several of those tribes. Executed by the little-known Mexican artist Lino Sánchez y Tapia during the mid-1830s, nearly all of these pictures were after originals drawn by José Maria Sánchez y Tapia or Jean Louis Berlandier while they were members of an official Mexican scientific expedition into Texas in 1828.[9] With the aid of these pictorial documents, other contemporary pictures, some extant specimens, and dated observations by field investigators published in the widely scattered literature, let us try to trace both the history and distribution of this two-piece, two-garment costume—the simple poncho and skirt.

Tapia's series of watercolors clearly point up the differential acculturation that had taken place among the Indian tribes of Texas prior to 1830. Its effects were most marked on those easternmost tribes who were in closest contact with the advancing frontier of white settlement. By that time, however, none of the true Plains tribes had been affected to the extent that they discarded their traditional skin clothing for cloth garments resembling those worn by whites. At that time the Caddo Indians of East Texas wore colorful cloth garments influenced by non-Indian models. Tapia's watercolor shows a Caddo woman clad in a thigh-length yellow skirt with ruffled neck, calf-length blue skirt, and long-sleeved red coat all of cloth.[10] Richard E. Ahlborn has expressed the opinion that this costume was derived from European clothing of the eighteenth century.[11]

Nevertheless, missionaries and travelers among the Caddo Indians during the late seventeenth and early eighteenth centuries observed that their women then wore skin clothing which was of the skirt and poncho type. As early as the spring of 1687 Henri Joutel, of La Salle's ill-fated colony, noted that the Cenis women "wear nothing but a skin, mat or clout, hanging round them like a petticoat, and reaching down halfway their legs, which hides their nakedness before and behind." Their exposed upper bodies were tattooed: "thereof they make a particular show of their bosom, and those who have the most are reckoned the handsomest, though the pricking in that part be extremely painful to them."[12]

Father Casañas, the pioneer Spanish missionary among the Caddo, wrote in August, 1691: "During the hot season, the men generally go about the house naked; but the women, even when very young, are always covered from the waist down."[13]

Father Espinosa's account of the Hasinai prior to 1722 mentions women's skin ponchos as well as skirts.

> From another large skin, carefully dressed, and with an opening in the middle large enough for the head, they cover their shoulders and breasts to the waist. They cut all the edges in fringe so the garment is very pretty."[14]

Ethnologists classify the Caddo as a marginal southeastern people, but in the matter of traditional women's costume they appear to have been the easternmost wearers of the skirt and poncho. Some evidence suggests that the little-known Atakapa, south of Caddo in Louisiana and Texas, also shared this clothing trait. William Newcomb quotes a fragmentary account of the Atakapa of Lake Charles, Louisiana, during the years 1817–20 which describes a woman's garment thus: "A skin was trimmed into a circular shape, in its center a circular hole was cut, and the garment was slipped over the head and fastened around the waist with thongs."[15]

The skirt and poncho style survived much longer among the Caddoan-speaking tribes of the southern plains who were not missionized during the colonial period and who were not closely touched by the expansion of white settlements until after the mid-nineteenth century. Tapia's watercolor of a Tawakoni couple harvesting corn in the 1830 period clearly pictures the woman wearing two skin garments—a miniskirt and an abbreviated poncho barely long enough to cover the wearer's breasts (see sketch in fig. 7.3b).

The nineteenth-century Tawakoni, like the earlier Caddo women, dispensed with the poncho in warm weather, exposing their tattooed breasts. W. B. Parker, who accompanied Capt. Randolph B. Marcy's expedition to present western Oklahoma in 1852, visited a Waco and Tawakoni camp in the month of July. He observed: "The squaws were tattooed on the breast and face; in lines on the face, and circles on the breasts." He was intrigued by the sight of one Indian woman who "had not an article of clothing on her except an old filthy rag round her loins, and a gay calico sun bonnet on her head."[16]

During the frontier years the Wichita, Caddoan-speaking allies and northern neighbors of the Tawakoni, were known to whites as Pawnee Picts or Tattooed Pawnees. The tribal sign for this tribe in the Plains Indian gesture language was given with a circular motion and referred to the painted or tattooed rings around the women's breasts.[17] When members of Col. Henry Dodge's Dragoon Expedition met the Wichita in late July 1834, they saw the women of the tribe "naked save for a skirt of deer skin or red cloth extending from the waist to a little below the knee."[18] Josiah Gregg, well-known contemporary observer of Indians along the old Santa Fe Trail, described the Wichita women's tattooing as "a perfect calico of the whole underjaw, breast, and arms, and the mammae are fancifully ornamented with rings and rays." He mentioned their "primitive petticoat . . . of about a yard and a half of strouding or else a small dressed skin, suspended from the waist." He also noted: "The upper portion of the body remains uncovered except for a blanket or small skin thrown loosely over the shoulders."[19] Gregg's description of that upper garment may have been no more precise than was Edward Curtis's much later reference to it as a "deerskin shirt."[20] Both must have been referring to the skin poncho. The topless condition appears to have persisted among some Wichita women longer than among the women of other tribes on the southern plains. During the years 1869–74 William S. Soule, the pioneer photographer at Fort Sill, pictured women among many southern Plains tribes. Only his Wichita women appear bare-breasted, clad from the waist down in cloth skirts.[21] This was shortly before missionaries prevailed upon all Wichita women to cover themselves modestly above the waist. Col. Richard I. Dodge dated the demise of toplessness among the Wichita closely, when he wrote in 1882, "until within about ten years the women of the Wichita Indians wore in summer no covering on the body above the waist."[22]

In 1828 the Tonkawa lived south of the Tawakoni and west of the Caddo in Texas. They were marginal Plains Indians. When José Maria

Sánchez y Tapia visited a Tonkawa encampment on April 22, 1828, he saw that the women "wear nothing but a dirty piece of deer skin around the waist, leaving the rest of their bodies naked."[23] Each breast was decorated with concentric circles from the nipple to the base. Lino Sánchez y Tapia's watercolor after José's original drawing depicts the short skin skirt and the elaborate tattooing in circles on the breasts and in vertical lines on the center of the abdomen (fig. 7.3c).[24] That the women of this tribe on occasion also wore an upper garment is attested by a brief description of women who accompanied a Tonkawa delegation to the capitol of Texas in 1838. "Some of the women have a piece of leather or dressed skin around the waist. Some, an additional piece around the shoulders."[25] Likely that "additional piece" was a poncho.

At Laredo on the Rio Grande in February 1828, José Maria Sánchez y Tapia saw a band of Lipan Apache under Chief Castro. Lino Sánchez y Tapia's watercolor of a Lipan man and woman probably was derived from a drawing or drawings executed by José at that time. The woman is depicted wearing a relatively large, fringed buckskin poncho and a long skin skirt falling well below the knees. The skirt is fringed in a horizontal band sewn to the garment as well as at the bottom (see fig. 7.3d).[26] This view appears to support Berlandier's observation that "Lipan women are the best turned out of all the nomadic women. Though they dress entirely in tanned deerskin, they are clean and elegant."[27]

The Lipan were aboriginal inhabitants of the southern plains who were driven southward by the Comanche during the eighteenth century. They may or may not have been the Teyas whom Coronado met in 1541, but it is most probable that those Teyas were Apaches. In the Zuni Pueblos of the Southwest one of the major chroniclers of the Coronado Expedition, Pedro de Castañeda, observed that the women wore "blankets which they tie or knot over the left shoulder leaving the right arm out." But the same observer reported that the Teyas women of the plains dressed quite differently. "The women wear cloaks over their small under petticoats, with sleeves gathered up at the shoulders, all of skin, and some wore something like little sanbenitos with a fringe, which reached halfway down the thigh over the petticoat." Editor George Parker Winship explained that the sanbenito was a broad piece of cloth hanging before and behind with a hole for the head.[28] By likening this upper garment worn by strange Indian women to a sanbenito, an Old World religious garment known to his readers, this Spanish explorer has informed us that he was describing a simple poncho, which Teyas women wore with a skin skirt. This reference to the wearing of the skin skirt and poncho by Apache women at the time of first recorded contact between Indians and whites on the southern plains assures us that this was the aboriginal women's costume in this region.

During the summer of 1601 Don Juan de Oñate met the Escanjaques Indians on the Arkansas River. The identity of those Indians is not certain, but they were more probably Apache than the Kansa they were thought to have been some seventy years ago.[29] Oñate recorded that the weather was hot and the men "went about nearly naked," but the "women were clothed from the waist down."[30] At the inquiry which followed that expedition, two participants testified that the Escanjaques women painted (or more likely tattooed) stripes on their faces, breasts, and arms and covered their privy parts with small skins. One of them testified that "some wore a cloak."[31] This evidence is in agreement with that already cited for the Comanche, the Caddoan tribes, and the Tonkawa in more recent years to the effect that southern Plains Indian women traditionally tended to go topless in warm weather and that many of them tattooed their breasts.

The skirt and poncho continued in favor among both Eastern and Western Apache tribes until after the Civil War. Theodore Gentilz's painting, *Camp of the Lipans*, executed about 1845 and preserved in the Witte Museum in San Antonio, portrays women wearing fringed ponchos and skirts of skin.[32] Gordon Baldwin's study of the Western Apache of southern New Mexico and Arizona claims that this traditional style prevailed until the women of those tribes began to imitate the styles of cloth garments worn by the wives of army personnel stationed at frontier posts in the Southwest.[33] Yet the traditional skirt and poncho persisted among the old women of the San Carlos Apache in 1890, when an observer described their clothing as "a skirt about the loins reaching below the knees; with a piece of cloth fastened loosely about the shoulders." He noted, however, that the younger women wore "full calico skirt, and blouse with sleeves."[34]

During the decade of the 1890s the wearing of the long-fringed skin poncho and skirt became a status symbol among young women of prominent families of Chiricahua Apache residing at Fort Sill, Oklahoma. A photograph of a daughter of Naiche, son of the famed Cochise, and leader of the Fort Sill Apache, shows her in an elaborately decorated skin poncho and skirt (fig. 7.4). A buckskin skirt and poncho attributed to the daughter of Geronimo is in the U.S. Military Academy Museum at West Point. The skirt and poncho has survived as a favored ensemble for Apache girls' wear in the traditional puberty ceremony of their people.

Lino Sánchez y Tapia's watercolors of Karankawa and Cocos may be the only pictures executed of those tribes of the Texas Gulf Coast before they became extinct prior to 1860.[35] They are of value to our study because they show that the skin skirt and poncho both in abbreviated forms—were worn by tribes living to the southward of the Great Plains circa 1830 (fig. 7.3e,f).

Looking still farther afield in order to determine the distribution of the skirt and poncho as a style of Indian women's wear, we find evidence of its occurrence in the Southwest and in northern Mexico during the sixteenth century and in Vera Cruz in prehistoric times.

Diego Perez de Luxan's account of the Espejo Expedition into New Mexico surely describes this costume worn by women of the Patarabueyes (a Shuman tribe) on the Conchos River, a southern tributary of the Rio Grande in Mexico. In his description of these Indians, seen in December 1582, Luxan states: "The women wear tanned deerskin bodices of some sort, resembling scapularies, for covering their breasts, and other tanned deerskins as skirts, using as cloaks hides of the cattle."[36] By cattle he meant bison. Scapularies were sleeveless, Old World religious garments which hung from

133

Fig. 7.4. Skin poncho and skirt worn by Dorothy, daughter of Naiche, leader of the Fort Sill Apache, ante 1900. (National Anthropological Archives, Smithsonian Institution)

the shoulders, as do ponchos.

Still farther southwest, in the thickly populated villages on the Sonora River in extreme northwestern Mexico, Castañeda in 1541 noted that the Indian women wore "petticoats of dressed deerskin, and little sanbenitos reaching halfway down the body."[37]

The only evidence I have found that the skirt and poncho were woven of cotton by Indians north of Mexico appears in Espejo's description of the Piro Pueblo Indians of eastern New Mexico in 1583: "The women have cotton skirts, often embroidered with colored thread, and over the shoulders a blanket like that worn by the Mexican Indians, fastened at the waist by a strip of embroidered material, with tassels, resembling a towel. The skirts are worn like slips next to the skin, the lower portion loose and swishing. Each woman displays such an outfit to the best of her ability."[38] That reference to a "blanket like that worn by the Mexican Indians" is most intriguing! Was Espejo referring to the *huipil* most common in southern Mexico, or to the woven *quechquemitl* (a Nahuatl word meaning "neck garment") which is still worn in many villages in north-central Mexico? I believe the latter interpretation is more probable. The Cordrys, in their recent book, *Mexican Indian Costumes*, explain that the quechquemitl is usually, but not always, worn with a blouse, and always with a skirt. In researching the history of the quechquemitl they found that it "seems to be a garment originally worn in warm or temperate regions, and then taken over by people of the Valley of Mexico from the Totonacs or Huastecs."[39] They refer to those short, curved-bottomed upper garments portrayed on finely modeled pottery figurines of young women from the Classic Period ca. A.D. 300–900 in Vera Cruz as quechquemitls. Many of these figurines are preserved in museums in the United States and Western Europe, as well as in Mexico. One fine example, from the collections of the Museum of the American Indian, Heye Foundation, is here illustrated as figure 7.5. It clearly shows the short, curved poncho worn with a long skirt, and exposing a bare midriff. A few of the figurines from Vera Cruz portray young women clad only in skirts, suggesting that the upper garment was seasonal or optional as it was among the historic tribes of the southern plains. To me this prehistoric costume of the Totonac Indians of Vera Cruz was very like the poncho and skirt of the historic tribes of the southern plains. It may be significant, too, that the Indians of Vera Cruz lived near the northern limit of textile weaving in old Mexico, as defined by Beals.[40] He found that Indians who lived in the Gulf Coast north of the Huastec dressed in skins rather

Fig. 7.5. Poncho and skirt portrayed on a female figurine from Vera Cruz, Mexico. Period A.D. 300–900. (Courtesy National Museum of the American Indian, Smithsonian Institution, Cat. no. 22,2310)

than in cotton garments.

I venture to suggest that the prehistoric woven quechquemitl of Mexico and the skin poncho of the tribes of the southern plains were historically related and that the original form was the simple poncho made by cutting a transverse slit in the center of a single deer or antelope skin to provide a covering for the shoulders and breasts. This garment was replaced by a woven one by the Indians of Central Mexico after they became weavers of cotton, but it persisted in its original material among the Indians of the southern plains until after the middle of the nineteenth century. To me this is a more logical explanation of the origin of this garment than is the idea that the poncho made from a whole animal skin was adopted from the more sophisticated woven quechquemitl worn by Indians in Mexico.

I shall not attempt to plot the known occurrences of the quechquemitl in Mexico, but I have added prehistoric Vera Cruz to my map of known distribution of the skirt and poncho farther north as I have documented this woman's costume in this paper (map 7.2). The map reveals a historic distribution of this trait among both horticultural and nomadic tribes from the Caddo in Louisiana to the western divisions of the Apache in Arizona, and from the Southern Cheyenne and Arapaho on the Arkansas, southward into Mexico—with the exception of the great majority of the Pueblo tribes of the Southwest. I suggest that this style of woman's wear originated somewhere within this area of distribution, but not necessarily at its center. Nor should we consider its occurrence among the historic tribes of the southern plains necessarily a marginal survival.

Climate may well have been an important factor in defining the northern limit of this style of woman's wear. To the map 7.2 I have added the northern limit of 180 frost-free days as located on the map appearing in the *Atlas of American Agriculture* (1936). It is significant that nearly all wearers of the skirt and poncho lived south of this line where winters were shorter and less severe than they were farther north on the plains or at higher elevations, and where there was less need for an upper garment that more closely enveloped the body than there was in the country of the more northern tribes of the Great Plains.

The milder year-round climate and longer periods of warm weather favored the invention and use of the short poncho which could be discarded readily in the warmer season. The availability of deer and antelope throughout the area of distribution of this style favored the use of those skins in the making of the poncho. Nor is there any reason to believe this costume must have originated outside the bison area. Throughout the Great Plains Indians favored the skins of mammals smaller than the bison for body clothing prior to their adoption of garments of trade cloth. The fact that women who wore the poncho and skirt appeared topless both indoors and outdoors throughout a goodly portion of the year must have encouraged the women of many tribes to decorate their breasts, abdomens, arms, and shoulders elaborately with tattooed or painted designs. That was not the custom of the women among the tribes of the northern plains who were more fully clothed throughout the year.

137

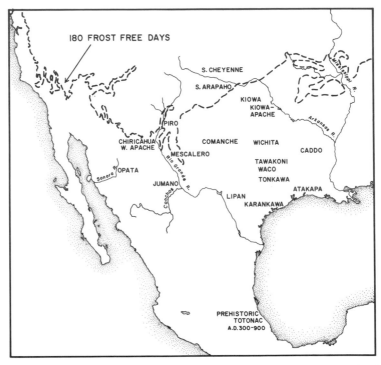

Map 7.2. Distribution of the woman's poncho and skirt as determined by this study. Dashed line shows northern limit of 180 frost-free days annually.

Early Use of Trade Cloth. The tribes of the southern plains neither grew nor wore cotton. Their first use of textiles for women's garments appears to have been in the substitution of trade cloth for skins in the fashioning of their traditional skirts and ponchos. Such use by the Wichita and Apache has been cited in some field observers' descriptions of those tribes cited in this paper. That trade cloth was used by other tribes of the southern plains at least a half century before those tribes were confined to reservations is attested in Say's description of the clothing worn by some of the women in the combined Kiowa,

138

Kiowa-Apache, Cheyenne, and Arapaho encampment he visited on the Arkansas in 1820. After he described the skin skirt and poncho worn by the majority of the women in that camp, he added:

A few are covered by the more costly attire of coarse red or blue cloth, ornamented with a profusion of blue and white beads; the short gown of this dress has the addition of wide sleeves descending below the elbow. Its body is of a square form with a transverse slit in the upper edge for the head to pass through; around this aperture and on the upper side of the sleeves is a continuous stripe, the breadth of the hand, of blue and white beads, tastefully arranged in contact with each other, and adding considerable weight, as well as ornament to this part of the dress; around the petticoat, and on a line with the knees, as an even row of oblong conic bells, made of sheet copper, each about an inch and a half in length, suspended vertically by short leathern thongs as near to each other as possible, so that when the person is in motion they strike upon each other and produce a tinkling sound."[41]

Say's description suggests that this elaborately decorated trade cloth outfit was worn only by the wives and/or daughters of the most affluent Indians in 1820. The description also indicates that the substitution of trade goods for animal skins resulted in some change in the form of the upper garment, including the addition of elbow-length "wide sleeves."

THE MULTIPIECE TRADE CLOTH DRESS

The use of trade cloth by southern Plains Indian women to fashion a true dress—a garment which covered the wearer from the shoulders to below the knees—may not have antedated the middle years of the nineteenth century. The earliest reference to a trade cloth dress among these Indians that I have found appears in an exquisite watercolor portrait of an attractive young Indian woman executed by the talented German artist, Friedrich Richard Petri, during the years 1852–57 (fig. 7.6). The woman's name and tribe are not recorded. We know, however, that the artist emigrated from Germany to Texas for his health in 1852, and that he lived in the German settlement of Fredericksburg on

139

Fig. 7.6. Comanche or Lipan Apache woman wearing a trade cloth dress. Watercolor by Friedrich Richard Petri, 1852–57. (Courtesy Mrs. Hunter P. Harris)

the Indian frontier in the valley of the Pedernales River until his death in 1857. The German settlers were at peace with both the Comanche and Lipan Apache. This young lady might have been of either tribe.

Notice that this dress is entirely of cloth. The central portion is of dark blue cloth. The short, elbow-length kimono sleeves are sewn to the dress, but the arm holes and sleeves are unshaped straight pieces of material and the sleeve seam is left open. A gore is sewn to the side to add fullness to the lower portion of the dress—a necessity to an active horsewoman. Both sleeves and gore are red. (A color reproduction of this watercolor appears as plate 29 in Newcomb 1978.)

It is noteworthy that this trade cloth dress appeared among the Indians two decades before the last Comanche hostiles were confined to reservations. It was *not* a reservation period innovation. Indeed, its sleeves may have been anticipated by those of the upper garments of cloth described by Say as early as 1820. Whether this dress was entirely an Indian invention, or whether white traders, settlers, or captives played some role in its design we do not know.

That this style of dress may have been quite new among the Comanche and/or Lipan in the middle 1850s is suggested by the fact that the very attractive young woman who wears it might be considered to be a style-setter among her people, and that Indian women of the period portrayed in other of Petri's illustrations wore skin ponchos and knee-length skirts of an earlier style.[42] And still another woman, a young mother, wore a poncho and skirt of figured yellow cloth.[43]

That the trade cloth dress was fashionable among the wives and daughters of prominent men among the Comanche, Southern Cheyenne, and Arapaho prior to 1876 appears in photographs of those women preserved in the National Anthropological Archives. Wives of Comanche and Kiowa leaders wore them when they accompanied their husbands to Washington in 1872. The trade cloth dress is well represented in the field photographs taken by William Soule at Fort Dodge and Fort Sill during the years 1867–75. His portrait of a daughter of the famed Kiowa chief, Satanta, shows her in a trade cloth dress decorated with five horizontal rows of elk teeth across the breasts and sleeves, beside her warrior husband.[44] Soule's studio portrait of an Arapaho woman illustrates how the trade cloth dress was worn with an elaborate belt decorated with silver discs, and beaded hightop moccasins of skin, during this period (fig. 7.7).

Kiowa and Cheyenne artists who were members of that unique art colony that developed among the young southern Plains Indian prisoners of war at Fort Marion, St. Augustine, Florida, created nostalgic pictorial memories of life in their home camps during their incarceration in the late 1870s. They tended to picture women in their best clothes—even when engaged in the bloody task of butchering buffalo. And those women invariably were shown in trade cloth dresses with

141

Fig. 7.7. Southern Arapaho woman wearing a trade cloth dress. Studio portrait by William S. Soule, 1869–75. (National Anthropological Archives, Smithsonian Institution)

kimono sleeves and vertical gores of contrasting colors to the bodies of the dresses.[45]

Greater use of cloth for both dress clothing and daily wear was encouraged by the distribution of large quantities of yard goods as annuities to the Southern Cheyenne and Arapaho, Kiowa, Kiowa-Apache, and Comanche during the years immediately following the Medicine Lodge Treaties with those tribes in 1867. An article in each of those treaties specifically provided "for each female over twelve years of age a flannel skirt, or the goods necessary to make it, a pair of woolen hose, twelve yards of calico and twelve yards of cotton domestics."[46]

Calico-clad women appear in numerous field photographs of southern Plains Indian women taken during the years immediately following those treaties. Ticking was included in the "cotton domestics" distributed in the annuities. An old woman's upper garment collected among the Comanche by Dr. Edward Palmer in 1868 is made entirely of blue and red striped ticking. Blue is used for both the body and the gores, while the short sleeves are of red ticking (cat. no. 6, 993 U.S. National Museum).

In 1893 Rev. H. R. Voth, who had been a Mennonite missionary among the Southern Cheyenne and Arapaho at Darlington since 1883, added a child's flannel dress to the Smithsonian collections (cat. no. 165, 775 U.S. National Museum). This is a veritable miniature of the fashionable women's dress of the 1870s. It reminds us of the Plains Indians' love of dressing their little girls in the same styles of clothing that were favored by women. In this specimen the gores and sleeves are red, and the body is blue. This dress is of further interest because the white cloth binding, applied to keep the edges of the flannel from fraying, was machine-sewn. Perhaps this dress was made in a school or mission sewing class.

The pictorial record of field photographs suggests that by the decade of the 1890s the trade cloth dress with short sleeves and gores in contrasting colors to the body had passed out of style among the women of the southern Plains Indians in Anadarko. My photograph of one of those dresses, modeled by a young Indian woman and taken on the grounds of that museum in 1948, shows that the old blue and red color scheme was retained.

THE THREE-PIECE BUCKSKIN DRESS

The buckskin dress, which came to replace the trade cloth dress as the favored "Indian costume" among southern Plains Indian women who could afford it, was not a new style of dress during the 1890s. Nor did it evolve from the aboriginal skin poncho and skirt ensemble. Rather it involved a new concept of the use of buckskin in dress design as well as some elementary tailoring—the piecing and sewing together of three buckskins to form a true dress which covered the wearer from the shoulders to well below the calves of the legs. One skin, with a slit in the center of the head, covered the shoulders, upper arms, and breasts—as had the old poncho. But this skin was trimmed and sewn in a horizontal seam at the midriff to *two* other skins—one of which formed the front and the other the back of the middle and lower portions of the garment. Advantage was taken of the broad natural extensions of the rear legs of the deerskins to provide needed fullness to the lower portion of this dress. The two lower deerskins were sewn or tied together at the sides. The oldest well-documented example of this true skin dress that I have seen from the southern plains is in the collections of the U.S. National Museum (cat. no. 59, 592). It was given to Mr. F. V. Calver, one of the two U.S. commissioners who negotiated the Treaty of Fort Wise in mid-February 1861, by Little Raven, the first Southern Arapaho chief to sign that treaty. If the woman who made this dress was the one who executed the beadwork on its yoke, she may not have been a fullblood Indian. The double-curved and conventionalized floral designs are thought to have been introduced into Plains Indian beadwork by half-breeds, and it is doubtful if fullblood Arapaho women were using these designs as early as 1860 (fig. 7.8).

Even so, the pictorial record suggests that the true skin dress was worn by some Indian women on the southern plains before 1861. Lt. James W. Abert's watercolor portrait of the Cheyenne Indian wife of William Bent, the noted trader who operated famed Bent's Fort on the Upper Arkansas, appears to picture that woman wearing a skin dress, presumably of the three-piece pattern, decorated with panels of geometric beadwork. That watercolor was executed in 1845.[47]

Perhaps a wider use of the skin dress among the tribes of the southern plains was inhibited during the late 1850s and the 1860s by the growing popularity of the trade cloth dress. But there is ample evidence that by

144

Fig. 7.8. Three–piece skin dress, Southern Arapaho. Collected in 1861. (Cat. no. 59, 592, Department of Anthropology, U.S. National Museum)

the 1890s both Comanche and Kiowa women had come to prefer the three-piece skin dress for wear on occasions when "dressing Indian" was appropriate. By that time buckskin had become more difficult to obtain, and the possession of a well-made, elaborately decorated skin dress had become something of a status symbol.

James Mooney's field photographs taken during the 1890s show a number of Kiowa women and small girls wearing buckskin dresses.

Comanche and Kiowa skin dresses collected by Mooney and others during the early 1890s are in the Smithsonian collections. The most handsome of these, collected by Dr. James D. Glennan, Army Medical Officer, while on duty at Fort Sill, is Kiowa, and is now exhibited in the Plains Indian section of the U.S. National Museum (cat. no. 385, 892) (Fig. 7.9). The horizontal midriff seam of this dress is covered by a curved peplum, and the skin surface is elaborately but tastefully decorated with paint, beadwork, and rows of elk tooth pendants.

By the turn of the century Kiowa women were loading their best skin dresses with row upon row of elk teeth, and because elk teeth were rare, some Kiowa dresses came to have high monetary values. Millie Oytant was photographed in 1900 wearing an elk tooth dress valued at $1,000.[48] On May 15, 1902, the *King-Fisher Free Press* reported the recent sale of a Kiowa "squaw dress" at El Reno, Oklahoma, for $1,600. The article explained that the dress was so lavishly adorned with elk teeth that "the Indian woman who owned it thought that $1,600 was too much money to be invested in a dress." But the purchaser "thought he was lucky to get it at that price."

In 1948 I sought to purchase a fine example of an older Kiowa buckskin dress for exhibition in the then new Museum of the Southern Plains Indian from a dealer near Oklahoma City who displayed it rather prominently on the wall behind a sales counter. His Indian wife promptly informed me, "That dress is not for sale. It is very rare. We bought it from a dealer in Brooklyn."

Even so, less lavishly embellished buckskin dresses have continued to be made by women of the southern Plains tribes for wear on special occasions when these symbols of Indianness are displayed. I observed that the pretty young ladies from the Plains Indian tribes of western Oklahoma—the Southern Cheyenne, Southern Arapaho, Comanche, Kiowa, and Kiowa-Apache—who were selected to represent their respective tribes as "princesses" in the 17th Annual American Indian Exposition at Anadarko during August 1948 all wore buckskin dresses. All were painstakingly made, tastefully decorated, and spotlessly white, and were in the basic three-piece style their grandmothers

Fig. 7.9. Three–piece skin dress, Kiowa. Collected in 1890s. (Cat. no. 385,892, Department of Anthropology, U.S. National Museum, Smithsonian Institution)

Fig. 7.10. Princesses representing five different tribes of Oklahoma at the 17th Annual American Indian Exposition, Anadarko 1948. Left to right: Arapaho, Kiowa, Comanche, Delaware, Seminole. (After a photograph by John C. Ewers.)

might have worn during the 1890s. The Comanche princess was a descendant of renowned chief, Quanah Parker, and the other princesses were from prominent families in their tribes (fig. 7.10). The princesses who represented the tribes of eastern Oklahoma—whose ancestors had been accustomed to wear cloth clothing even before they were removed to Oklahoma from the Eastern Woodlands—tribes such as the Seminole and Delaware—wore different styles of cloth dresses.

CONCLUSION

If my findings with regard to the history of the southern Plains Indian women's clothing differ markedly from Wissler's conclusions of 1915 it is not because I have failed to follow my former teacher's suggestion: "For perishable objects, such as costume, real historical data are

148

usually available." They are, and they clearly indicate that the skin dress, made from *three* not two, *skins*, was a nineteenth-century innovation among the tribes of the southern plains, which began to appear among these Indians at about the same time as did the trade cloth dress. The earlier and aboriginal woman's ensemble among the tribes of this region was of two skins, comprising two garments—a skirt and a poncho. The poncho was commonly dispensed with in warm weather. This costume was like that worn by other Indian tribes living to the south and west during the early historic period, and like that worn by Indian women of Vera Cruz, Mexico, during the Classic Period, A.D. 300–900.

This style of clothing was quite *unlike* that worn by Indian women of the northern plains at the time of first white contact or at any other time of which we have any record. From the viewpoint of women's clothing, the Great Plains was *not* a single culture area, but part of several clothing areas. I am confident that this fact will be made abundantly clear when a comprehensive history of North American Indian women's clothing is written. In that history, factors of climate and of resource availability over the broad expanses and factors of acculturation resulting from Indian-white contacts should emerge as important ones, while the boundaries of the classic culture areas will pale into insignificance.

※ ≡ ※ ≡ ※

CHAPTER EIGHT

Folk Art
in the Fur Trade
of the Upper Missouri

DURING MUCH of the nineteenth century the Upper Missouri region, from the mouth of the Platte to the Rocky Mountains, was still remote Indian country peopled by numerous warring tribes. Until 1855 the only white settlements in this vast area were isolated fur trading posts, compact groupings of a few buildings surrounded by tall, strong palisades which provided protection from Indian raids. It may be difficult to visualize these trading posts as centers of artistic activity, or to consider the practical men who managed and manned them as sponsors or creators of art. Yet written and pictorial evidence does exist to support such views.

The largest and most successful firms engaged in the fur trade of the Upper Missouri during this period were the American Fur Company and its successor, Pierre Chouteau, Jr., and Company. With headquarters in St. Louis, they operated a chain of posts that stretched up the Missouri as far as the mouth of the Marias in Blackfoot country and the territory of the Crow Indians in the middle Yellowstone Valley. By 1832 the American Fur Company had inaugurated steamboat service as far as Fort Union at the mouth of the Yellowstone, some fifteen hundred miles up the Missouri. These company boats not only carried employees and supplies but also occasionally transported artists who wished to picture the Indians, the wildlife, and the varied landscape of the Upper Missouri region. The artists were housed and fed at company posts for periods of a few days to several months. Post managers, clerks, and interpreters introduced the artists to the chiefs, warriors, women, and children of the many Indian tribes that came to trade and thus made it possible for the artists to portray picturesque red men and women from life. Traders also arranged for the artists to visit nearby Indian camps and villages, to witness Indian ceremonies, and to picture various activities in Indian life. Hunters at the posts took artists on exciting buffalo chases and showed them the smaller wild animals of the region.

Had it not been for the kind attentions of the fur traders such artists as George Catlin, Karl Bodmer, and John James Audubon could not have created their rich pictorial record of the Upper Missouri country. No other section of the trans-Mississippi West was portrayed so extensively and so vividly by artists during the days before the development of photography.

But the artistic interests of these companies were not limited to the encouragement of transient artist-explorers. The companies employed men who possessed artistic talent to embellish their wilderness posts in order to make them more attractive to Indian customers and to create decorative objects to give or to sell to prominent Indians. Few original works are extant, and not many of the artists can be identified by name, but contemporary writings and drawings attest to the existence of a lively folk art among the fur traders of the Upper Missouri country prior to 1855.

The largest, handsomest, and busiest trading post on the Upper Missouri was Fort Union. It was constructed in 1829 at the mouth of the Yellowstone in the territory of the Assiniboine, reputedly at the request of Iron Arrow Point, a prominent chief of the tribe. The post soon attracted trading parties of Plains Cree and Plains Ojibwa from the north and east, Crow from the Yellowstone Valley, occasional parties of Gros Ventre, Piegan, and Blood Indians from higher up the Missouri, and even half-breeds from the Red River Valley during their extended buffalo-hunting excursions westward. Competition for the trade of these nomadic tribes was keen among the smaller American firms and the powerful Hudson's Bay Company.

At Fort Union in 1833 the German scientist-explorer Maximilian,

151

Fig. 8.1. Certificate of good conduct by Jean Baptiste Moncravie, 1833. Given to the Assiniboine, Le Brechu, by Kenneth McKenzie. (Courtesy Joslyn Art Museum, Omaha, Nebraska; Gift of the Enron Art Foundation)

prince of Wied-Neuwied, obtained a copy of an artistic device used by the American Fur Company to attract and hold its Indian customers. This earliest known record of fur trader art was an elaborately and colorfully decorated certificate, designed by Jean Baptiste Moncravie (also known to his contemporaries as Montcrévier, or Moncrévie) and presented to Le Brechu, an Assiniboine chief, by Kenneth McKenzie, the enterprising factor of Fort Union (see fig. 8.1).

A cartoonlike bubble between the white trader and the Indian in the act of shaking hands advises the Indian: "Give your hand to the white man, offer him food and conduct him on his road and you will always find friends in your time of need." At the lower right is the further admonition: "Respect your Trader and he will always keep your pipe filled and make your heart glad." In the center of the American flag are the words: "Le Brechu an Assiniboin receives this testimonial of his good conduct, from K. McKenzie, 1833." Doubtless the astute McKenzie took pains to interpret the text of the document when he presented it to the illiterate chief. The Indian's "good conduct" implied not only that he was friendly to whites, but that he often brought his band to Fort Union to trade.[1]

A decade later the artist-naturalist John James Audubon spent two months at Fort Union. His journal contains a detailed description of the fort written by Edwin T. Denig, then chief clerk at the post. The account mentions a "painting of a treaty of peace between the Indians and whites executed by J. B. Moncrévier, Esq." which was prominently displayed above the twelve-foot-wide main gate. Although no date is given for the painting, it may have commemorated the 1831 treaty Kenneth McKenzie negotiated between the Assiniboine and their traditional enemies, the Blackfeet. This was a diplomatic coup for the American Fur Company since it paved the way for the establishment of the first American trading post in the country of the Blackfeet who previously had been hostile to American traders and trappers.[2]

An unsigned and undated watercolor painting of Fort Union, preserved in the Jesuit Missouri Province Archives in St. Louis, clearly shows Moncravie's portal painting framed and in place over the main gate. Whether this panoramic view was created by Moncravie or another artist, it appears to have been the work of an ambitious amateur who had some difficulty with perspective. We can be sure it was executed at some time before the roof of the main building was raised, in 1850. (See fig. 8.2.)

Jean Baptiste Moncravie was born in Bordeaux, France, about 1797. He emigrated to the United States and enlisted in the army at Philadelphia in 1820, serving until 1829 when he was honorably discharged. His original enlistment papers describe him as twenty-three years old, five feet three inches tall, with a light complexion, hazel eyes, and light brown hair, and a musician by profession. Moncravie must have

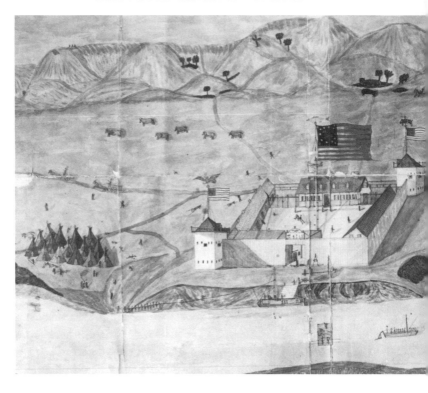

entered the employment of the American Fur Company shortly after
he left the army since his name appears in the company ledger books
as early as April 15, 1830, and Maximilian knew him as a clerk at
Fort Union in the fall of 1833. Audubon found him to be a helpful
and enjoyable companion, referring to Moncravie as "one of the most
skillfull of the hunters" at the fort. Audubon accompanied him on
buffalo hunts and arranged for the cooperative Frenchman to procure
other animals for his collection. The great naturalist was impressed
by Moncravie's keen sense of humor and storytelling skill. He wrote
on August 7, 1843: "We had a sort of show by Moncrévier which was
funny, and well performed; he has much versatility, great powers of
mimicry, and is a far better actor than many who have made names for

154

Fig. 8.2. Panoramic view of Fort Union, showing Moncravie's painting over the main gate. Unsigned, undated watercolor antc 1850. (Courtesy Jesuit Missouri Province Archives, St. Louis, Missouri)

themselves in that line."[3]

Moncravie's weaknesses were liquor and women. Charles Larpenteur, a fellow trader of very jealous nature, criticized his inept supervision of the reconstruction of Fort William by laborers from Fort Union during the fall of 1834, claiming that "he was a little too fond of whisky, and much too fond of the squaws, to do this work or any other as it should be done." While in charge of keelboatmen transporting company supplies and trade goods upriver to the Blackfoot post in June 1844, Moncravie reputedly drank too much and gave twenty gallons of company liquor to his men. The convivial Frenchman survived a threatened firing by reimbursing the company for the $400 worth of liquor. Moncravie continued in company service on the Missouri near

Fig. 8.3. Jean Baptiste Moncravie. Portrait by Albert Bierstadt in 1863. (From Fitz Hugh Ludlow, *The Heart of the Continent*, 1870)

Fort Pierre until the summer of 1849 when he was transferred to the Platte. Two years later he was said to be in the Pawnee country.

Albert Bierstadt, the famous painter of western scenery, met and executed a pen-and-ink portrait of Jean Baptiste Moncravie while traveling across Nebraska in 1863 in the company of Fitz Hugh Ludlow on their way to the Rockies (fig. 8.3). In his 1870 book, *The Heart of the Continent*, Ludlow identified Moncravie as an Indian interpreter and described him as "sixty-eight years of age yet looks scarcely over fifty, full of French grace, fire and vivacity, grafted with American humor." Ludlow added incorrectly that Moncravie "went west with Audubon, and became so well acquainted with frontier life that at the close of the ornithological tour he determined to stay among the Indians." Ludlow was greatly impressed by Moncravie's linguistic accomplishments, writing: "He is now perfectly conversant with six different Indian languages—the Sious, Pawnee, Arapaho, Blackfeet, Crow, and Flathead. . . . He furnished me with some vocabularies, valuable not only in the practical, but the philological point of view." Ludlow sent these vocabularies to George Gibbs at the Smithsonian Institution, where they still are preserved in the National Anthropological Archives.

Apparently Ludlow did not know that this many-talented Frenchman was also an artist, or that he arrived on the Upper Missouri in 1831, a year before George Catlin visited that region. So Moncravie really was Fort Union's first white artist.

There is no evidence that Moncravie returned to the Upper Missouri; he died in Brownsville, Nebraska, July 18, 1885, at the age of eighty-eight.[4]

Moncravie's major known artwork, that painting over the main gate to Fort Union, may not have survived his departure from the Upper Missouri. The framing of the painting does appear in a distant view of the fort in a pen-and-ink drawing by Alexander Murray, another artist-employee of the fur company, executed in 1845 (fig. 8.4).

However, there are no later references to this painting. It must have been removed within the next six years,[5] for there are no references to Moncravie's work in the lengthy diary and numerous drawings of the fort by Rudolph Friederich Kurz, who spent the fall and winter of 1851 at the post. A Paris-trained artist and a friend of Karl Bodmer, Kurz had journeyed from his home in Switzerland to draw and to paint Indians in the American wilderness. To support himself while pursuing his artistic objectives Kurz worked as a clerk at the fort.

Soon after Kurz arrived at Fort Union, Edwin T. Denig, now post manager, found a number of practical uses for the artist's talents. He directed Kurz to paint a portrait of Pierre Chouteau, Jr., the major

157

Fig. 8.4. View of Fort Union. Pen–and–ink drawing by Alexander Hunter Murray in 1845. (Reproduced in *Field and Stream* 70, 1908)

shareholder in the firm that bore his name, in the gable above the entrance to the imposing main building. Kurz copied Chouteau's likeness from a medal typical of those the company presented to Indian leaders. A Chouteau medal, dated 1843, is shown with Kurz's own drawing of the larger-than-life portrait in place, embellished with a decorative frame painted on the building in figure 8.5.

At Denig's request Kurz also painted a knee-length, life-size portrait of the post manager to hang in his office where it would be seen by prominent Indian visitors. The Swiss artist also designed decorative cotton flags, which the Indians could obtain for twenty dressed buffalo robes. The striped flags, resembling banners, were approximately fifteen feet long and three to four feet wide, with an eagle, wings outspread, holding an Indian calumet in its claws. One of these flags appears on the left wall in Kurz's sketch of Denig in council on October 19, 1851, with Le Tout Pique, a Cree chief; on the rear wall hangs Kurz's portrait of Denig (fig. 8.6).[6]

The most important company post between Fort Union and St. Louis was Fort Pierre situated on the west side of the Missouri above the mouth of the Teton or Bad River and across the river from the present city of Pierre. Fort Pierre was the principal trading center in the country

Fig. 8.5. View of the main building at Fort Union, with portrait of Pierre Chouteau, Jr., under the gable, by Rudolph F. Kurz, 1851 (Courtesy of the Bernisches Historisches Museum, Bern, Switzerland) Kurz copied the portrait from the 1843 trade medal as shown in the insert. (Courtesy Missouri Historical Society, St. Louis)

of the strong and aggressive tribes of the Teton Sioux. When Thaddeus Culbertson, brother of Alexander Culbertson, a partner in the company, visited the fort on May 26, 1850, he briefly described in his journal "two large gates over each of which there is a large picture intended to represent scenes of interest to the Indian."[7]

These portal paintings must have been executed sometime between 1847 and 1850. Father Point's pencil sketch of Fort Pierre in 1847 shows no superstructures above the gates. Kurz's panoramic view of Fort Pierre, sketched on July 4, 1851, shows the panels above both gates and roughly indicates that there were human figures on the one above the main gate.[8]

Fig. 8.6. Rudolph F. Kurz sketch of Cree chief Le Tout Pique and trader Edwin T. Denig in council at Fort Union, 1851. (Courtesy the Gilcrease Museum, Tulsa, Oklahoma)

More detailed renderings of these portal paintings appear in a large watercolor of the fort, signed by "F. Behman, Del." (fig. 8.7), which is preserved in the National Archives. This view, accompanied by a brief written description of the fort, in which the buildings are identified by the numbers appearing on the drawing, was sent to the quartermaster general by Pierre Chouteau, Jr., and Company on April 7, 1855. The neat and sturdy appearance of the fort in this watercolor may not have truly reflected its condition at the time. But the picture must have been useful to the company in selling Fort Pierre to the United States in 1855 for $36,500 as the first military post on the Missouri in the Dakotas. Army officers who took possession of the fort that summer found both the stockade and buildings badly in need of repair. The fate of the portal paintings is not known.[9]

Behman's watercolor depicts both the compositions and the subjects of the paintings. The enlarged details from this rendering show that the scene over the main gate (fig. 8.8a) was surmounted by a decorative eagle with outspread wings. The scene is obviously an interior occupied by six seated and two standing figures. The man standing in the center is presenting something to the man seated nearest him. This may be either a trading or a treaty-making scene. The gate on the right (fig. 8.8b) opens into the fort's corral and stables. The painting over this gate depicts a mounted Indian or white man chasing three buffalo against a background of rounded hills.

These must have been the "scenes of interest to the Indians" first mentioned so laconically by Culbertson in his description of Fort Pierre in the spring of 1850. The council scene is reminiscent of the brief description of Moncravie's earlier portal painting at Fort Union. Perhaps he executed these paintings also before he left Fort Pierre in 1849, or possibly they were the work of Frederick Behman, who was employed by the Chouteau company as a clerk on the Upper Missouri from 1843 to 1856.[10] Behman's watercolor view of Fort Pierre demonstrates that he possessed sufficient artistic talent to have executed the Fort Pierre portal paintings.

This evidence for the existence of a white man's folk art on the Upper Missouri during the period 1830 to 1855 is sufficient to demonstrate that folk art preceded agricultural settlement in this region. Decorative certificates, trade flags, and portal paintings, as well as pictures of trading posts, were created by at least four clerks in the employ of the major company engaged in the Indian trade of the region.

Precedents for each type of art can be found. Certainly George Catlin and Karl Bodmer executed views of Fort Pierre and Fort Union some years before Murray, Kurz, and Behman pictured either of them. During the 1790s St. Louis traders, seeking to extend their business to the tribes of the Upper Missouri, presented colorful Spanish flags, decorated certificates, and medals bearing the likeness of the Spanish king to prominent Indian chiefs of the region. These presents, furnished by the governor of Spanish Louisiana in New Orleans, were intended to encourage Indian loyalty to Spain and to stimulate the business of

Fig. 8.7. Panoramic view of Fort Pierre. Watercolor by F. Behman, 1855 or ante. (Courtesy the National Archives)

Spanish subjects, licensed to trade with the Indians on the Missouri. Soon after Upper Louisiana was transferred to the United States in 1804, Lewis and Clark ascended the Missouri on their overland exploration to the Pacific. They held councils with tribal chiefs at various points on the river, during which they formally presented American flags, certificates, and medals bearing the likeness of President Jefferson to Indian leaders.[11] These were intended to replace similar symbols of peace and friendship which these Indians had received from Spain and England.

162

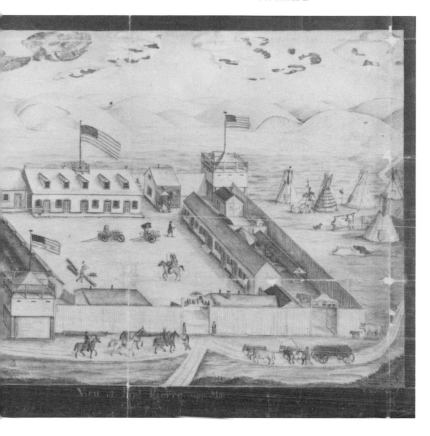

Officials of the American Fur Company observed that Indian leaders prized these gifts as symbols of status which enhanced their standing with their people. Possessors of these symbols expected to be treated with respect by the whites. The traders, following the precedent set by three governments and using American flags or modifications thereof and eagles in the design of these articles, expected that the recipients would bring fine furs and buffalo robes to trade at the company posts rather than to its competitors. The traders must have regarded these relatively inexpensive symbols as justifiable business expenses.

163

Fig. 8.8A. Detail of painting over main gate, Fort Pierre, from Behman watercolor.

Fig. 8.8B. Detail painting over corral gate, Fort Pierre, from Behman watercolor.

The large portal paintings prominently displayed over the gates of Forts Union and Pierre can be traced to different sources. They should be considered, perhaps, as extensions into the remote Indian country of an advertising medium that had been employed in American towns and cities since colonial days. Literacy had not been required to comprehend the pictorial signs over the entrances to colonial shops and taverns. The unschooled Indians of the Upper Missouri must have understood clearly the message of the colorful scenes over the trading post gates: "See here, this is the place. You can see that we are your friends. Come in and trade with us."

※ ▆▆ ※ ▆▆ ※

CHAPTER NINE

Intertribal Warfare
as the Precursor
of Indian-White Warfare
on the Northern Great Plains

ONE HUNDRED SEVENTY-FIVE YEARS AGO Alexander Henry, Northwest Company trader, built a post on Park River, a western tributary of the Red River near the present international boundary in eastern North Dakota. Looking westward from that isolated post on September 18, 1800, he saw the plains covered with buffalo as far as he could see. This practical businessman wrote in his journal for that day: "This is a delightful country, and were it not for perpetual wars, the natives might be the happiest people on earth."[1]

What Henry observed of the Park River region might have been said of the entire northern Great Plains at that time. The region between the Mississippi and Red River on the east to the Rocky Mountains, and from the valley of the Saskatchewan southward toward the Platte, was rich in buffalo and other natural resources for the support of an Indian population that numbered considerably less than one person per square mile. That Indian population was divided and subdivided into a host of small societies in which the major political unit was the tribe. The sedentary, horticultural tribes were further divided into politically autonomous villages, and the nomadic tribes into hunting bands, each with its chief or chiefs. The individual Indian owed his loyalty to his tribe. He boasted, "I am a Crow," or "I am a Cree," depending on his tribal membership.

The roots of intertribal warfare in this region can be found in the very nature of tribalism itself—in the common disposition of the members

of each tribe to regard *their* tribe as "the people," and to look upon outsiders with suspicion. This is not to deny that other and more specific
causes for intertribal conflict existed—competition for choice hunting
grounds, capture of women, or horses, or inanimate property, and individual desire for recognition and status through the winning of war
honors. But in an atmosphere charged with intertribal distrust even an
imagined slight by an outsider could lead to retaliation against other
members of his tribe, while more violent acts of aggression could lead
to revenge raids in force. The history of intertribal warfare in this region seems to show that it was much easier to start a war than it was
to end one, and that hostilities between neighboring tribes persisted
from generation to generation.

Certainly the northern Great Plains constituted a vast and complex
theater of intertribal warfare from prehistoric times until after the last
of the great buffalo herds was exterminated in the western portion
of this region during the mid-1880s. Archaeological evidence cannot
pinpoint the beginnings of intertribal warfare in this region. But it
certainly reveals the existence of warfare in prehistoric times.

Along the Missouri River in the Dakotas numerous pre-Columbian
village sites have been identified. Their occupants lived in semiperma
nent earth lodges, and gained their subsistence by raising crops in the
fertile river bottoms and by hunting on the open plains. Painstaking
excavations of many of these sites since World War II have revealed
that the villages were fortified by ditches and palisades, and that some
of them were protected by more elaborate defensive works which included bastions constructed at carefully calculated intervals. A few of
these fortified villages were the homes of some of the earliest agri-
culturalists in the region—settlers who preceded Columbus by four
or more centuries. Later prehistoric villages were inhabited by ancestors of the Arikara, Mandan, and Hidatsa, who continued to surround
their villages with strong palisades until the end of intertribal warfare
in this region. George Catlin and Karl Bodmer pictured the fortified villages of the Arikara, Hidatsa, and Mandan during their travels
up the Missouri in 1832–34. Donald Lehmer has described both the

167

prehistoric and historic fortified villages as they have become known to archaeologists, and has presented typical fortification plans of several varieties.[2]

Surely the prehistoric villagers would not have taken elaborate steps to fortify their settlements had they not been endangered by enemies. Whoever those enemies were, we can be sure that they were other Indians.

Farther west evidences of prehistoric warfare as practiced by presumably nomadic Indians appear in the paintings of armed warriors on the walls of Pictograph Cave, south of Billings, Montana. These warriors carry large, circular shields which were considerably larger in proportion to the men who bear them than were the rawhide shields used by mounted Indian warriors of this region during the nineteenth century. The shields were decorated with designs that probably represented the supernatural helpers and protectors of the warriors who carried them. William Mulloy, who excavated and interpreted this site, has assigned these shield-bearing warriors to the Late Prehistoric Period, A.D. 500–1800.[3]

That intertribal warfare was rife in this region at the time these Indians first became known to whites is evident in the writings of the pioneer explorers. French explorers of the western Great Lakes during the mid-seventeenth century heard of Indians living to the west whom the Algonquian tribes called "Nadoessis," that is, "Enemies." That name has survived in the abbreviated form of Sioux for the Dakota tribes. When Father Allouez met some of these Sioux at the head of Lake Superior during the mid-1660s he described them as "warlike" and reported that they "have conducted hostilities against all their enemies, by whom they are held in extreme fear."[4]

Other whites who met tribes of the easternmost portion of this region before those Indians acquired horses commented on the intertribal warfare of the time. Henry Kelsey, a young Hudson's Bay Company employee, was the first white man known to have written an account of his travels with Indians on the northern Great Plains. During the summer of 1691 he accompanied some Assiniboine and Cree Indians onto the buffalo plains west of Lake Winnipeg seeking to extend his firm's trade to a more distant tribe who were enemies of both the Assiniboine and the Cree—the "Naywatome," or "Mountain Poets." The identity of that tribe is still uncertain. Kelsey had difficulty persuading his Indian companions to enter the "Enemies Country," for those enemies had killed three Cree women the previous spring. When he met the "Naywatome" chief, that leader protested that the Cree had killed six lodges of his people. But after Kelsey gave him a gun and other presents, the chief agreed to meet the trader the following spring and to go with him to Hudson's Bay to trade. In the end he did not do this because the Cree killed two more men of his tribe before spring arrived.

Brief observations appended to Kelsey's journal mention two specific war customs of the Assiniboine and Cree—the wearing of a feathered bonnet which "they put to use when the enemies are in sight believing yt will save yin from being killed," and the carrying of a sacred pipestem "upon any expedition as when they go to seek out their Enemies' tracks." Mention of these items by Kelsey in 1691 assures us that war medicines played important psychological roles in the intertribal warfare of this region at the time of first Indian-white contact.[5]

Pierre La Vérendrye, the French trader from Montreal, had tried unsuccessfully for several years to end the warfare between the Assiniboine-Cree and the Sioux before he wrote in 1743, "It will take a long time to pacify all these tribes who from time immemorial have been deadly enemies."[6]

Some idea of the scale of this intertribal warfare during the early 1740s may be gleaned from Father Couquart's report of an attack on the "Sioux of the Prairies" by a combined Cree-Assiniboine force in 1742. In a four-day battle more than two hundred Cree and Assiniboine warriors killed seventy Sioux, "without counting women and children." Their Sioux captives "occupied in their march more than four arpents," that is, over eight hundred feet. Even if those captives were marched in single file as much as four feet apart, that would yield a figure of some two hundred captives taken in a single battle. The 270 or more Sioux killed or captured in that action may have equaled or exceeded the entire population of a hunting band of thirty lodges.[7]

The Blackfoot tribes farther west had acquired horses when David Thompson first met them in the shadow of the Rockies during the 1780s. But older men told him of Piegan warfare with the Shoshoni in the days when their people were still afoot. They said that the greatest damage was done when a large war party surprised, attacked, and wiped out a small hunting camp of ten to thirty lodges, but that casualties were few in pitched battles between relatively equal numbers of warriors. There was no close contact in those larger battles. The opposing forces formed lines facing each other, barely within arrow range. They protected themselves behind large rawhide shields, and shot arrows from their long bows. They also wore body armor of several thicknesses of rawhide which restricted their movements. Darkness generally brought an end to the battle.[8]

During the middle decades of the eighteenth century the tribes of the northern Great Plains began to acquire horses from the south. After the nomadic tribes gained enough well-trained horses to enable them to ride to battle, the static, primarily defensive action became obsolete. No longer could warriors hide behind their shields in safety. Cumbersome hide armor was discarded; shields were reduced in size to cover only the vital parts of the body of the mounted warrior; and bows were shortened for easier use on horseback. The mounted charge brought combatants quickly into close contact, where they wielded lances, clubs, and knives in man-to-man combat. Warriors had more opportunities to distinguish themselves—to win coveted war honors, or to be killed. And casualties increased.

Even so, large-scale battles between nearly equal forces, numbering more than one hundred on each side, do not appear to have been very common in nineteenth-century intertribal warfare in this region. Reliable figures on casualties in those battles are almost impossible to find. Indians tended to overestimate the numbers of enemies and the damage they inflicted on them. Body counts may have been even less accurate in this warfare than in actions in Vietnam. Nevertheless, there were some battles that have been fairly well documented from both sides, battles in which Indian losses probably exceeded the Indian casualties in the oft-described tragic action at Wounded Knee in 1890.

In a battle near the Cypress Hills during the summer of 1866 the Piegan are reputed to have killed more than three hundred Crow and Gros Ventres. Shortly before that engagement the Gros Ventres had killed Many Horses, the Piegan head chief. His followers were seeking revenge. The ferocity of their charge caused their enemies to panic, and the killing is said to have ended only when the victors decided they had enough of it. Piegan survivors remembered this as a great victory; the Gros Ventres recalled it as their most disastrous defeat.[9]

Horse raids against enemy camps came to be the most numerous military actions. A thorough study of the vast literature on all the tribes of this region would yield references to hundreds of horse raids in which they participated. Even so, the great majority of horse raids probably were never referred to in the literature. Horse raids were well-organized, small-scale military expeditions, similar to the commando raids of World War II. Their limited objective was to capture horses from the enemy without loss to themselves. (My elderly Indian informants who had participated in these raids preferred the word "capture" to "steal.") Yet these parties sometimes found more action than they anticipated, either on their outward journey, while trying to take horses from enemy camps, or on their hurried rides homeward. Some whole parties were wiped out; others lost one or more members. Some raiders survived forty or more of these dangerous expeditions; others lost their lives in their first effort.[10]

It seems probable that, during the nineteenth century, more Indians of this region lost their lives on horse raids than on large-scale revenge or scalp raids, simply because the horse raids were many times more numerous. Nor is there reason to doubt that, during the historic period, many more Indians of this region were killed by other Indians in intertribal wars than by white soldiers or civilians in more fully documented Indian-white warfare.

Had each of the tribes of this region continued to stand alone, fighting all neighboring tribes, it is probable that many of the smaller tribes either would have been exterminated or their few survivors would have been adopted into the larger tribes, thereby increasing the latters' military potential. Tribes survived, maintained their identity, and strengthened their own war effort by forming alliances with one or more neighboring tribes. The allied tribes had common enemies, and sometimes launched joint expeditions against them. The sharing of common enemies appears to have been a stronger motive for some alliances than the fact that the tribes involved spoke related languages. One of the major alliances during the historic period was that of the Siouan-speaking Assiniboine and the Algonquian-speaking Plains Cree. One of the best-documented intertribal battles in this region was the Assiniboine-Cree attack on a small Piegan camp outside Fort McKenzie on August 28, 1833. Prince Maximilian and Karl Bodmer witnessed, described, and illustrated this battle.[11]

We can better understand the complex history of Indian warfare on the northern Great Plains if we view it in terms of a history of the four major alliances of tribes and their struggles to maintain a balance of power in the intertribal warfare of this region. All of these alliances were established before the United States acquired Louisiana in 1803, and all predate the Lewis and Clark Expedition. Different numbers of tribes were included in these alliances. At its height each alliance may have included tribes totaling from about 15,000 to more than 25,000 people. During the nineteenth century a few tribes, or portions of tribes, changed their alliances in response to changing conditions, such as the threat of remaining at war with an aggressive, nearby enemy alliance. Some tribes tried to go it alone over a period of years with almost disastrous results. The four major alliances are here named after their core tribes—the tribes that remained together throughout the historic period without shifting alliances. But we should understand that other tribes were members of those alliances for extended periods.

On the northwestern plains were the tribes of the Blackfoot alliance, of which the core tribes were the Piegan, Blood, and North Blackfoot (Siksika), who shared a common language and customs and were often

172

referred to collectively as Blackfoot or Blackfeet. These tribes moved westward and then southward during the eighteenth century, and in so doing displaced the Kootenai, Flathead, and part of the Shoshoni from lands near the Rockies in southern Alberta and northern Montana. Their alliance, at the height of its power during the first half of the nineteenth century, also included the small Athapascan tribe of Sarsi and the larger Algonquian-speaking Gros Ventres. The members of this alliance raided the smaller tribes west of the Rockies and tried to prevent them from hunting buffalo on the plains east of those mountains. They aggressively raided the Crow Indians in the Yellowstone Valley; and they stemmed the westward push of the Plains Cree and Assiniboine on their eastern flank. They also made life miserable for white mountain men, who sought to trap beaver in the Missouri headwaters region, twice driving them from Montana before 1825. There is no indication that the tribes of the Blackfoot alliance coveted more hunting grounds after about 1830 as they then occupied one of the finest buffalo-hunting areas on the plains, an area twice the size of New England.

Yet six years after they negotiated their first treaty with the United States in 1855 as members of the "Blackfoot Nation," the Gros Ventres, in a dispute over stolen horses, left the Blackfoot alliance and became allies of their former enemies, the River Crow and Assiniboine.

During the decade of the 1860s small Blackfoot parties attacked miners, ranchers, and freighters in Montana. But after Col. E. M. Baker's punitive expedition killed some 173 Indians of Heavy Runner's peaceful band on the Marias on January 23, 1870, the tribes of the Blackfoot alliance posed no serious threat to white settlement in either Montana or Alberta. Weakened by a smallpox epidemic and demoralized by whiskey, they were in no condition to organize a war against the whites. Their chiefs found that peace with the whites was in the best interest of their people. The North Blackfoot head chief, Crowfoot, refused both Sitting Bull's invitation to join him against the whites after the Battle of the Little Big Horn, and the Métis's offer to join them in the Riel Rebellion on the Saskatchewan in 1885.[12]

To the east of the tribes of the Blackfoot alliance in Canada and Montana were the tribes of the Assiniboine-Cree alliance. There can be little doubt that military considerations motivated the initial alliance of these core tribes. In 1700 Pierre-Charles Le Sueur, the French trader among the Sioux, explained the formation of that alliance. "The Christinaux (Cree) have obtained the use of firearms before the Scioux did, by means of the English at Hudson's Bay, continually waged war against the Assinipoils, who were their nearest neighbors. The latter, finding themselves weak, asked for peace, and to render it more firm, allied themselves to the Christinaux, taking their women to wife."[13]

Together these tribes pushed westward, exerting strong pressure on the tribes of the Blackfoot alliance. The Assiniboine extended their hunting grounds into the valley of the Missouri above the Mandan villages and as far west as Milk River, and the Cree moved up the Saskatchewan north of the present international boundary. These tribes both traded and fought with the Mandan and Hidatsa. They fought the Crow until after midcentury. Until 1851 they were at war with all of the tribes of the Blackfoot alliance.

Then the Upper Assiniboine made peace with the Gros Ventres, and mingled and intermarried with them on Milk River. During the waning years of intertribal warfare these two tribes also were friendly to the River Crow, while they launched joint war parties against the Piegan.[14]

The westernmost band of Ojibwa on Red River became part of the Assiniboine-Cree alliance because they shared a powerful common enemy, the Sioux. As these people moved westward to become known as the Plains Ojibwa early in the nineteenth century, they mingled with the Cree and Assiniboine. Some warriors of these three tribes also accompanied the large, well-organized buffalo-hunting excursions of the Red River Métis southward into Sioux country in later years. Some of the Cree also aided the Métis in the short-lived and unsuccessful Riel Rebellion on the Saskatchewan in 1885.

During the 1850s and early 1860s, as the buffalo range contracted westward, the Yanktonai Sioux aggressively overran the eastern portion of the Assiniboine hunting grounds in North Dakota and Montana, and some 150 lodges of the Lower Assiniboine living in closest proximity to the invading Sioux found it expedient to make peace with them. Even so, those Assiniboine who came to share the same agency and later the same reservation of Fort Peck with the Yanktonai, did not join their longtime Sioux enemies in their conflicts with the Army of the United States.[15]

Doubtless the third alliance, the Mandan-Hidatsa alliance, was an old one which antedated the separation of the Crow Indians from the Hidatsa and their movement westward to become a nomadic tribe. Tradition has it that the Crow and Hidatsa quarreled over buffalo, but by the beginning of the nineteenth century they certainly had patched up their differences, and during the eight remaining decades of intertribal warfare in this region the Crow and Hidatsa frequently exchanged friendly visits.

South of the Mandan and Hidatsa on the Missouri were the Arikara, Caddoan-speaking relatives of the Pawnee of Nebraska. During the early years of the nineteenth century the Arikara were sometimes friends and at other times enemies of the Mandan and Hidatsa. But they shared one powerful enemy, the Sioux. In their efforts to go it alone against the Sioux, the Arikara failed. In 1832 they were forced to abandon their earth lodge villages, and the Sioux burned them. The Arikara survived by eventually moving upriver and firmly joining the Mandan-Hidatsa alliance. During the last two decades of intertribal warfare in this region the Mandan-Hidatsa-Arikara shared a common fortified village, Like-a-Fishhook, on the Missouri in North Dakota, where they, with difficulty, survived repeated Sioux attacks.[16]

No tribe of the northern Great Plains held a more precarious military position than did the Crow after they drove the Shoshoni from the middle Yellowstone Valley late in the eighteenth century. Never a large tribe, the Crow were surrounded by powerful enemies—the tribes of the Blackfoot alliance and the Assiniboine-Cree alliance on the north, the Sioux on the east, the Cheyenne on the south, and the Shoshoni on the west. The Crow were too far from their old allies, the Mandan and Hidatsa on the Missouri, to benefit from their help in the fight for survival. From the 1830s on white men who knew and admired the Crow Indians gloomily predicted their extermination by their more numerous enemies. For several years during the 1850s their country was so overrun by enemies that white traders abandoned their posts in Crow country. Yet the Crow Indians survived, due to their courage and military prowess, and their diplomacy. The Crow succeeded in making their own alliances not only with such tribes as the Nez Percé from west of the Rockies, the Gros Ventres, and the Assiniboine, but also with the whites. Thirty years ago, various elderly Blackfoot informants expressed the opinion that the Crow were saved from extermination by their alliance with the whites.[17]

The word Dakota translates as "allies"; the word Sioux as "enemies." During the historic period of intertribal warfare on the northern Great Plains the tribes of the Dakota, or Sioux, alliance came to be regarded as aggressive enemies by more tribes than did any other Indian people of the American West. Close-knit by language, and by the tradition that they comprised "seven council fires," the seven major divisions of the Dakota included about 25,000 people in 1790. The four eastern divisions were known collectively as the Santee. The membership of the middle division consisted of the Yankton and Yanktonai. The western division, known as the Teton or Western Sioux, included some 40 percent of the total population of the Sioux alliance.

The Dakota movement—from the time the Dakota first became known to white men in the middle seventeenth century until the decade of the 1870s—was westward from the Great Lakes and the Mississippi Valley across the Dakotas, southward into Iowa and Nebraska, and westward into Montana and Wyoming. Pressures from the Ojibwa and other Woodland tribes, as well as the attractions of buffalo hunting on the Great Plains, encouraged the early Sioux movement westward. The pace of this movement accelerated after the Sioux obtained both firearms and horses. Some of them reached the Missouri before 1750. Some Teton bands may have been hunting as far west as the Black Hills a century before Custer found gold in that region. Before the end of intertribal warfare they were raiding the Shoshoni near the Rockies.

During this period of nearly two centuries the Dakota fought at least twenty-six other Indian tribes, as well as the Red River Métis and the Army of the United States. Their enemies included at least ten Woodland tribes, and all the tribes of the Assiniboine-Cree alliance and the Mandan-Hidatsa alliance, and much less frequently some of the tribes of the Blackfoot alliance. They also fought the Iowa, Omaha, Oto, Ponca, and Pawnee south of the area we are considering.

During their westward movement the Dakota displaced many tribes from portions of their hunting grounds: the Iowa, Omaha, Ponca, Pawnee, Arikara, Mandan, Hidatsa, Assiniboine, and Crow all lost some territory to the Dakota. There can be little doubt that the continued westward push of the Teton and Yanktonai during the 1850s and 1860s was stimulated by the contraction of the buffalo range westward and the increasing scarcity of game in former Dakota hunting grounds farther east. Yet too few historians appear to be aware that this movement onto lands described as Mandan, Hidatsa, Arikara, Assiniboine, and Crow in the Fort Laramie Treaty of 1851 helped to make a shambles of that treaty. Furthermore, it should be noted that the most dramatic battles fought between the army and the Dakota were on lands those Indians had taken from other tribes since 1851.[18]

Actually the Dakota had been allies of the army in its first Indian campaign on the Great Plains—against the Arikara villages in 1823. When the soldiers and the Dakota reached the fortified Arikara settlements the Dakota were eager to attack. But Colonel Leavenworth was reluctant to do so. While he delayed, the Arikara escaped during the night. Edwin T. Denig, who knew the Dakota well for over twenty years prior to 1855, attributed their disdain for the courage of white soldiers to their memory of the army's failure to attack the Arikara villages in 1823.[19]

The Teton regard for the Crow Indians as worthy, longtime enemies is revealed in their own records—their pictorial winter counts—in which many years were remembered for specific actions in their prolonged war with the Crow. Indeed, the first entry in the famed Lone Dog Winter Count recorded, "thirty Dakotas were killed by Crow Indians" in 1800–1801.[20] In addition to winter counts, the autobiographical drawings by Sioux chiefs and warriors also tell of actions against other tribes. Drawings by Running Antelope, a famous Hunkpapa chief, reveal that he counted coup most frequently upon the Arikara during the decade of the 1850s. In one action he killed two Arikara chiefs, while in another ten men and three women died at his hand.[21]

After the Fort Laramie treaties of 1851 and 1868, chiefs of the Crow and of the village tribes complained repeatedly to their agents of Dakota aggression. These tribal leaders petitioned for the aid of whites to help redress their grievances against the aggressive Dakota. In 1864 the Arikara chief, White Shield, reminded Agent Mahlon Wilkinson that the Arikara and Hidatsa chiefs who had signed the Fort Laramie Treaty in 1851 had since been killed by the Dakota, and called upon the Great Father to keep his promise of sending soldiers "to help us keep the Dakotas out of our country."[22]

At a council with their agent in 1870 two old chiefs of the village tribes called upon the whites to punish the Sioux. White Shield forcefully expressed his opinion that "the Sioux will never listen to the Great Father until the soldiers stick their bayonets in their ears and make them." The Hidatsa chief, Crow's Breast, further advised, "If the Great Father wants to be obeyed by the Sioux he must give them some prompt punishment. We are Indians and know how to deal with Indians. They will not keep the peace until they are severely punished. Either keep them a year without gifts or provisions, or cut off some camp, killing all, and the rest will then listen."[23]

In view of these reactions to the Dakota, is it any wonder that the tribes of the old Mandan-Hidatsa alliance became allies of the whites in their wars with the Sioux? On the other hand, is it surprising that the Sioux, unable to induce any of their traditional enemies among the tribes of the Dakotas and Montana to join them, found allies in the Cheyenne and Arapaho farther south?

Most white historians have been accustomed to approach the subject of the Indian wars of the American West from an ethnocentric viewpoint. To them, "the Indian wars" have meant only "Indian-white wars"—wars which interrupted the steady flow of the expansion of white settlement. Thus, in 1934, Paul I. Wellman began his *Death on the Prairie* with an account of the Minnesota Massacre of 1862. Dee Brown's better-known *Bury My Heart at Wounded Knee* (1970) began at the same point in its discussion of the Great Plains Indian wars. Even though he subtitled his book "An Indian History of the American West," Brown ignored the fact that Indians of different tribes had very different views of that history. He sought to interpret the Indian wars of the northern Great Plains only as Indian-white wars, and described them only from the viewpoint of the Sioux hostiles. Brown brushed off as "mercenaries" those tribes that became allies of the whites against the Sioux.

To view the Crow and Arikara as "mercenaries" of the whites is to overlook the long history of Indian-Indian warfare in this region. The Crow, Arikara, and other tribes had been fighting the Sioux for generations before they received any effective aid from the whites. They still suffered from Sioux aggression during the 1860s and 1870s. Surely the history of Indian-white warfare of the northern Great Plains cannot be understood without an awareness of the history of intertribal warfare in this region.

179

CHAPTER TEN

The Making
and Uses of Maps
by Plains Indian Warriors

EARLY IN MAY, 1877 a young lieutenant, less than a year out of West Point, marched up the valley of the Yellowstone River from Fort Buford to Fort Keogh as an officer in Troop I, Seventh Cavalry. It was less than a year since Sitting Bull's warriors overwhelmed the Seventh Cavalry on the Little Bighorn. Sitting Bull was still at large, and the buffalo range on the northern plains was contracting relentlessly.

Years later that young lieutenant became General Hugh L. Scott, Chief of Staff of the U.S. Army. He recalled that on that march in the spring of 1877 an Indian traveled with his party for protection against the Sioux. His name was Poor Wolf (sometimes translated as Lean Wolf; fig. 10.1). He rode an old pony, and carried both a lance and a muzzle-loading gun. Scott remembered that Poor Wolf also "made for me a very good map of the location of Sitting Bull's camp at that time and of the country where buffalo were."[1]

Poor Wolf was then second chief of the Hidatsa, a small tribe of farming Indians who had been fighting the nomadic Sioux since long before Poor Wolf or Sitting Bull was born. Poor Wolf's maternal uncle had been chief of one of the Hidatsa villages before the destructive smallpox epidemic of 1837. That plague nearly wiped out the Mandan and greatly reduced the numbers of the Hidatsa. In succeeding years the Hidatsa earth lodge dwellers continued to give ground to the much more numerous Sioux. They moved up the Missouri, and united with remnants of the Mandan and Arikara tribes in one large village, known as Like-a-Fishhook, for their mutual preservation. Much of the

Fig. 10.1. Poor Wolf, second chief of the Hidatsa, in 1881. (Courtesy National Anthropological Archives, Smithsonian Institution)

land that was defined as the hunting grounds of the Arikara, Mandan, and Hidatsa at the Fort Laramie Treaty of 1851 was overrun by the aggressive Sioux during the next decade.

During the 1860s and early 1870s, Poor Wolf and his fellow chiefs of the Arikara-Mandan-Hidatsa alliance repeatedly sought government aid in their conflict with the Sioux. In 1869 they reckoned that "if the Great Father will supply us with arms and ammunition, so that we can defend our fields against the hostile Sioux, we will plant and raise enough to support ourselves."[2] But by 1870 the Arikara chief, White Shield, was urging more drastic and aggressive action by the whites, saying, "The Sioux will never listen to the Great Father until the soldiers stick their bayonets in their ears and make them."[3]

Whites who knew him regarded Poor Wolf as a "modest speaker" in council, but he was very proud of his personal war record against the Sioux. During a visit to Washington in 1881, he drew several pictures on paper illustrating his leadership of war parties and his counting of coups in battle with those traditional enemies. (See fig. 10.2 for an example of Poor Wolf's art.) He also drew on a small piece of cardboard a lightly penciled map depicting one of his horse-raiding exploits against the Sioux. It is here reproduced, redrawn from the faint original in the National Anthropological Archives at the Smithsonian Institution. So, even though that map Poor Wolf drew for Lieutenant Scott in 1877 may no longer be extant, we do have an example of his cartographic skill and his clever use of graphic symbols (Map 10.1).

Poor Wolf was not content merely to record the geographic setting of that horse raid, he tried to convey the action as well. This raid must have taken place some time after the establishment of Fort Buford in 1866, for it was a successful theft of a horse from a Sioux encampment near that fort. In Map 10.1, *a* clearly identifies Poor Wolf as the successful horse raider by the pictographic signature of a lean wolf above his head. He designated his home village *b* by a cluster of circles representing earth lodges at the far right. He shows his outward-bound upriver course afoot by a series of dotted lines. He reveals the complexity of the settlement at Fort Buford by a square *d* representing the government buildings, circles *e* indicating lodges occupied by some Hidatsa married to Sioux, and crosses *f* identifying an encampment of Sioux living in the tipis nearby. The cross within the square *g* identifies still another element in the community at that time, a white man married to a Sioux woman. Poor Wolf recorded his successful return journey astride his captured horse by a line of hoofprints. The larger watercourses between Forts Berthold and Buford—the Missouri River

Fig. 10.2. Poor Wolf's drawing of his fight with the Sioux at age twenty–three. (Courtesy National Anthropological Archives, Smithsonian Institution)

(1), and its major tributaries—are designated by solid lines. Poor Wolf showed that he traveled south of the Missouri, crossing Dancing Bear Creek *p*, the Little Missouri *o*, and the Yellowstone River *n*, rather than the northern tributaries of Tule Creek *j*, Little Knife River *k*, White Earth River *l*, and Muddy Creek *m*.

Long before the United States Army became involved in military actions against the largest and most aggressive Plains Indian tribes— the Sioux, Blackfoot, and Comanche—French, English, and American explorers and traders learned of the skill of some Indian leaders in mapping more extended areas. Indeed, it is most probable that the first Plains Indian drawings on white men's paper were maps. Some of these were executed quite early in the colonial period to help pale-faced explorers who had no previous knowledge of the country they were about to traverse.

As early as 1680, Father Louis Hennepin was much impressed by

183

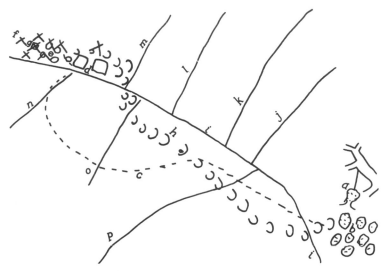

Map 10.1. Poor Wolf's map of his capture of a horse during his raid on the Sioux near Fort Buford. After his original pencil drawing in the National Anthropological Archives, Smithsonian Institution.

the cartographic skill of the Sioux chief, Ouasicoude, who "with a Pencil, mark'd down on a Sheet of Paper, which I had left, the Course that we were to keep for four hundred Leagues together. In short this natural Geographer described our Way so exactly, that this Chart served as well as my Compass could have done. For by observing it punctually, we arrived at the Place which we design'd, without losing our way in the least."[4]

Apparently that map covered the route from the Mississippi River near the Falls of St. Anthony (present St. Paul, Minnesota) to the Jesuit mission at Green Bay by way of the Wisconsin and Fox rivers. Hennepin made no reference to a scale on this map, but the observant Italian, Beltrami, who traveled among the Sioux in Minnesota in 1823 was not only impressed by the fact that those Indians made maps on tree bark, but that "these maps want only the degrees of latitude and longitude to be more correct than those of some of our visionary geographers. They measure only by the number of days required to travel over them; and as they are very well acquainted with the territories they inhabit, immense as they are, they can fix on their maps the precise time requisite to attack an enemy's post, or for a new and more excursive chase."[5]

On February 7, 1801, a Blackfoot Indian chief, named The Feather, drew a rough map for Peter Fidler, Hudson's Bay Company trader-explorer, at Chesterfield House on the Red Deer River near the border of the present Canadian provinces of Saskatchewan and Alberta. That Indian cartographer drew a double line to show the southward extension of the main chain of the Rocky Mountains for more than thirty-three day's travel by a Blackfoot war party. He delineated by solid lines the major rivers, by a series of inverted-U symbols the prominent uplifts on the plains east of the Rockies, and located by small ovals some thirty-one tribes living to the southward, both east and west of the Continental Divide, which were known to him. Fidler added the names of the rivers and landmarks indicated on the map. He also numbered each oval and provided an explanatory key in which both the Blackfoot name and the English translation were given for each Indian tribe or major grouping located on this map.

This map, preserved in the Archives of the Hudson's Bay Company, and reproduced in the *American Heritage Book of Indians* (1961: 324–25), is a very significant historical document. It reveals that a Blackfoot Indian helped a British trader to map the plains and the Rockies of present-day Montana fully four years *before* the Lewis and Clark Expedition traversed this region on their epic overland trek to the shores of the Pacific Ocean. Fidler claimed that at the time this map was drawn only 2 of the 31 tribes located on it had visited the English trading posts. Because the very great majority of the tribes named on the map were enemies of the Blackfoot at the time, the map reveals the very extensive knowledge of enemy territory possessed by a Blackfoot Indian at that time—at least as far to the southward as the Shoshoni in present-day Wyoming. That winter Fidler noted that Blackfoot war parties who embarked on raids against the Shoshoni expected to return fully "two moons" later.

It is obvious that this map was executed according to a notion of scale. That scale was based on a unit of a day's march or "number of nights the Inds. slept in going from one place to the other."[6]

Josiah Gregg, the experienced overland trader to Santa Fe, found that an old Comanche chief, Big Eagle, was able to map an even wider area. The Comanche, renowned as the largest and most aggressive tribe on the southern plains, raided southward from their home camps in present western Oklahoma and Texas deep into Old Mexico. In mid-May 1839 Gregg met Big Eagle at Chouteau's trading post on the Canadian River. Gregg was bound for Chihuahua, but had never been there. He was delighted to find that Big Eagle was well acquainted with the whole Mexican frontier, from Santa Fe to Chihuahua, and even to the Gulf. He gave Big Eagle a sheet of paper and a pencil and asked him to draw a map of the prairies. Gregg assures us, "This was very promptly executed; and although the draft was somewhat rough, it bore, much to my astonishment, quite a map-like appearance, with a far more accurate delineation of all the principal rivers and the plains—the road from Missouri to Santa Fe and the different Mexican settlements—than is to be found in many of the engraved maps of these regions."[7]

But what of the Indians' making of maps for use in planning their own travels or conduct of their own military operations?

A detailed description of Comanche mapmaking as an aid to the conduct of their raiding operations was obtained by Col. Richard I. Dodge. While on duty at frontier posts in Texas during the 1850s, Dodge became well acquainted with Pedro Espinosa, a Mexican scout and guide, who had been captured by the Comanche when he was a boy of about nine in ca. 1820, was adopted into the tribe, and lived some nineteen years among them.

Dodge wrote that Espinosa

told me that when he was a boy-prisoner among the Comanches, and the youngsters wished to go on a raid into a country unknown to them, it was customary for the older men to assemble the boys for instruction a few days before the time that was fixed for starting.

All being seated in a circle, a bundle of sticks was produced, marked with notches to represent the days. Commencing with the stick with one notch, an old man drew on the ground with his finger, a rude map illustrating the journey of the first day. The rivers, streams, hills, valleys, ravines, hidden water-holes, were all indicated with reference to prominent and carefully described landmarks. When this was thoroughly understood, the stick representing the next day's march was illustrated in the same way, and so to the end. He further stated that he had known one party of young men and boys, the eldest not over nineteen, none of whom had ever been in Mexico, to start from the main camp on Brady's Creek, Texas, and make a raid into Mexico as far as the city of Monterey, solely by memory of information represented and fixed in their minds by these sticks.[8]

Edwin T. Denig, who traded with the Sioux, Assiniboine, and their Indian neighbors on the Upper Missouri for two decades prior to 1855, was impressed by the tendency of most elderly Indians to illustrate their oral accounts of travels, battles, and other events by "drawing maps on the ground, on bark with charcoal, or on paper if they can get it."[9]

He collected three examples of Assiniboine mapmaking on paper, one of which covers a very large area and is reproduced here (Map 10.2). He titled that map "Map of the north side of the Missouri river from Fort Union, mouth of the Yellowstone, to Fort Benton mouth of the Maria, drawn by a Assiniboine warrior at Fort Union Dec. 27, 1853. The artist was not acquainted with the country on the south side of the Mo. The dotted line is their usual war path to the Blackfeet. Names of rivers etc. were written under his direction and explanation." Presumably Mr. Denig added the compass rose.

Actually this map covers an even larger area than its title indicates—westward from Fort Union to the Rocky Mountains, a distance of some four hundred or more miles. If one will compare this map with a modern map of the state of Montana he can gain some conception of the strengths and weaknesses of Indian mapping. Perhaps the most obvious discrepancy in the Indian map appears in the orientation of some river courses and mountain masses–especially the course of the upper portion of Milk River, of the Missouri River west of Fort Benton, and of the main chain of the Rocky Mountains. This Indian map may illustrate a fairly common tendency in Indian mapping to become less accurate the farther they were carried from the common hunting grounds of the tribe to which the mapmaker belonged.

Even so, a knowledge of this map would be generally useful to an Assiniboine warrior bound westward to steal horses from a Blackfoot camp somewhere in the neighborhood of the Big Belt–Little Belt–Big Snowy Mountains region, and who desired to avoid any concentrations of enemy Indians near the major trading post of Fort Benton. It shows the succession of southward-flowing tributaries of the Missouri to be crossed in the early stages of his journey and the mountain masses from which to take his bearings as he proceeds westward—the Bear Paws, Sweetgrass Hills, and the main chain of the Rockies. Even though the Rocky Mountains are skewed the map suggests that after the traveler comes in sight of them he should proceed southward and parallel to the Rockies until he approaches the target area after crossing the Missouri. Raiding parties could not anticipate that a small map of so large an area would lead them directly to an enemy camp of nomadic Indians. It was customary for such parties, as they neared their general target area, to send scouts ahead to search out the enemy camp and report back to the main party.

Doubtless, too, many Indian maps have been criticized unjustly for not providing detailed information which the Indian cartographer had no desire to include. It is easy to criticize the Sioux Chief Red Horse's

---

Map 10.2. *On facing page,* an Assiniboine Indian Map Showing the Route War Parties Followed Westward When Raiding Blackfoot Camps for Horses. Fort Union, December 27, 1853. (Courtesy National Anthropological Archives, Smithsonian Institution)

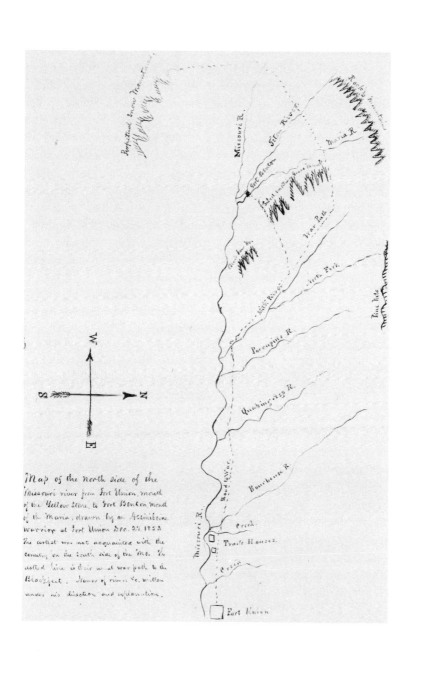

Map of the North side of the
Missouri river from Fort Union, mouth
of the Yellow Stone, to Fort Benton mouth
of the Maria, drawn by an Assiniboine
Warrior at Fort Union Dec. 27, 1853
The artist was not acquainted with the
country on the south side of the Mo. The
dotted line is their usual war path to the
Blackfeet. Names of rivers &c. written
under his direction and explanation.

map, unfortunately captioned "Map of the Little Big Horn Battlefield," for not showing topographical details of the battlefield. But this hardly appears to have been the purpose of the Indian cartographer. Rather, it appears that Red Horse was trying to locate this historic action within the *entire theater of warfare* in which the Western Sioux operated at that time—extending westward as far as the Wind River Mountains and beyond to include the lands of their distant enemies, the Shoshoni.[10]

Our data on Indian mapping seems to suggest that Plains Indians did create maps for their own use before the end of their intertribal wars and their conflicts with whites. Perhaps most of these maps were executed with more ephemeral materials than pencils on paper. Many were traced in the earth or sand with a stick or a human finger. Consequently they were short-lived phenomena—not the kind of document to be preserved in archives, libraries, or museums.

We have found repeated references to Indian use of a scale in their mapmaking. However, the unit of measurement in that scale was not the mile or the kilometer but the day's journey. That, in itself, may account for some of the apparent distortions in Indian maps, for the day's journey was a variable unit. It varied with the nature of the terrain to be traversed—level or hilly, open or wooded, dry or broken by several stream crossings of varying difficulties, or combinations of these factors.

Surely Plains Indians created maps for planning military operations as well as for recounting past military accomplishments. Perhaps we may never know the extent to which experienced Indian war leaders, familiar with the topography and the natural landmarks of the region in which they fought whites, drew maps to assist them in planning their operations and informing their followers of those plans. It would seem strange indeed if Indians who had made and used maps as visual aids in intertribal warfare had not also employed them in fighting non-Indians in the same theater of warfare.

※ ▄▄▄ ※ ▄▄▄ ※

CHAPTER ELEVEN

Women's Roles
in Plains Indian Warfare

MOST STUDENTS of Plains Indians have recognized warfare as a significant aspect of Plains life in the eighteenth and nineteenth centuries, and they have tended to treat warfare as a men's activity. Well then, what about the drawing by a Cheyenne Indian in a ledger book (fig. 11.1)? It pictures an Indian woman, nude to the waist and clutching her rifle. But how accurate is it as an interpretation of women's roles in Plains Indian warfare?

Evidence demonstrates that women were much involved in a number of ways besides providing encouragement to their menfolk. Women's roles were both passive and active ones. They exulted in the thrill and excitement of victory; they also suffered the humiliation and agony of defeat.

In 1832 the American artist George Catlin found it difficult to accept the accuracy of the war honors story of the Mandan Four Bears, told on a painted robe he gave to Catlin (fig. 11.2a). Could Four Bears have been so lacking in chivalry as to kill enemy women? Indeed Catlin reported: "I incurred his ill-will for a while by asking him whether it was manly to boast of taking the scalps of women? And his pride prevented him from giving me any explanation or apology. The interpreter, however, explained to me that he had secreted himself in the most daring manner, in full sight of the Ojibbeway [Chippewa] village, seeking to avenge a murder, where he remained six days without sustenance, and then killed two women in full view of the tribe, and made his escape, which entitled him to the credit of a victory,

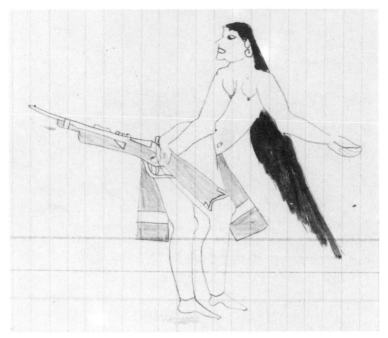

Fig. 11.1. A woman warrior drawn by a Cheyenne artist before 1899. (Manuscript 166,032, National Anthropological Archives, Smithsonian Institution)

though his victims were women."[1]

Four Bears was not the only prominent chief to record with pride his killing of enemy women. Running Antelope, one of the chiefs among the Hunkpapa Sioux before Sitting Bull gained a prominent position in that tribe, compiled a record of killing ten men and three women in the year 1856 (fig. 11.2b).

Ledger drawings by late nineteenth-century Cheyenne warriors portray women's deaths in warfare. A drawing in the Crazy Dog Ledger portrays a mounted Cheyenne warrior delivering an apparently fatal lance thrust to the breast of a Crow woman.[2] Another drawing pictures a Cheyenne warrior chasing and killing two Kiowa women (fig. 11.3).

Fig. 11.2A. Mandan chief Four Bears killing two Chippewa women, as painted on a buffalo robe before 1832. (From Catlin, 1841, vol. 1, facing p. 154)

Fig. 11.2B. Hunkpapa chief Running Antelope's pictorial record of his killing ten enemy men and three women in 1856. (Mallery, 1893. fig. 816)

Fig. 11.3. Cheyenne killing of two Kiowa women, as pictured in a Cheyenne ledger book, pencil and crayon, 1881. (Courtesy The Frontier Army Museum, Fort Leavenworth, Kansas. Leave 66.50.1)

There is an earlier reference to a shift from the killing to the capture of enemy women during the historic period. David Thompson, a pioneer fur trader on the Canadian plains, told of a meeting of Piegan chiefs and warriors in 1783 or 1784 after that tribe had suffered population losses in the smallpox epidemic of 1781. At that meeting a chief stated that smallpox was a punishment for their having killed so many in warfare.

> The chief suggested that in the future enemy women [young women] must all be saved and adopted i.e. brought to our camps, and be adopted amongst us, to be our people, and make us more numerous and stronger than we are. Thus the Great Spirit will see that when we make war we will kill only those who are dangerous to us, and make no more ground red with blood than we can help, and the Bad Spirit will have no more power over us. . . . Everyone signified his assent to the Old Chief, and since that time, it has sometimes been acted

on, but more with the women than the boys and while it weakens our enemies it makes us stronger.[3]

Observe that David Thompson reported that the old chief's sage advice "has sometimes been acted on." Actually the killing of women persisted in intertribal warfare on the northern plains into the second half of the nineteenth century.

The fur trader Edwin T. Denig, while in charge of the American Fur Company's post of Fort Union at the mouth of the Yellowstone River during the 1850s, wrote: "The Assiniboin, Blackfeet, Sioux, Cree, and Arikara also kill women and children and dance as much for their scalps as for those of men."[4] At the same time Denig recognized that the Crows didn't kill enemy women and children. Why this difference? At that time the Crows were a relatively small tribe, but they occupied one of the best hunting grounds on the northern plains. They were surrounded by four larger enemy tribes—the Sioux, Blackfeet, Cheyenne, and Eastern Shoshone. They needed to increase their number while they fought desperately for survival. So they captured rather than killed the women and children of enemy tribes who fell into their hands.

Nevertheless, it is probably true throughout most of the historic period of intertribal warfare on the Great Plains that Indian women had more reason to fear being taken captive than being killed. Early in the historic period young Indian women captives became valuable pawns in intertribal trade, passing from the west to the more easterly tribes and to white traders at their early outposts in the wilderness.

There were said to have been Blackfeet and Gros Ventre women captives among the English on Hudson's Bay before Anthony Henday became the first Englishman to explore westward to the Upper Saskatchewan River in 1754.[5] He reported seeing "many fine girls who were captives" in the camps of those Indians. In 1772 Mathew Cocking found young people of both sexes taken as slaves and adopted into Gros Ventre families "who have lost their children, either by war of sickness."[6] During the 1770s the elder Alexander Henry saw Blackfeet

195

women and children who were slaves among the Assiniboine.[7] And during the first decade of the nineteenth century the younger Alexander Henry found that the Cree and Assiniboine still referred to the Blackfeet and Gros Ventre as "Slaves."[8]

During the late seventeenth and early eighteenth centuries, the Illinois Indians made something of a business of capturing women and children from the Plains tribes and passing them on to other Indians and French outposts farther east. These captives came to be known by the French word *pani*, often translated as Pawnee. However, the *pana* women and boy who were given to René-Robert Cavelier, Sieur De LaSalle, in 1682 were probably members of the Wichita tribe. The boy claimed that he had been passed eastward as a captive from tribe to tribe over a period of years before he was given to LaSalle.[9]

The Wichita, too, captured enemy women. "The chief object of [their] war expeditions was the taking of scalps and capture of women to be used as slaves. The hereditary enemies of the Wichita were the Apache, Osage, and Tonkawa."[10]

In the southwestern plains the Kiowa and Comanche took many captives from enemy tribes and from the Mexicans to strengthen their diminishing numbers during the nineteenth century. During the 1850s Indian Agent Robert S. Neighbors observed that the "Comanche sometimes take women prisoners, in which case their chastity is uniformly not respected."[11] At nearly the same time the Lipan Apache women were "noted for their prettiness and good features. On this account the Comanches have often made war upon the Lipans so as to take their women as prisoners."[12]

The best and most detailed description of intertribal slave raiding of Plains Indian women appears in the accounts of Illinois Indian raids on the Pawnee and Quapaw, about the year 1700.[13] Similarities in the organization and procedures between those early slave raids and the later horse raids of Plains Indians suggest that the raid for captives may have furnished the model for the horse raid of the Plains Indians.[14]

Although all Plains Indian women may have had reason to fear being killed or captured by the enemy, not all of them were content to stay home and pray for the safe return of their fathers, brothers, or husbands while the men were off raiding their enemies. There is ample evidence that a number of women of many tribes joined raiding parties and took active parts in them.

As early as 1751 the governor of New France, in a letter to the French minister, described a combined Comanche and Wichita attack on the Osage in which he stated "their women go to war with them."[15] In 1820 Capt. John Bell of Maj. Stephen H. Long's exploring expedition, returning overland from the Rocky Mountains down the Arkansas River valley, reported meeting three returning war parties from three different tribes of the southern plains. The first, composed of eight men and a woman of the Arapaho, was returning from an unsuccessful horse raid upon the Pawnee. The second, "about 40 men and 4 or 5 squaws" of Cheyenne, was returning with a Pawnee scalp. And the third, a party of "30 men and 5 squaws," were Comanche who had been badly beaten in a fight with the Otoe.[16]

A journal written at Fort Clark on the Upper Missouri for the date of April 24, 1839, reported the arrival at that trading post of "a war party of Arikaras on their way to the Pawnees to steal horses composed of 42 men and 2 women."[17]

A Kiowa woman accompanied her husband on a raid into Mexico in 1854, and another woman of that tribe joined a party of thirty-seven men to avenge an enemy killing of her husband.[18] The literature provides numerous references to women of the so-called hostile tribes who fought alongside men against the Army of the United States during the 1860s and 1870s.[19]

The Sioux artist, Amos Bad Heart Bull, drew the picture of an outward-bound Sioux war party leaving their home camp on foot (fig. 11.4). The partisan in the lead carries the pipe. The two women bringing up the rear carry packs on their backs as do the men. A note on this drawing in Lakota translates "women also go along." This was a small war party, comprising only six men and two women. The two women were probably wives of two of the men on the expedition.

Graphic portrayals of women warriors in action against their

197

Fig. 11.4. An outward-bound Sioux war party of six men and two women pictured by Amos Bad Heart Bull, detail. (Reproduced from *A Pictographic History of the Oglala Sioux*, by Amos Bad Heart Bull, text by Helen H. Blish, by permission of the University of Nebraska Press. Copyright © 1967 by the University of Nebraska Press. Copyright © renewed 1995 by the University of Nebraska Press)

enemies are exceedingly rare. Father Nicholas Point, a pioneer Roman Catholic missionary among the tribes of the northern Rockies during the 1840s, learned of Quilix, "a young Pend d'Oreille woman renowned for intrepidity in battle," who led a party of men of her tribe in the destruction of a Blackfeet war party.[20] Father Point's drawing of a woman warrior in action may have been intended to picture Quilix.[21]

Members of several Plains Indian tribes recalled successful women leaders of war parties. Two outstanding examples have become heroines of historical novels—Woman Chief[22] and Running Eagle.[23] There can be no doubt that both these women were successful war leaders. The trader Edwin T. Denig knew Woman Chief well during the 1850s and was the first to write of her successes as a war leader.[24] A Gros Ventre by birth, she was taken prisoner by the Crow Indians at the age of twelve and grew up to become a Crow war leader and to gain chiefly recognition in that tribe, only to be killed by her own people when she attempted to pay them a friendly visit. Denig learned that an Assiniboine woman who sought to emulate Woman Chief's success as a warrior was killed on her first expedition against the enemy.

The Piegan war leader, Running Eagle, came into prominence somewhat later. Weasel Tail, a Blood Indian, gained some knowledge of her through Old Chief White Grass, who had accompanied Running Eagle on several expeditions. Weasel Tail's account did not jibe with that of Schultz (1919) on a number of points. He said that when she was young, she married a Piegan, but her husband was killed by the Crows. She sought help from Sun to avenge her husband's death. Sun told her, "I will give you great power in war, but if you have intercourse with any other man, you will be killed."

Running Eagle was a large woman. On the warpath she wore men's leggings, a sort of undershirt doubled over like a diaper, a woman's dress, and a blanket coat.

Weasel Tail said that the men who followed her on war parties respected her highly. She was not proud. She always insisted that she was a woman, and she cooked for her war parties and mended the men's moccasins. When one of the men protested that it was not right for the party leader to do that kind of work she replied, "I am a woman. Men don't know how to sew."

Weasel Tail said that Running Eagle was successful on repeated raids on the horse herds of the Flathead Indians west of the Rockies. When those Indians learned that it was a woman who had been leading those raids, they determined to kill her. One time she entered a Flathead camp for horses when the Flatheads were on the lookout for a strange woman. A man saw her, and in his Salish language asked her name. She did not answer but backed away. He lifted his gun and shot her dead.

Some Blackfeet claimed that Running Eagle had not been faithful to her vow to the Sun: that she had sexual relations with one of the men of her war parties. "That was why she was killed."[25]

Marked differences of opinion have been expressed about the social roles of these women warriors. Capps said that Woman Chief "defied the limitations placed upon her sex and made the fierce warriors of the northern plains respect her."[26] On the other hand, Beatrice Medicine, a Sioux anthropologist, after reviewing the literature on Plains Indian woman warriors, concluded that the warrior role was not an unwomanly one, but it was an alternative one which the individual woman might accept if she so chose.[27]

What is known of these woman warriors does not suggest that they were sexual deviants. They did have to be powerfully motivated to assume a warrior's role in a culture where the great majority of women did not. A strong motivation was an important factor in the making of outstanding male warriors also. For example, White Quiver, who became a successful horse raider, was spurred on by the fact that his father was killed by Crow Indians; most of his daring raids were on Crow camps.[28]

An examination of the literature on Plains Indians reveals relatively little evidence of the torture of prisoners such as was common among the tribes east of the Mississippi in historic times. There is considerable evidence of the mutilation of dead enemies by Plains Indians and of women playing active roles in that mutilation.

The classic case involved the Blackfeet in their defense of an Assiniboine-Cree dawn attack on a small camp of Piegan just outside the walls of the American Fur Company's post of Fort McKenzie near the mouth of the Marias on August 28, 1833. This was the action the German naturalist, Prince Maximilian of Wied-Neuwied and his artist companion, Karl Bodmer, witnessed from the raised platform behind the stockade, and the one Bodmer illustrated in a view that portrays the intensity of the action and the use of a variety of deadly weapons at very close range.

After the attackers were driven off, Maximilian sought to obtain the skull of one of the enemy who had been killed. He found "The scalp had already been taken off, and several Blackfeet had engaged in venting their rage on the dead body. The men fired their guns at it; the women and children beat it with clubs, and pelted it with stones, the

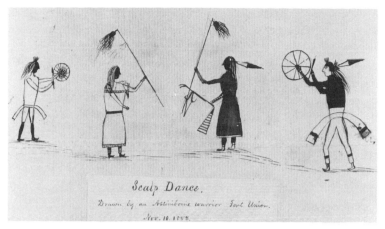

Fig. 11.5. Scalp Dance, drawn by an Assiniboine warrior at Fort Union, 1853. Pen–and–ink. (Courtesy National Anthropological Archives, Smithsonian Institution)

fury of the latter was particularly directed against the privy parts."[29]

The action of older women in emasculating the dead bodies of enemy males was well documented in the writings of other careful observers of Plains Indian warfare as far back as the 1790s. Jean-Baptiste Truteau, an experienced French trader and keen observer of the tribes of the Middle Missouri, described the frenzied mutilation of dead enemies by elderly Indian women: "I have seen these furious old hags near their dwelling themselves cut off the hands, limbs, [and] the virile parts of the dead enemies, hang them around the neck and at the ears, and dance thus at all the lodge doors of the village."[30]

The literature contains numerous references to the roles Plains Indian women played in the postraid victory celebration of their people. In the scalp dance it was customary for women to stand in the center displaying the trophies their husbands or other male relatives had taken in the recently concluded action. The scalps were held high, attached to the upper ends of slender willow poles (fig. 11.5).

Despite the heavy emphasis on the scalp, it was not the only part of an enemy that Plains Indians took as a trophy. Other extremities—most commonly hands—were severed from the fallen body, carried home, displayed in the victory dance, then thrown away. In a Cheyenne drawing of a scalp dance that followed the Indian victory over Gen. George Custer's cavalry on the Little Bighorn in June 1876, one woman holds a hand tied to the upper end of her pole.[31]

The widow of a warrior who failed to return from a raid against the enemy took no part in the public celebrations. Left alone, she went into extended mourning, cutting her long hair, and in some cases sacrificing a finger or scarifying her legs and arms. She would encourage her male relatives to avenge her loss in raids against the tribe that took her husband's life. She herself might accompany one of those revenge raids.

Weasel Tail, my aged Blood Indian informant, possessed a remarkably accurate memory of the details of his experiences:

> A lot of the old timers took their wives on war parties. Their wives wanted to go. But usually only a woman who as yet had no children would go on a war party with her husband. My wife was in five fights with me. She carried a revolver—a six shooter. Once she took a horse with a saddle, a bag of ammunition, and a war club on it. She said she loved me, and if I was to be killed she wanted to be killed with me.
>
> I was frequently a leader of war parties. On those parties my wife didn't have to do the cooking or other chores. We took boys 14 to 20 years old who cooked, rustled food and firewood for us in my day.[32]

Weasel Tail recalled that Red Crow, a Blood head chief, had a wife named Sings Before who took a gun from the enemy while on a war party with her husband. Weasel Tail named several Piegan men who took their wives on war parties. One of them was Young Bear Chief, whose wife, Annie Elk Hollering in the Water Bear Chief, accompanied him on several war parties and had taken things from the enemy (fig. 11.6).[33]

Wades in the Water, a fullblood Piegan, was probably the last man of

Fig. 11.6. Annie Bear Chief, a Piegan Indian who, as a young woman, accompanied her husband on war parties. (Photograph by John C. Ewers, 1943)

his tribe to take an enemy scalp in intertribal warfare. He was a young teenager at the time, and the action was a small-scale one against some Assiniboines. After he took the scalp of a fallen Assiniboine, his older brother, who was close by, told him to cut off the enemy's hand at the wrist. This he did, and his brother tied the wrist trophy to the bridle of Wades in the Water's horse for the return to camp. The hand was

203

carried in a victory dance, and then thrown away.[34]

Weasel Tail stated that the Blackfeet tribes did not ordinarily mutilate the dead. "If a man had a brother or a son killed by the enemy, and he went on a war party to avenge that killing, and one of the enemy was killed, this relative would mutilate the dead body. . . . But if there was no revenge [motive] there was no mutilation."

During World War II, the sun dance experienced a revival on the Blackfeet Reservation. Traditionally the pledger of the sun dance was a woman of unquestionable virtue who vowed to Sun that she would give the ceremony in return for Sun's help to her. During those war years, the pledger asked Sun for the safe return of the young Blackfeet who were serving in the armed forces. The wife of Swims Under, the pledger of the sun dance in 1943, on the climactic day of the ceremony, faced the sun in the western sky, held toward it a piece of the sacred tongue, and prayed for the welfare of her people and the safe return of their servicemen.

But what of those Blackfeet men who did not return? The old people consoled the mothers of those young men with a traditional saying: "It is better for a man to die in battle than of old age or sickness."

Proof that that belief was an old and widespread one among Plains Indians appears in the 1796 writings of Jean-Baptiste Truteau:

I myself have seen, when I resided for three consecutive years at the home of the nation of *Panis Republicains* [Pawnee] fathers and mothers sing near the bodies of their sons that had been brought back to the village to be interred, sons who had been killed in a battle between the *Halitannes* [Comanche] and the *Republicains* on open prairie at some distance from their summer hunting camp, which episode I witnessed. These women, mothers of the young men who were killed, holding a bow in one hand and an arrow in the other, sang near the bodies of their sons an air both gay and martial, thanking them for having given them [the mothers] the satisfaction of seeing them die at the hands of the enemy while fighting valiantly for the defense of their country, a death a thousand times preferable to the fate of him who on a wretched mat expires consumed by some deadly disease.[35]

CHAPTER TWELVE

The White Man's Strongest Medicine

On sunday, october 28, 1804, the Corps of Volunteers for North-Western Discovery neared the villages of the Hidatsa Indians at the mouth of Knife River on the Missouri. Those Indians were eager to see the strange Americans and their large twenty-oared keelboat, and Meriwether Lewis and William Clark obliged them by trying to satisfy the Indians' curiosity. The captains reported, "We entertained our visitors by showing them what was new to them in the boat; all which, as well as our black servant, they called Great Medicine, the meaning of which we afterward learnt."[1]

Some five weeks later Lewis and Clark observed that the Mandan Indians, close neighbors of the Hidatsa, applied the term "Great Medicine" to "every thing which they do not comprehend."[2]

Thus rather early in their twenty-eight months of travel in the western Indian country, Lewis and Clark became aware of a fundamental concept of primitive Indian religion—the belief that men, animals, and even strange objects of unknown origin possessed supernatural powers which were superior to the natural powers of men. All the western tribes shared this concept of medicine, and it was this belief in medicine that conditioned their attitudes toward the early white explorers and traders, and that distinguished Indian reactions to whites from white men's reactions to Indians in the early American West. Despite the fact that pale-faced explorers and traders did not fully understand all of the aspects of Indian life they encountered in the field, their approach to the Indians and their cultures was essentially secular, and their observations, for the most part, were objective. For Indians who believed in "medicine," however, early contacts with white men and the many strange and wonderful things they introduced into the Indian country provided a succession of deeply religious experiences. Indian reactions to whites and the manifestations of their culture tended to be quite subjective.

I know that some historians take the position that our records of early Indian-white relations must be biased because we have only the white man's written accounts of these interracial and intercultural contacts. This position sounds very logical, for there must also have been an Indian side to this story. In recent years ethnohistorians have been taking great pains to ascertain and to evaluate the Indians' role in Indian-white relations. We must nevertheless recognize that the Indians' belief in "medicine" complicates this problem. It pervades their oral traditions, and obscures and even falsifies the record of what actually happened in the early contacts between two quite different cultures in the remote Indian country in the early days.

Let me illustrate this point. We know that the European horse was diffused northward from the American Southwest so rapidly that the tribes living on the northwestern plains obtained horses *before* the first white explorers arrived in their country, but nevertheless it seems improbable that the Blackfoot tribes of present-day Alberta acquired their first horses more than two-hundred-fifty years ago. Logically, these Indians could have received their first horses in one of only four ways. They could have received these animals as gifts from or in trade with people who obtained horses before they did. Or they could have stolen their first horses from such a people. Or they could have captured their first horses as strays or runaways from the herds of a people who already possessed horses.

A quarter of a century ago I asked nearly a dozen aged Blackfoot Indians how their ancestors acquired their first horses. Only one of them gave an explanation which might be termed a historically logical answer. Other informants recited versions of one or another of several beautiful legends of the gift of horses to a member of their tribe by sky spirits or underwater spirits. Extreme ethnocentrism alone does not explain these Indian substitutions of mythological explanations for historical ones. These Indians regarded the horse as much more than a very useful domesticated animal. To them the horse was sacred—a godsend, whose origin demanded an explanation in the same mythical terms as they employed in their origin myths for their most revered Indian ceremonies—the sun dance, the medicine pipe, or the beaver bundle. In Blackfoot belief, these were gifts to their people from sky or water spirits. So it was that in less than two centuries the European horse became so completely integrated into the religious beliefs of these Indians that historically acceptable traditions of its first acquisition were lost.[3]

Other tribes of the Great Plains also regarded the horse as strong medicine. Witness the Sioux name for this animal—*shonka wakan*, "medicine dog." Witness also the existence among the Plains tribes of a secret and powerful horse medicine cult, whose members claimed to have acquired supernatural powers from horses which enabled them to control the actions of their own and their enemies' mounts, and to cure both sick horses and humans. The horse medicine cult may now be defunct among the Indians of the Blackfeet Reservation in Montana, but it was just twenty-four years ago that I left an all-night ceremony of that cult in which I witnessed the invocation of horse power through prayers, songs, and mimic dances, to cure several Indians who had been sickly that winter.[4]

Of the many inanimate objects from the white man's world which Indians came to regard as "medicine," one of the most highly and widely venerated was the gun. This curious hollow rod, which made such a frightening noise when the little trigger was pulled, and hurled a tiny missile so swiftly that the human eye could not follow its flight, and with such force that it could kill or cripple wild game or an enemy at a distance, inspired both terror and awe in the minds of primitive Indians. Three centuries ago Nicholas Perrot observed that "guns so astonished" the Indians of the Lake Superior region that they declared "there was a spirit within the gun, which caused the loud noise made when it was fired." At that time the Sioux possessed no firearms. When a delegation from that tribe visited the Ottawa and witnessed their firing of some guns, "the report of these weapons so terrified the Sioux that they imagined it was the thunder or lightning, of which the Outaouas had made themselves master in order to exterminate whomsoever they would."[5]

In 1673 Father Jacques Marquette learned that the Illinois used guns "especially to inspire, through their noise and smoke, terror in their enemies" to the west, who did not as yet possess firearms.[6] Other references in the white man's literature describe the panic created in the ranks of primitive tribesmen when they first encountered Indian enemies who fired guns at them. The noise and smoke of these strange weapons appear to have done more harm than their bullets. Indians gained a respect for the old muzzle-loading, smoothbore trade musket which was out of all proportion to its effectiveness as a lethal instrument.

Even after Indian tribes owned considerable numbers of guns some of them attributed their success or failure in the use of these weapons to "medicine" rather than to their abilities as marksmen. The Crow were well armed when the French trader, François Larocque, accompanied a hunting party of that tribe during the summer of 1805. He reported that when they killed no game, the chief complained that "someone had thrown bad medicine on our guns and that if he could know him he would surely die."[7]

Nearly three decades later Maximilian, Prince of Wied-Neuwied, learned of a Mandan ceremony for consecrating firearms. His description of this ritual indicates that it followed traditional patterns for Mandan religious ceremonies. The gun owner invited a group of men to a feast, and after eating and singing to the accompaniment of drums and rattles, "the host then takes the gun, cuts a piece of flesh, and with it rubs the barrel, and flings the meat into the fire; this is repeated thrice. He then takes up some of the water in which the meat was boiled, rubs the whole length of the barrel with it, pours the rest of the broth into the fire; and, lastly, takes fat, with which he rubs the whole gun, and then throws the remainder in the fire."[8]

There can be little doubt that both the European horse and the white man's gun became strong medicines for the Indians of the Great Plains. Nevertheless, taking a long view of this matter of great medicine among these Indians, it appears to me that the white man's strongest medicine was something more complex; something the primitive Indian became aware of only through close association with white men in his country, but something which he himself was not able to master. I refer to the ability of white men to record what they saw or experienced in the Indian country in precise detail through drawings, paintings, photographs, and the written word, and their ability to preserve these records for study by future generations of students. If the white man had *not* possessed these powers—if his art had not advanced beyond the stage of picture writing, if his literature had been limited to the recital of oral traditions which passed from generation to generation by word of mouth, and were distorted or elaborated on in the course of their retelling; and if he had no libraries, archives, and museums in which to preserve his records of the past—most of our record of Indian life and customs, and of Indian white relations of more than a century ago would have been lost.

But did the Indians themselves look upon these white men's skills as "medicine"? They most assuredly did. And one of the reasons these white men's powers so impressed the Indians was the limited development of their own skills in recording history.

Examples of picture writing by Plains Indians of more than a century ago are not uncommon. Some of them may still be seen in the form of crudely drawn human and animal figures in caves or on exposed rock surfaces in isolated localities widely scattered from Texas to Alberta. In the summer encampments of the Blackfoot tribes one may still see colorful mural paintings on the sides of tipi covers representing the sacred animals from which the tipi owners obtained their supernatural powers. These painted lodges have been transferred from one generation to another, and the designs transferred from buffalo hides to canvas, but there is a growing body of evidence to suggest that

209

the designs themselves are old, supporting aged Indian informants' contentions that these designs are much older than they are. In many museums are preserved pictographic biographies of Indian warriors. These are simplified pictorial records of the warriors' most heroic battle actions, or coups, painted on the inner surfaces of buffalo robes they wore as outer garments more than a century ago. A limited number of Indian "winter counts" also have been preserved. In these Indian records, one pictograph was drawn to represent a memorable event for each year. Arranged in chronological order, some of these "winter counts" begin with the late years of the eighteenth century—before the Lewis and Clark explorations. The crude pictographs on these Indian calendars, however, served primarily as mnemonic devices. They were not self-explanatory even to Indians, and unless they are accompanied by written explanations many of the pictographs appearing in these "winter counts" are as meaningless to present-day Indians as they are to non-Indians. These "winter counts" are the most precisely ordered of all Plains Indian records, but I am by no means sure that they were not inspired by mixed-bloods who had some knowledge of the white man's concept of the calendar.

I have found no evidence to indicate that before white artists visited the Plains tribes the Indian painters of this region had any knowledge of perspective, of color modeling, or of how to combine a number of pictorial elements into an integrated composition. They represented the human being by a featureless, knoblike head atop a blocky body, from which projected linear, sticklike arms and legs. This was a sort of pictorial shorthand. And there was *no* concept of portraiture.

Is it any wonder then that these Indians were awed by the magic of a George Catlin or a Karl Bodmer who painted lifelike two-dimensional images of individual Indians? Catlin, the first white artist known to have pictured the Mandan Indians, wrote from their village on the Upper Missouri to the New York *Commercial Advertiser* on August 5, 1832:

Perhaps nothing ever more completely astonished these people than

210

the operations of my brush. Soon after arriving in their village, I invited and painted the two principal chiefs; in a very few minutes after having exhibited them, it seemed as if the whole village was crowding upon me to see them. I was obliged to stop painting and place them in a conspicuous place where all could see them. The likenesses were recognized, and some commenced yelling, some singing and others crying. The next curiosity was to see *me*, and so great was the rush upon me that I was in danger of suffocation. The eager curiosity and expression of astonishment with which they gazed upon me, plainly showed that they considered me some strange being. They soon resolved that I was the greatest *medicine man* in the world, for they said I had made living beings.[9]

During the following summer (1833) the young Swiss artist, Karl Bodmer, gained a medicine man's reputation among the warlike Blackfoot tribes. He executed a fine likeness of the old warrior Bear Chief, shortly before that Indian took part in a battle with the Assiniboine and Cree outside Fort McKenzie. Prince Maximilian reported that Bear Chief returned to the fort "full of joy, and told us that no ball had touched him; doubtless because Mr. Bodmer had taken his portrait a few days before."[10]

During the summer of 1851 another Swiss artist, Rudolph Friederich Kurz, was picturing Hidatsa Indians at Fort Berthold when a cholera epidemic broke out among them. Recalling that a smallpox scourge had more than decimated the Mandans in 1837, only a few years after Catlin and Bodmer's portrait-making experiences with those Indians, the superstitious Hidatsa blamed Kurz for their current misfortune. Threatened with death if he remained at Fort Berthold, Kurz moved up the river to Fort Union. There he gained a reputation as a medicine man among the Assiniboine. He painted a portrait of the bourgeois of Fort Union, Edwin T. Denig. When one of Denig's Assiniboine wives viewed this portrait, it seemed to her that her husband's eyes followed her wherever she moved about the room, and she called out, "Ehah wakan! What witchcraft is this?"[11]

Six years later fun-loving Henry A. Boller, a young Philadelphian, was serving as a clerk at Fort Atkinson close to the Hidatsa and Mandan village of Like-a-Fishhook. He decorated the log walls of his quarters with colored prints of buffalo hunts which his Indian friends admired. When buffalo appeared near the fort, he convinced these Indians that his pictures were "strong medicine, and so long as I kept them on the walls buffaloes would be close and plenty." Boller did not identify the artist who executed these prints, but we know that Boller was a great admirer of Catlin and that lithographs of Catlin's paintings of buffalo hunts were available as early as 1844. It seems most probable, therefore, that colored reproductions of the works of that "medicine man" of the early 1830s were returned to the Indian country a quarter of a century later to assume the role of a buffalo-calling medicine among the Mandan and Hidatsa.[12]

The early Indians were accustomed to picture writing, but had no knowledge of any alphabet. Prince Maximilian noted that when the Blackfoot Indians commented on Bodmer's portraits, they said, "Bodmer could write very correctly," because "they have no proper word for drawing."[13]

In the 1850s Denig reported that "the writings, paintings, and pictures done by whites are considered great charms by some Indians, particularly the Crows, and are eagerly sought after as such."[14]

And Boller wrote home from Fort Atkinson on August 18, 1858:

> I never sit down to write, but what the, to them, mysterious movements of my pen do not attract the greatest attention, and wonder from the Gros Ventres some of whom are always on hand. They pick up the few books we have and look at the pictures and turn over the leaves as if they understood it perfectly. One morning I caught three gentlemen, among whom was the great fat "Rotten Bear," with an open book, upside down before them, which they gazed at as if they were actually reading for a long time—more than an hour! Perhaps they thought it was a medicine for the eyes.[15]

If you have followed me this far, I hope that we may take the next logical step together. If the white man's abilities accurately to record life and events in the Indian country were the white man's

strongest medicine, then surely we can extend this metaphor and refer to this century-old Missouri Historical Society—which houses
so many important records of the Indian country—as a uniquely
significant "medicine lodge," without committing any sacrilege.

I wish I knew exactly how many serious students of our western
Indians have found inspiration and information in the collections and
study rooms of your institution. Surely that number would be a most
impressive one. Although I cannot adequately express the indebted-
ness of all of these students to the Missouri Historical Society, I am
not going to miss this opportunity to "speak for myself, John," for I
have found in your Society sources of inspiration in research during
the last thirty years of your first century. Mention of a few ways in
which you have helped me may serve as examples of the kinds and
qualities of assistance this Society and its staff have offered to students
of ethnology and ethnohistory in the past.

Early in February 1949, I saw and read portions of a manuscript
in the collections of your Society which had been obtained from the
heirs of Alexander Culbertson, noted Upper Missouri Indian trader.
It was rich in detailed descriptions of life among five Indian tribes
of the Upper Missouri during the two decades *following* Catlin's and
Maximilian's explorations in that region, and it contained many references to prominent Indians whom Catlin and Bodmer had pictured in
the years 1832–34. The author's style, and some of the specific data
in this manuscript appeared to me to resemble closely that of Edwin
T. Denig's *Indian Tribes of the Upper Missouri*, which the Bureau
of American Ethnology had published in 1930. Your Society kindly
furnished photostats of pages from this manuscript which handwriting
experts of the FBI Laboratory in Washington compared with the handwriting in photographs of Edwin T. Denig's will. They concluded that
the handwriting of the two documents was that of the same individual.

Charles van Ravenswaay, then director of your Society, kindly
granted me the privilege of editing this newly identified Denig
manuscript, and the greater part of it was published in your *Bulletin*.
Later the entire manuscript appeared in book form under the title *Five*

Indian Tribes of the Upper Missouri. Your collection of American Fur Company papers provided salient facts about Denig's career of twenty-three years as a fur trader in the employ of that company on the Upper Missouri which I needed for my biographical introduction. I do not believe that any scholar has disputed my appraisal of Denig as "the most prolific and the most knowledgeable writer on the Indian tribes of the Upper Missouri in the mid-nineteenth century.[16]

A few years later I was preparing a monograph on those long, tubular shell (and later bone) ornaments worn by Plains Indians, and known to Lewis and Clark and generations of fur traders as "hair pipes." This study covered the manufacture, the distribution, and the varied uses of these trade ornaments by the Indians. Although my research took me to a number of museums and archives in this country and Canada, as well as to several Indian reservations, it was right here in St. Louis, in the Chouteau Papers of your Society, that I found the earliest reference to trade in hair pipes west of the Mississippi—a year before the Louisiana Purchase.[17]

More recently I was invited to write a chapter on William Clark's Indian Museum here in St. Louis, the first museum west of the Mississippi, for a book on the history of American museums which is now in press. The most helpful published accounts of Clark's Museum were the two excellent articles on the subject by John Francis McDermott which appeared in your *Bulletin*.[18] And the most valuable unpublished document proved to be the handwritten catalog of Indian artifacts in Clark's Museum compiled by William Clark himself and by his son Meriwether Lewis Clark. Where is this document? In the Archives of the Missouri Historical Society, of course.

No one can prophesy the breadth or extent of your Society's assistance to ethnohistorians during the next hundred years, but one thing appears certain. Ethnohistorians should be making greater use of your resources in the future than they have in the past. Until very recent years aged Indian informants on Plains Indian reservations were fruitful sources of detailed information on Indian life in buffalo days, much of which had not been recorded by contemporary observers, but since

World War II the last generation of Indians who participated fully in that life and possessed lively memories of it has passed away. The veterans of the intertribal wars and of the buffalo chase on horseback are gone. Now the scholar who wants to learn about Indian life on the Great Plains before the buffalo were exterminated *must* turn to books and documents, to collections of artworks and photographs, and to museum specimens collected in the field before the middle 1880s.

Much work remains to be done. If we consider *only* studies which involve the Indian tribes of the Upper Missouri, there is much gold that has not been mined. In 1902, Hiram M. Chittenden published his monumental *The American Fur Trade of the Far West* which was based in large part on the archives of this Society. He did not, however, consider the trade of the Upper Missouri after the early 1840s. Sixty-three years later John E. Sunder published *The Fur Trade on the Upper Missouri, 1840–1865*, also relying heavily on the records of your Society. I hope that another six decades will not pass before an able scholar carries the story of the Indian trade of the Upper Missouri on for another two decades and until the extermination of the buffalo in that region in the middle 1880s.

We now have adequate tribal ethnohistories for only a few of the Upper Missouri tribes. There is need for more studies which skillfully interweave the findings of ethnology and of history to trace the experiences of the other tribes from the time of their first mention by explorers to the present. A study of the Mandan, for example, would be a real challenge to a scholar who is equal to the difficult task of examining and evaluating the vast collections of fascinating ethnological and historical documents and published writings on the Mandan since Pierre La Vérendrye first heard of these strange Indians living in settled villages on the Missouri from Canadian Indians more than 230 years ago.

There is also a need for thorough biographical studies of prominent Indian leaders among the Upper Missouri tribes *prior* to the 1860s. There were many able chiefs among these tribes long before Sitting Bull, Red Cloud, and Crazy Horse gained national prominence. They

215

played important roles in the histories of their respective tribes, in intertribal wars, and in Indian-white relations and deserve to be better known. Likenesses of many of them were painted or drawn by white artists.

As an example I will cite Big Elk, the Omaha chief who was the first signer of his tribe's first treaty with the United States in 1815, was Thomas Say's principal Indian informant on Omaha customs at Engineer Cantonment during the winter of 1819–20, and visited Washington in 1821. Big Elk was renowned as an orator, and a number of examples of his picturesque speeches have been preserved, beginning at least as early as his moving funeral oration for the Teton Sioux chief, Black Buffalo, at Portage des Sioux in 1815. His portrait was painted by at least three artists. The extensive but widely scattered information on the career and character of Big Elk deserves to be brought together in a biography of this chief which might assume book-length proportions.

Far too little study has been made of the trade goods employed in the Indian trade of the Upper Missouri. We know that it was the opportunity to obtain these items that made the Indians active participants in the fur trade. The records of your Society are rich in lists of goods St. Louis merchants offered to Indians at their distant posts far up the Missouri. I hope a way will be found to correlate studies of these records with descriptions and illustrations of trade objects found by archaeologists at historic trading post and Indian village sites so that a comprehensive account of the material culture of the fur trade can be made available, and will enable us to see what the objects mentioned in the contemporary records looked like.

In my partial examination of your records I have been impressed by the number and variety of articles for the Upper Missouri Indian trade which were made right here in St. Louis. A thorough study of this theme would be a contribution to the history of St. Louis as well as to fur trade studies.

There has been a phenomenal growth of interest in the artists and photographers who pictured the Old West. Examples of their works

216

are widely scattered in public and private collections. As yet no comprehensive catalog of these pictures has been prepared; indeed, many important collections of these vivid pictorial documents have not been described and evaluated. One of these, surely, is the fine series of field sketches executed by Charles Wimar during his travels up the Missouri before 1860. They are right here in the collections of your Society.

These, then, are a few of the challenges in the field of Indian studies which should be met in the future, and those who undertake these studies will find many of their most enlightening source materials here in the rich collections of your Society.

I cannot close without expressing my deep appreciation of this opportunity to join you in commemorating this landmark in the history of the Missouri Historical Society. You should be proud of your record of accomplishment during the Society's first century, and you should look forward to a brilliant future. In the spirit of the primitive Indians, who attributed strong supernatural power to the white man's methods of record keeping, may I say—"More power to you."

×≣×≣×

Notes

CHAPTER ONE

1. Felix S. Cohen, *Handbook of Federal Indian Law, with Reference Tables and Index* (Washington, D.C., 1942).

2. See the chapter "Achievements and Contributions," in Harold E. Driver, *Indians of North America* (Chicago, 1961). The Indians' contributions to medicine have been well presented in Virgil J. Vogel, *American Indian Medicine* (Norman, Okla., 1970).

3. "Peter Fidler's Journal of a Journey Overland from Buckingham House to the Rocky Mountains in 1792 and 3," manuscript E.3/2, Hudson's Bay Company Archives, published by permission of the Governor and Committee of the Hudson's Bay Company.

4. I have referred to a number of these medicines in "The White Man's Strongest Medicine," *Bulletin of the Missouri Historical Society* 24 (October 1967): 36–46.

5. Edwin T. Denig, *Indian Tribes of the Upper Missouri*, Forty-sixth Annual Report of the Bureau of American Ethnology, 1928–29 (Washington, D.C., 1930), 528.

6. John C. Ewers, *Indian Life on the Upper Missouri* (Norman, Okla., 1968), 34–44.

7. Pierre-Jean De Smet, S.J., *Life, Letters and Travels of Father Pierre-Jean De Smet, S.J., 1801–1873: Missionary Labors and Adventures Among the Wild Tribes of the North American Indians . . .* , ed. Hiram M. Chittenden and A. T. Richardson (New York, 1905), 3: 953–54.

8. Paul Kane, *Wanderings of an Artist Among the Indians of North America from Canada to Vancouver's Island and Oregon, Through the*

Hudson's Bay Company's Territory and Back Again (Toronto, 1925), 275.

9. Thisba H. Morgan, "Reminiscences of My Days in the Land of the Ogallala Sioux," *Report and Historical Collections of the South Dakota State Historical Society* 29 (1958): 32.

10. Thomas L. Riggs, "Sunset to Sunset," *Report and Historical Collections of the South Dakota State Historical Society*, 29 (1958): 256.

11. Dabney Otis Collins, "A Happening at Oglala," *American West Magazine* 6 (March 1969): 15–19; Peter John Powell, *Sweet Medicine: The Continuing Role of the Sacred Arrows, the Sun Dance, and the Sacred Buffalo Hat in Northern Cheyenne History*, 2 vols. (Norman, Okla., 1969).

12. John C. Ewers, "Primitive American Commandos," *Masterkey* 17 (July 1943): 117–25.

13. Denig's "Indian Tribes of the Upper Missouri," 544–56, provides an excellent description of intertribal warfare on the northern plains during the mid–nineteenth century by an observant fur trader of that period.

14. John C. Ewers, *The Blackfeet: Raiders on the Northwestern Plains* (Norman, Okla., 1958), 244–53.

15. Lo is taken as a proper name in the phrase "Lo, the poor Indian," in *Essay on Man* by the English poet Alexander Pope.

16. The first five of the famed annual reports of the Bureau of American Ethnology, published 1881–7, contain six important monographs by army officers H. C. Yarrow, Garrick Mallery, and Washington Matthews. Capt. John G. Bourke's *The Medicine–Man of the Apache* appeared in the ninth annual report (1887–88) of that bureau.

17. Captain Bourke's manuscript in the library at West Point indicates that Sheridan gave him the opportunity to pursue his Indian studies while on active duty.

18. Thomas Wilson, "Arrow Wounds," *American Anthropologist* n.s., 3 (July–September 1901), 517–31 and illustrations. Many of the specimens of Indian handicrafts in the Army Medical Museum were transferred to the Smithsonian Institution in 1869 and subsequent years.

CHAPTER TWO

1. W. Raymond Wood, "Northern Plains Village Cultures Internal Stability and External Relationships," *Journal of Anthropological Research*

(University of New Mexico, Albuquerque) 30, no. 1 (Spring 1974): 1–16.

2. Lawrence J. Burpee, ed., *Journals and Letters of Pierre Gaultier de Varennes de la Vérendrye and His Sons* (Toronto, 1927), 332.

3. John C. Ewers, "The Influence of the Fur Trade upon the Indians of the Northern Plains," in *People and Pelts: Selected Papers from the North American Fur Trade Conference*, ed. Malvina Bolus (Winnipeg, 1972), 1–26.

4. Edwin T. Denig, *Indian Tribes of the Upper Missouri*, ed. J. N. B. Hewitt, 46th Annual Report of the Bureau of American Ethnology (Washington, D.C., 1930), 528; John C. Ewers, "When Red and White Men Met," *Western Historical Quarterly* 2, no. 2 (April 1971): 136–38.

5. Lawrence J. Burpee, ed., *Journal of Larocque from the Assiniboine to the Yellowstone*, 1805. Publications of the Canadian Archives, no. 3 (Ottawa, 1910), 62–66.

6. Pierre-Jean De Smet, *Western Missions and Missionaries* (New York, 1862), 46.

7. Louis Hennepin, *A New Discovery of the Vast Country in America*, ed. Reuben Gold Thwaites (Chicago, 1903), 1: 292; Mildred Mott Wedel, "Le Sueur and the Dakota Sioux," in *Aspects of Upper Great Lakes Anthropology: Papers in Honor of Lloyd A. Wilford*, Minnesota Historical Society (St. Paul, 1974), 171.

8. Alexander Philip Maximilian, Prince of Wied–Neuwied, "Travels in the Interior of North America," in *Early Western Travels, 1748–1846*, ed. Reuben Gold Thwaites, (Cleveland, 1906), 24: 246.

9. Abraham P. Nasatir, ed., *Before Lewis and Clark: Documents Illustrating the History of the Missouri, 1785–1804* (St. Louis, 1952), 2: 382.

10. Alexander Henry and David Thompson, *New Light on the Early History of the Greater Northwest*, ed. Elliott Coues (New York, 1897), 2: 731.

11. John Bradbury, "Travels in the Interior of America, in the Years 1809, 1810, and 1811," in *Early Western Travels*, 5: 132–33.

12. Pierre-Jean De Smet, S.J., *Life, Letters, and Travels of Father Pierre-Jean De Smet, S.J.* ed. Hiram M. Chittenden and A. T. Richardson (New York, 1905), 3: 953–54.

13. Maximilian, "Travels," 23: 140–42; testimony to author of Richard Sanderville, Piegan (1940s).

14. Annie Heloise Abel, ed., *Tabeau's Narrative of Loisel's Expedition to the Upper Missouri* (Norman, Okla., 1939), 200–201.

15. *Ibid.*, 201.

16. *Ibid.*, 196–97. In 1833, Prince Maximilian was invited by a Hidatsa woman to assume the role of ceremonial father in that tribe's buffalo calling ceremony. See Maximilian, "Travels," 24: 30.

17. Charles Mackenzie, "The Missouri Indians, 1804–1805," in Louis R. Masson, *Les bourgeois de la Compagnie du Nord-Ouest* (Quebec, 1889–90), 1: 330.

18. John C. Ewers, "Images of the White Man in 19th-Century Plains Indian Art," in *The Visual Arts, Plastic and Graphic*, ed. Justin M. Cordell (The Hague: Mouton, 1979), 411–29; Garrick Mallery, *Picture-Writing of the American Indians*, 10th Annual Report of the Bureau of American Ethnology (Washington, D.C., 1893), 313, 653.

19. George Catlin, in *New York Commercial Advertiser*, November 23, 1832. Maximilian, "Travels," 23: 152, 319; 24: 35.

20. J. Russell Harper, ed., *Paul Kane's Frontier* (Austin, 1971), 144.

21. J. N. B. Hewitt, ed., *Journal of Rudolph Friederich Kurz . . . 1846–1852*, trans. Myrtis Jarrell Bureau of American Ethnology Bulletin no. 115 (Washington, D.C., 1937), 76–77, 98, 215.

22. John C. Ewers, "Plains Indian Painting: The History and Development of an American Art Form," *American West* 5, no. 2 (March 1968): 4–10.

23. Lawrence J. Burpee, ed., *Journals and Letters of Pierre Gaultier de Varennes de la Vérendrye and His Sons*, 262–64.

24. Ewers, "The Influence of the Fur Trade," 4.

25. Edwin T. Denig, "Of the Arikaras," in *Five Indian Tribes of the Upper Missouri*, ed. John C. Ewers (Norman, Okla., 1961), 41–62.

26. John C. Ewers, *The Blackfeet: Raiders on the Northwestern Plains* (Norman, Okla., 1958), 45–57.

27. John C. Ewers, "The Influence of the Fur Trade," 7–11.

28. For further biographical information on Four Bears and The Light, see John C. Ewers, *Indian Life on the Upper Missouri* (Norman, Okla., 1968), 75–90, 103–9.

29. Ibid., 57–67.

30. Maximilian, "Travels," 23: 288.

31. Denig, *Indian Tribes of the Upper Missouri*, 486–87.

CHAPTER THREE

1. Waldo R. Wedel, *Prehistoric Man on the Great Plains* (Norman, Okla., 1961), 176, 274; W. Raymond Wood, *An Interpretation of Mandan Culture History*, Bureau of American Ethnology Bulletin no. 198 (Washington, D.C., 1967), 18–19, 154–55, 166.

2. Lawrence J. Burpee, ed., *Journals and Letters of Pierre Gaultier de Varennes de la Vérendrye and His Sons* (Toronto, 1927), 153, 160; John C. Ewers, "The Indian Trade of the Upper Missouri before Lewis and Clark: An Interpretation," *Bulletin of the Missouri Historical Society* 10, no. 4 (St. Louis, 1954), 432–35.

3. Burpee, *Journals . . . of Vérendrye*, 332.

4. Ewers, "Indian Trade of the Upper Missouri," 436–40.

5. J. B. Tyrrell, ed., *David Thompson's Narrative of His Explorations in Western America, 1784–1812* (Toronto, 1916), 12: 212; Lawrence J. Burpee, ed., *Journal of Larocque from the Assiniboine to the Yellowstone, 1805*, Publications of the Canadian Archives, no. 3 (Ottawa, 1910), 16–21.

6. Ewers, "Indian Trade of the Upper Missouri," 445; Reuben Gold Thwaites, ed., *Original Journals of the Lewis and Clark Expedition* (New York, 1904–5), 3: 190.

7. John C. Ewers, *The Blackfeet: Raiders on the Northwestern Plains* (Norman, Okla., 1958), 45–57.

8. Henry A. Boller, *Among the Indians: Eight Years in the Far West, 1858–1866*, ed. Milo M. Quaife (Chicago, 1959), 177–78.

9. Prince Maximillian witnessed the burial of two Indians whose bodies had been prepared by the American Fur Company at Fort McKenzie in August 1833, at the request of the chief. Alexander Philip Maximilian, Prince of Wied-Neuwied, "Travels in the Interior of North America," in *Early Western Travels, 1748–1846*, ed. Reuben Gold Thwaites (Cleveland, 1906), 23: 141.

10. Paul Kane, John James Audubon, George Catlin, and Karl Bodmer are but the best known of the many artists who enjoyed the hospitality of the trading posts. The American Fur Company actually employed two little-known artists on the Upper Missouri, Jean Baptiste Moncravie and Alexander Murray. The Swiss artist, Rudolph Friederich Kurz, spent the winter of 1851–52 in that company's employ at Fort Union.

11. Abraham P. Nasatir, ed., *Before Lewis and Clark: Documents Illus-*

trating the History of the Missouri, 1785–1804 (St. Louis, 1952), 1: 275, 288.

12. W. S. Wallace, "Notes of an 18th-Century Northerner," *The Beaver*, Outfit 283, June 1952, 41.

13. Office Purveyor of Public Supplies, Letters Sent, Book 16, April 1805 to July 1807, 233–34, National Archives, Washington, D.C.

14. Hiram M. Chittenden, *The American Fur Trade of the Far West*, 2d ed. (New York, 1902), 1: 22.

15. John C. Ewers, *The Horse in Blackfoot Indian Culture*, Bureau of American Ethnology Bulletin no. 159 (Washington, D.C., 1955), 181 and fig. 28.

16. Glyndwr Williams, ed., *Andrew Graham's Observations on Hudson's Bay, 1767–91*, Hudson's Bay Record Society, vol. 27 (London, 1969), 276.

17. A. M. Johnson, "Mons. Maugenest Suggests," *The Beaver*, Summer 1956, 49–53.

18. Nasatir, *Before Lewis and Clark*, 1: 246.

19. Hudson's Bay Company Archives, Manchester House Journal, 1786–87, Manuscript B.121/a/1, fos. 28, 33.

20. Erwin N. Thompson, "Fort Union Trading Post," *Historic Structures Report, Part II*, Historical Data Section. National Park Service (Washington, D.C., 1968), 144.

21. *Ibid.*, 139.

22. Hudson's Bay Company Archives, manuscript E.3/2, fo. 17.

23. Burpee, *Journal of Larocque*, 71.

24. Ewers, *The Horse in Blackfoot Indian Culture*, 114–16.

25. Edwin T. Denig, *Indian Tribes of the Upper Missouri*, ed. J. N. B. Hewitt, 46th Annual Report of the Bureau of American Ethnology (Washington, D.C., 1930), 591.

26. *Ibid.*, 591.

27. John C. Ewers, "Hair Pipes in Plains Indian Adornment: A Study in Indian and White Ingenuity." Bureau of American Ethnology, Anthropological Papers no. 50 (Washington, D.C., 1957).

28. The best description of the most common type of trade gun is Charles E. Hanson, Jr., "The Northwest Gun," Nebraska State Historical Society Publications in Anthropology, no. 2 (Lincoln, 1955).

29. John C. Ewers and William Wildschut, "Crow Indian Beadwork:

A Descriptive and Historical Study," Contributions 16, Museum of the American Indian Heye Foundation (New York, 1959), 32, figs. 33, 34.

30. Ewers, *The Horse in Blackfoot Indian Culture*, 50.

31. Alexander Henry and David Thompson, *New Light on the Early History of the Greater Northwest*, ed. Elliott Coues (New York, 1897), 1: 432; George Catlin, *Letters and Notes on the Manners, Customs, and Condition of the North American Indian* (London, 1841), 1: 38.

32. Lawrence J. Burpee, ed., "York Factory to the Blackfeet Country: The Journal of Anthony Hendry, 1754–55," *Transactions of the Royal Society of Canada, ser. 3*, vol. 1 (1907), 338–39; Hudson's Bay Company Archives, manuscript E.3/2, fo. 1.

33. *Tyrrell, David Thompson's Narrative*, 365; James W. Schultz and Jessie L. Donaldson, *The Sun God's Children* (Boston, 1930), 122–58.

34. J. N. B. Hewitt, ed., *Journal of Rudolph Friederich Kurz . . . 1846–1852*," Bureau of American Ethnology *Bulletin* no. 115 (Washington, D.C., 1937), 234; F. W. Hodge, ed., *Handbook of American Indians North of Mexico*, Bureau of American Ethnology Bulletin no. 30 (Washington, D.C., 1910), 1: 219.

35. James H. Bradley, *Characteristics, Habits, and Customs of the Blackfoot Indians*, Montana Historical Society Contributions, vol. 9 (Helena, 1923), 258.

36. Nicholas, Garry, "Diary of Nicholas Garry, Deputy–Governor of the Hudson's Bay Company," *Proceedings and Transactions, Royal Society of Canada*, 2d ser., vol. 6 (Toronto, 1900), 195.

37. Arthur S. Morton, ed., *The Journal of Duncan M'Gillivray of the Northwest Company at Fort George of the Saskatchewan, 1794–1795* (Toronto, 1929), 75; Maximilian, "Travels," 23: 124–26.

38. John C. Ewers, "Mothers of the Mixed–Bloods: The Marginal Woman in the History of the Upper Missouri," in *Probing the American West* (Santa Fe, New Mex., 1962), 65–69.

39. Examples of Indians who held these positions were The Light (Catlin's Pigeon's Egg Head) and Four Bears, of the Assiniboine and Mandan tribes, two of the best–known Indians of the Upper Missouri in the period 1832–34.

40. Hudson's Bay Company Archives, manuscript B.121/a/1, fo. 39.

41. Henry and Thompson, *New Light*, 2: 723.

42. Chittenden, *The American Fur Trade of the Far West*, 1: 23 ff.

43. Correspondence Blackfeet Agency, winter 1874–75. Indian Office Records, National Archives, Washington, D.C.

44. Edwin T. Denig, *Five Indian Tribes of the Upper Missouri: Sioux, Arickaras, Assiniboines, Crees, Crows,* ed. John C. Ewers (Norman, Okla., 1961), 204; Denig, *Indian Tribes of the Upper Missouri,* 530.

45. Ewers, *The Blackfeet,* 200–201.

46. Manuscript notes accompanying the William Bragge Collection, British Museum, London.

47. Sir Cecil Edward Denny, *The Law Marches West* (Toronto, 1939), 116–19.

48. Edwin James, *Account of an Expedition from Pittsburgh to the Rocky Mountains, Performed in the Years 1819 and 1820.* (London, 1823), 1: 482.

49. Catlin, *Letters and Notes,* 1: 261–62.

50. Pierre-Jean De Smet, "Oregon Missions and Travels over the Rocky Mountains in 1846–87," in *Early Western Travels, 1748–1846,* ed. Reuben Gold Thwaites (Cleveland, 1906), 29: 364–65.

51. The classic study of the destruction of the great buffalo herds remains William T. Hornaday, "The Extermination of the American Bison," *U.S. National Museum Annual Report for 1886–1887* (Washington, D.C., 1889).

52. Andrew Garcia, *Tough Trip Through Paradise,* ed. Bennett H. Stern (Boston, 1967).

53. The life of these people at midcentury is well described by Alexander Ross in *The Red River Settlement, Its Rise, Progress, and Present State* (London, 1856).

54. Verne Dusenberry, "Waiting for a Day that Never Comes: Story of the Dispossessed Métis of Montana," *Montana: The Magazine of Western History* 8, no. 2 (1958): 26–39.

55. A carefully researched, sympathetic account of Louis Riel and his cause is Joseph Kinsey Howard, *Strange Empire* (Westport, Conn., 1952).

CHAPTER FOUR

1. R. Ellis and C. Steen, "An Indian Delegation in France, 1725," *Journal of the Illinois State Historical Society* 64, no. 4 (1974): 385–405.

2. John C. Ewers, *Indian Art in Pipestone: George Catlin's Portfolio in the British Museum* (London and Washington, D.C., 1979), 62 and

pl. 21.

3. John C. Ewers, "Three Effigy Pipes by an Eastern Dakota Master Carver," *American Indian Art* 3, no. 4(1978): 51–55.

4. Herbert E. Bolton, *Spanish Explorations in the Southwest 1542–1706*, (New York, 1916), 226–27.

5. George Catlin, *Catlin's Notes of Eight Years Travels and Residence in Europe with His North American Indian Collection*, 2 vols. (London, 1848).

6. Alfred Barnabas Thomas, *Forgotten Frontiers: A Study of the Spanish Indian Policy of Don Juan Bautista de Anza, Governor of New Mexico, 1777–1778* (Norman, Okla., 1932), 134–36.

7. John C. Ewers, "A Crow Chief's Tribute to the Unknown Soldier," *American West* Magazine 8, no. 6 (1971): 30–35.

8. John C. Ewers, "The Gun of Sitting Bull," *The Beaver*, Outfit 287: 20–23.

9. Ray H. Matteson, ed. "Henry A. Boller, Missouri River Fur Trader." *North Dakota History* 33(2): 80.

10. John C. Ewers, "William Clark's Indian Museum in St. Louis, 1816–1832," in *A Cabinet of Curiosities, Five Episodes in the Evolution of American Museums*, ed. Walter M. Whitehill (Charlottesville, Va., 1967), 49–72.

11. Clark Wissler, *Ceremonial Bundles of the Blackfoot Indians*, American Museum of Natural History, Anthropological Papers 7, pt. 2: figs. 10, 32, 35.

12. Hugh L. Scott, "Notes on the Kado, or Sun Dance of the Kiowa Indians," *American Anthropologist*, n.s. 13, no. 3 (1911): 345–79.

CHAPTER FIVE

1. James Mooney, *Calendar History of the Kiowa Indians*, 17th Annual Report of the Bureau of American Ethnology (Washington, D.C., 1898), 235.

2. Ibid., 236.

3. Robert E. Bell, Edward B. Jelks, and W. W. Newcomb, *A Pilot Study of Wichita Indian Archeology and Ethnology* (n.p., 1967), 340.

4. James Mooney, *The Aboriginal Population of America North of Mexico*, Smithsonian Miscellaneous Collections 80, no. 7 (Washington, D.C., 1928).

5. Alfred L. Kroeber, *Cultural and Natural Areas of Native North America* (Berkeley, 1939), 133–34.

6. Ibid., 133, 158.

7. John R. Swanton, *Source Material on the History and Ethnology of the Caddo Indians*, Bureau of America Ethnology Bulletin no. 132 (Washington, D.C., 1942), 25; John R. Swanton, *The Indian Tribes of North America*, Bureau of American Ethnology Bulletin no. 145 (Washington, D.C., 1952), 321.

8. Bell, Jelks, and Newcomb, *Pilot Study*, 347–49.

9. Mexican estimates of 20,000 to 30,000 for the Comanche in the early decades of the nineteenth century may reflect the Mexican authorities' fears of those aggressive Indians more accurately than they do the tribal population. Nevertheless, David Burnet, who knew the Comanche well in 1819, reckoned them at 10,000 to 12,000; and José Francisco Ruíz, who lived for eight years among them prior to 1821, estimated their population at 1,000 to 1,500 families twelve years after they suffered heavy losses in the smallpox epidemic of 1816. D. G. Burnet, "The Comanche and Other Tribes of Texas and the Policy to be Pursued Respecting Them," in Henry R. Schoolcraft, *Historical and Statistical Information Respecting the History and Prospects of the Indian Tribes of the United States* (Philadelphia, 1851), 1: 230; José Francisco Ruíz, untitled manuscript on several Indian tribes of Texas (Western Americana Collection, Beinecke Rare Book and Manuscript Library, Yale University, 1828).

10. The Kiowa–Apache, Mooney believed, "probably never numbered much over three hundred and fifty" (*Calendar History of the Kiowa Indians*, 253). Their unique ability to retain or enhance their population during the nineteenth century may have been due to additions from remnants of other Apache tribes, predominantly Lipan.

11. Mooney, *Aboriginal Population*, 12–13.

12. Pat Ireland Nixon, *The Medical Story of Early Texas, 1528–1853* (Lancaster, Pa., 1946), 8–15.

13. U.S. Census Office, 11th U.S. Census, 1890, *Report of the Indians Taxed and Indians Not Taxed in the United States* (Washington, D.C., 1894), 403.

14. Jean Louis Berlandier, *The Indians of Texas in 1830*, trans. Patricia Reading LeClercq, ed. and introd. John C. Ewers (Washington, D.C., 1964), 84.

15. Mooney, *Calendar History of the Kiowa Indians*, 164.

16. George B. Grinnell, *The Cheyenne Indians: Their History and Ways of Life*, 2 vols. (New York, 1962).

17. Commissioner of Indian Affairs, *Annual Report* (Washington, D.C., 1849).

18. Jedidiah Morse, *A Report to the Secretary of War of the United States on Indian Affairs* (New Haven, Conn., 1822), 260.

19. F. V. Hayden, *Contributions to the Ethnography and Philology of the Indian Tribes of the Missouri Valley*, Transactions of the American Philosophical Society, no. 12 (1862).

20. Nixon, *Medical History of Early Texas*, 53.

21. Mooney, *Calendar History of the Kiowa Indians*, 274, 289, 342, 391–433.

22. Fanny Bandelier, ed., *The Journey of Alvar Núñez Cabeza de Vaca* (Chicago, 1964).

23. Fray Francisco Casañas de Jesus Maria, "Fray Francisco Casañas de Jesus Maria to the Viceroy of Mexico, August 15, 1691," *Southwestern Historical Quarterly* 30, nos. 3–4 (1927): 294, 303.

24. M. E. Opler, *An Apache Life-Way: The Economic, Social, and Religious Institutions of the Chiricahua Indians* (Chicago, 1941), 187, 241, 278.

25. G. A. Dorsey, "Caddo Customs of Childhood," *Journal of American Folk-Lore Society* 18 (1906).

26. Burnet, "The Comanches and Other Tribes," 1: 234.

27. Commissioner of Indian Affairs, *Annual Report* (1892), 374.

28. Bandelier, *Journey*, 64; Casañas, "Casañas to the Victory of Mexico," 302–3; Berlandier, *Indians of Texas,* " 96–97; R. S. Neighbors, "The Na-u-ni or Comanches of Texas," in Schoolcraft, *Historical and Statistical Information*, 2: 133.

29. Commissioner of Indian Affairs, *Annual Report* (1853), 363.

30. Mooney, *Calendar History of the Kiowa Indians*, 236.

31. Marcus A. Goldstein, "Anthropology of the Comanches," *American Journal of Physical Anthropology* 19, no. 2 (1934): 289–319.

32. Noah Smithwick, *The Evolution of a State, or Recollections of Old Texas Days* (Austin, 1900), 173.

33. U.S. Census Office, *Indians Taxed and Not Taxed*, 541.

34. Grinnell, *The Cheyenne Indians*, 1: 92–93.

35. Ernest Wallace and E. A. Hoebel, *The Comanche, Lords of the South Plains* (Norman, Okla., 1952), 140.

36. U.S. Census Office, *Indians Taxed and Not Taxed*, 541.

37. Grinnell, *The Cheyenne Indians*, 2: 164–65.

CHAPTER SIX

1. Louis Houck, ed., *The Spanish Régime in Missouri* (Chicago, 1909), 1: 11–12.

2. Lawrence Kinnaird, ed., *Spain in the Mississippi Valley, 1765–1794* (Washington, D.C., 1946–49), 1: 101–2.

3. Houck, *The Spanish Régime in Missouri*, 2: 170–71.

4. Abraham P. Nasatir, ed., *Before Lewis and Clark: Documents Illustrating the History of the Missouri, 1785–1804* (St. Louis, 1952), 2: 495–96.

5. Alfred Barnaby Thomas, ed., *Forgotten Frontiers: A Study of the Spanish Indian Policy of Don Juan Bautista de Anza, Governor of New Mexico, 1777–1778* (Norman, Okla., 1932), 300–20.

6. Houck, *The Spanish Régime in Missouri*, 1: 268–69.

7. Nasatir, *Before Lewis and Clark*, 2: 185, 420.

8. Houck, *The Spanish Régime in Missouri*, 2: 189.

9. Kinnaird, *The Spanish in the Mississippi Valley*, 1: 329–30.

10. *Ibid.*, 2: 235.

11. H. Bailey Carroll and J. Villasana Haggard, eds., *Three New Mexico Chronicles* (Albuquerque, 1942), 135; Kinnaird, *Spain in the Mississippi Valley*, 2: 199; Houck, *The Spanish Régime in Missouri*, 2: 52.

12. Robert E. Bell, Edward B. Jelks, and W. W. Newcomb, *A Pilot Study of Wichita Indian Archeology and Ethnology* (n.p., 1967), 277.

13. Herbert E. Bolton, ed., *Spanish Exploration in the Southwest, 1542–1706* (New York, 1916), 416.

14. Eleanor Claire Buckley, ed., "The Aguayo Expedition into Texas and Louisiana, 1719–1722," *Texas Historical Association Quarterly*, 1, no. 4 (1898): 46, 47, 49.

15. Herbert E. Bolton, ed., *Athanase de Mézières and the Louisiana-Texas Frontier, 1768–1780* (Cleveland, 1914), 1: 73–74, 132–33, 157, 201–2, 211, 262; 2: 85, 86, 94, 185, 252.

16. Nasatir, *Before Lewis and Clark*, 1: 305.

17. Melvin R. Gilmore, *Uses of Plants by the Indians of the Missouri*

River Region," 33d Annual Report, Bureau of American Ethnology (Washington, D.C., 1911), 66.

18. Nasatir, *Before Lewis and Clark,* 1: 309–10.

19. Kinnaird, *Spain in the Mississippi Valley,* 1: 236.

20. Ibid., 229–30, 299, 305, 330.

21. Ibid., 2: 171–72, 182–84, 196–97, 253–56.

22. Ibid., 1: 391–92.

23. Nasatir, *Before Lewis and Clark,* 1: 291.

24. Kinnaird, *Spain in the Mississippi valley,* 1: xxiv; 2: 183–84; 3: 107.

25. Carroll and Haggard, *Three New Mexico Chronicles,* 135–36.

26. Alvin M. Josephy, Jr., *The American Indian and the Bureau of Indian Affairs—1969,* Hearings, Subcommittee on Indian Education, Committee on Labor and Public Welfare, U.S. Senate, 91st Cong., 1st sess., pt. 2, app. (Washington, D.C., 1969), 1447.

CHAPTER SEVEN

1. Clark Wissler, *Costumes of the Plains Indians,* American Museum of Natural History, Anthropological Papers, vol. 17, pt. 2 (New York, 1915), 65 ff.

2. Ibid., 91.

3. Edwin James, *Account of an Expedition from Pittsburgh to the Rocky Mountains, Performed in the Years 1819 and 1820* (London, 1823), 2: 180 81.

4. Gudmund Hatt, "Arctic Skin Clothing in Eurasia and America: An Ethnographic Study," *Arctic Anthropology* 5, no. 2 (1969): pl. 1, fig. 6, pp. 24, 28–29.

5. Jean Louis Berlandier, *The Indians of Texas in 1830,* ed. and introd. John C. Ewers (Washington, D.C., 1969), pl. 2 and p. 51.

6. Fray Vicente Santa Maria, *Relácion historica de lal Colonia del Nuevo Santander y costa del San Mexicano,* Publicaciones del Archivo General de la Nación, vol. 4 (Mexico City, 1930), 422.

7. Don Pedro Bautista Pino, *Three New Mexico Chronicles,* ed. H. Bailey Carroll and J. Villasana Haggard (Albuquerque, 1942), 100.

8. Victor Tixier, *Tixier's Travels on the Osage Prairies,* ed. John Francis McDermott (Norman, Okla., 1940), 267.

9. Berlandier, *Indians of Texas in 1830,* 155–66, pls. 1–16, figs. 16 and 17.

10. The watercolor is plate 7 in Berlandier, *Indians of Texas in 1830.*

11. Richard C. Ahlborn, "European Dress in Texas, 1830: As Rendered by Lino Sánchez y Tapia," *American Scene* 13, no. 4 (1972): 6.

12. Isaac Joslin Cox, ed., *The Journeys of René Robert Cavelier Sieur de La Salle* (New York, 1905), 2: 140–41.

13. Mattie Austin Hatcher, trans. and ed., "Description of the Tejas or Asinai Indians, 1671 to 1722," *Southwestern Historical Quarterly* 31, pt. 4, no. 2 (1927): 176.

14. Ibid., 176–77.

15. William W. Newcomb, Jr., *The Indians of Texas, from Prehistoric to Modern Times* (Austin, 1961), 321.

16. W. B. Parker, *Notes Taken during the Expedition Commanded by Captain R. B. Marcy through Unexplored Texas, in the Summer and Fall of 1854* (Philadelphia, 1856), 114.

17. William Philo Clark, *The Indian Sign Language* (Philadelphia, 1885), 402.

18. Lt. T. R. Wheelock, *Journal of Colonel Dodge's Expedition from Fort Gibson to Pawnee Pic Village (1834)*, American State Papers, Military Affairs, vol. 5 (Washington, D.C., 1860), 377.

19. Josiah Gregg, *Commerce of the Prairies*, ed. Max L. Moorhead, (reprint; Norman, Okla., 1954), 431.

20. Edward Curtis, *The North American Indian*, vol. 19 (Norwood, 1930), 223.

21. A good example can be found in Wilbur S. Nye, *Plains Indian Raiders* (Norman, Okla., 1978).

22. Col. Richard I. Dodge, *Our Wild Indians* (Hartford, 1882), 308.

23. José Maria Sánchez y Tapia, "A Trip to Texas in 1828," trans. Carlos E. Castañeda, *Southwestern Historical Quarterly* 29, no. 4 (1926): 269.

24. Berlandier, *Indians of Texas in 1830*, p. 5.

25. William S. Red, ed., "Extracts from the Diary of W. Y. Allen, 1838–39," *Southwestern Historical Quarterly* 17, no. 1 (1914): 53.

26. Berlandier, *Indians of Texas in 1830*, pl. 1.

27. Ibid., 51.

28. George Parker Winship, ed., *The Coronado Expedition, 1540–1542*, 14th Annual Report of the Bureau of American Ethnology (Washington, D.C., 1896), pt. 1: 517, 507.

29. F. W. Hodge, ed., *Handbook of American Indians North of Mexico,*

Bureau of American Ethnology Bulletin no. 30 (Washington, D.C., 1910), pt. 1: 655.

30. Cited in Herbert E. Bolton, *Spanish Exploration in the Southwest, 1542–1706* (New York, 1916), 256.

31. George P. Hammond and Agapita Rey, eds., *Don Juan de Oñate, Colonizer of New Mexico, 1595–1628* (Albuquerque, 1953), 841, 854.

32. The painting appears in Pauline Pinckney, *Painting in Texas: The Nineteenth Century* (Austin, 1967), 58.

33. Gordon C. Baldwin, *The Warrior Apaches* (Tucson, 1955), 75–76, and drawings p. 73.

34. U.S. Census Office, 11th U.S. Census, 1890, *Report of Indians Taxed and Indians Not Taxed in the United States* (Washington, D.C., 1894), 151.

35. Berlandier, *Indians of Texas in 1830*, pls. 15, 16.

36. George P. Hammond and Agapita Rey, eds., *The Rediscovery of New Mexico* (Albuquerque, 1966), 161.

37. Winship, *The Coronado Expedition*, 515.

38. Hammond and Rey, *Rediscovery of New Mexico*, 220.

39. Donald Cordry and Dorothy Cordry, *Mexican Indian Costumes* (Austin, 1968), 84.

40. Ralph L. Beals, "The Comparative Ethnology of Northern Mexico before 1750," *Ibero-Americana* 2 (Berkeley, 1932), map 2, p. 135.

41. James, *Account of an Expedition*, 2: 181.

42. William W. Newcomb, Jr., *German Artist on the Texas Frontier: Friedrich Richard Petri* (Austin, 1978), pl. 29.

43. Ibid., pls. 31, 35.

44. Nye, *Plains Indian Raiders*, 359.

45. For examples, see Karen Daniels Peterson, *Howling Wolf: A Cheyenne Warrior's Graphic Interpretation of His People* (Palo Alto, Calif., 1968) and *Plains Indian Art from Fort Marion* (Norman, Okla., 1971).

46. Charles J. Kappler, comp. and ed., *Laws and Treaties*, vol. 2, *Treaties* (Washington, D.C., 1904), 87.

47. Lt. James W. Abert, *Through the Country of the Comanche Indians in the Fall of the Year 1845*, ed. John Galven (San Francisco, 1970), 28.

48. This photograph is reproduced in Muriel H. Wright, *A Guide to the Indian Tribes of Oklahoma* (Norman, Okla., 1951), 172.

CHAPTER EIGHT

1. This certificate is preserved in the Maximilian Collection, Joslyn Art Museum, Omaha, Neb. The name "Le Brechu, or Le Fils du Gros François" was signed to the treaty between the Assiniboines and Blackfeet in 1831. "Gros François" was the traders' nickname for Iron Arrow Point, chief of the Gens des Roches, a prominent Assiniboine band, and father of a very large family. His family probably had traded at Fort Union from the time of its establishment in 1829. One of his daughters married Edwin T. Denig, clerk and later manager of the fort and one of the most prolific writers on Assiniboine history and culture. Gros François's son The Light was the first Assiniboine to visit Washington in 1832. Another son, First to Fly, represented his tribe at the Fort Laramie Treaty in 1851 and was second only to the head chief, Crazy Bear, in the tribal political hierarchy. First to Fly's great–grandson Joshua Wetsit has served as chairman of the tribal council on the Fort Peck Reservation and was my interpreter in 1953. See Edwin T. Denig, *Five Indian Tribes of the Upper Missouri: Sioux, Arickaras, Assiniboines, Crees, Crows,* ed. John C. Ewers (Norman, Okla., 1961), 86–88.

2. Maria R. Audubon, *Audubon and His Journals,* ed. Elliot Coues (New York, 1897), 2: 185. The full text of the treaty appears in Maximilian, "Travels in the Interior of North America, 1832–1834," in *Early Western Travels, 1748–1846,* ed. Reuben Gold Thwaites (Cleveland, 1904–7), 24: 317.

3. Registers of Enlistment in the United States Army, 1798–1914, Records of the Adjutant General's Office, Record Group 94, National Archives Building; American Fur Company Ledger Books, Missouri Historical Society, St. Louis; Maximilian, "Travels in the Interior," 23: 188; Audubon, *Journals,* 2: 105, 109, 128, 138, 146.

4. Charles Larpenteur, *Forty Years a Trader on the Upper Missouri,* ed. Milo M. Quaife (Chicago, 1933), 58–59; Annie Heloise Abel, ed., *Chardon's Journal of Fort Clark, 1834–39* (Pierre, S.D., 1932), 238; J. N. B. Hewitt, ed., *Journal of Rudolph Friederich Kurz,* Bureau of American Ethnology Bulletin no. 115 (Washington, D.C., 1937), 169–70; Fitz Hugh Ludlow, *The Heart of the Continent,* (New York, 1870), 50. The most complete biographical sketch of Moncravie is Charles E. Hanson, Jr., "J. B. Moncravie," in Le Roy Hafen, *The Mountain Men and the Fur Trade of the Far West* (Glendale, Calif., 1972), 9: 288–98.

5. Murray's sketches of trading posts were reproduced in *Field and Stream* 70 (1908): 131, 210–12. As an artist he is best known for his pioneer drawings of Kutchin Indians on the Yukon reproduced in his *Journal of the Yukon, 1847–48*, ed. Lawrence J. Burpee, Publications of the Canadian Archives no. 4 (Ottawa, 1910).

6. Hewitt, *Journal of Rudolf Friederich Kurz*, 133–34, 141, 144, 156, 203–4.

7. Thaddeus Culbertson, *Journal of an Expedition to the Mauvaises Terres and the Upper Missouri in 1850*, ed. John Francis McDermott, Bureau of American Ethnology Bulletin no. 147 (Washington, D.C. 1952), 76.

8. Joseph Donnelly, ed., *Wilderness Kingdom: The Journals and Paintings of Father Nicholas Point* (New York, 1967), 151; Hewitt, *Journal of Rudolph Friederich Kurz*, pl. 42. The viewer may need a magnifying glass to distinguish these details in the reproduction of Kurz's much larger original sketch in the Bernisches Historisches Museum, Bern, Switzerland.

9. Letters Received Regarding Fort Pierre, 1855, Consolidated File, Records of the Office of the Quartermaster General, RG 92, NA.

10. Pierre Chouteau, Jr., and Company Records, Missouri Historical Society.

11. Abraham P. Nasatir, ed., *Before Lewis and Clark: Documents Illustrating the History of the Missouri, 1785–1804* (St. Louis, 1952), 1: 305, 309, 325–27, 359; 2: 429–30, 496; Milo M. Quaife, ed., *Sergeant Ordway's Journal*, Publication of the State Historical Society of Wisconsin (Madison, 1916), 22: 112, 121, 138, 150, 159.

CHAPTER NINE

1. Alexander Henry and David Thompson, *New Light on the Early History of the Greater Northwest*, ed. Elliott Coues (New York, 1897), 1: 99.

2. Donald J. Lehmer, *Introduction to Middle Missouri Archeology*, National Park Service Anthropological Papers no. 1 (Washington, D.C., 1971), 69, 71, 113, 116, 122, 141–42.

3. William Mulloy, *A Preliminary Historical Outline for the Northwestern Plains*, University of Wyoming Publications 22, nos. 1–2 (Laramie, 1958), 118–39, figs. 42–44.

4. Louise Phelps Kellogg, ed., *Early Narratives of the Northwest*,

1634–1699 (New York, 1917), 132.

5. Henry Kelsey, The Kelsey Papers, ed. A. G. Doughty and Chester Martin (Ottawa, 1929), 19–20.

6. Lawrence J. Burpee, ed., Journals and Letters of Pierre Gaultier de Varennes de la Vérendrye and His Sons, Champlain Society Publications, vol. 16 (Toronto, 1927), 418.

7. Reuben Gold Thwaites, ed., The French Regime in Wisconsin . . . 1634–1748, (Madison, 1906), 3: 418.

8. J. B. Tyrrell, ed., David Thompson's Narrative of His Explorations in Western America, 1784–1812. Champlain Society Publications, vol. 12 (Toronto, 1916), 328–32.

9. John C. Ewers, The Blackfeet: Raiders on the Northwestern Plains (Norman, Okla., 1958), 242–43; Alfred L. Kroeber, Ethnology of the Gros Ventres, American Museum of Natural History Anthropological Papers, vol. 1 (New York, 1908), 146.

10. John C. Ewers, The Horse in Blackfoot Indian Culture, with Comparative Materials from Other Western Tribes, Bureau of American Ethnology Bulletin no. 159 (Washington, D.C., 1955), 171–215.

11. Alexander Philip Maximilian, Prince of Wied–Neuwied, "Travels in the Interior of North America," in Early Western Travels, 1748–1846, ed. Reuben Gold Thwaites, (Cleveland, 1906), 23: 146–53.

12. Ewers, The Blackfeet, provides a history of the Blackfoot alliance.

13. Pierre–Charles Le Sueur, Le Sueur's Voyage up the Mississippi, Collections of the State Historical Society of Wisconsin, vol. 16 (Madison, 1902), 190.

14. David G. Mandelbaum, The Plains Cree, American Museum of Natural History Anthropological Papers, vol. 37, pt. 2 (New York, 1940); David Rodnick, The Fort Belknap Assiniboine of Montana (Philadelphia, 1938); John C. Ewers, Ethnological Report on the Blackfeet and Gros Ventres Tribes of Indians (New York, 1974).

15. Edwin T. Denig, Five Indian Tribes of the Upper Missouri: Sioux, Arickaras, Assiniboines, Crees, Crows, ed. John C. Ewers (Norman, Okla., 1961); Ewers, Ethnological Report on the Blackfeet and Gros Ventres Tribes of Indians (New York: Garland, 1974).

16. Denig, Five Indian Tribes, 41–62.

17. Denig, Five Indian Tribes, 137–204; Ewers, Report on the Blackfeet and Gros Ventres, 77, 164, passim.

18. John C. Ewers, *Teton Dakota Ethnology and History* (Berkeley, 1938); Doane Robinson, *A History of the Dakota or Sioux Indians from Their Earliest Traditions*, South Dakota Historical Society Collections, vol. 2, pt. 2 (Aberdeen, 1904).

19. Denig, *Five Indian Tribes*, 55–57.

20. Garrick Mallery, *Picture-Writing of the American Indians*, Tenth Annual Report of the Bureau of American Ethnology, 1888–89 (Washington, D.C., 1893), 273.

21. Mallery, *Picture-Writing*, 572–73.

22. Mahlon Wilkinson, Report Number 117 of Indian Agent M. Wilkinson in Report of the Commissioner of Indian Affairs (Washington, D.C., 1864), 264.

23. John A. Burbank, Report Number 67 of John A. Burbank, Governor and ex officio Superintendent of Indian Affairs, Dakota Territory, Annual Report, Commissioner of Indian Affairs for 1870, 209–10.

CHAPTER TEN

1. This information was written by General Scott in ink under a portrait of the Hidatsa chiefs, Crow's Breast and Poor Wolf, published opposite p 117 in his personal copy of Joseph Henry Taylor's *Sketches of Frontier Life* (Bismarck, 1897) now in the library of the Department of Anthropology at the Smithsonian Institution.

2. Report of Capt. W. Clifford, U.S.A., Indian Agent, Fort Berthold, Sept. 1, 1869, Annual Report, Commissioner of Indian Affairs for 1869 (Washington, D.C. 1870), 312.

3. Report of John A. Burbank, Governor and ex officio Superintendent of Indian Affairs, Dakota Territory, Annual Report, Commissioner of Indian Affairs for 1870 (Washington, D.C., 1870), 209–10.

4. Louis Hennepin, *A New Discovery of the Vast Country in America*, ed. Reuben Gold Thwaites (Chicago, 1903), 1: 299.

5. Giacomo C. Beltrami, *A Pilgrimage in Europe and America* (London, 1828), 2: 275–76.

6. This reference to a scale appears in Fidler's handwriting in the lower center of the map.

7. Josiah Gregg, *Commerce of the Prairies*, reprint ed., (Norman, Okla., 1954), 233.

8. Col. Richard I. Dodge, *Our Wild Indians* (Hartford, Conn., 1882),

552–53.

9. Edwin T. Denig, *Indian Tribes of the Upper Missouri*. Forty-sixth Annual Report of the Bureau of American Ethnology, 1928–29. (Washington, D.C. 1930), 605.

10. Red Horse's map is reproduced in color as plate 40 in Col. Garrick Mallery, *Picture–Writing of the American Indians* Tenth Annual Report of the Bureau of American Ethnology (Washington, D.C., 1893).

CHAPTER ELEVEN

1. George Catlin, *Letter and Notes on the Manners, Customs, and Condition of the North American Indians* (London, 1841), 1: 154.

2. Peter John Powell, *People of the Sacred Mountain* (New York, 1981), 1: 142.

3. J. B. Tyrrell, ed., *David Thompson's Narrative of His Explorations in Western America, 1784–1812*, Champlain Society Publications, vol. 12 (Toronto, 1916), 339.

4. Edwin T. Denig, *Indian Tribes of the Upper Missouri*, ed. J. N. B. Hewitt, 46th Annual Report of the Bureau of American Ethnology (Washington, D.C., 1930), 552.

5. Lawrence J. Burpee, ed., "York Factory to the Blackfeet Country: The Journal of Anthony Hendry, 1754–55," *Transactions of the Royal Society of Canada*, ser. 3, vol. 1 (1907), 339.

6. Lawrence J. Burpee, ed., "An Adventurer from Hudson Bay: Journal of Mathew Cocking from York Factory to the Blackfeet Country, 1772–1773," *Transactions of the Royal Society of Canada*, ser. 3, vol. 2 (1908), 111.

7. Alexander Henry, *Travels and Adventures in Canada, and the Indian Territories Between the Years 1760 and 1775* (New York: I. Riley), 312.

8. Alexander Henry and David Thompson, *New Light on the Early History of the Greater Northwest*, ed. Elliot Coues (New York, 1897), 312.

9. Mildred Mott Wedel, *The Wichita Indians, 1541–1750*, Ethnohistorical Essays, Reprints in Anthropology. no. 38 (Lincoln, Neb., 1988), 53–74.

10. George A. Dorsey, *The Mythology of the Wichita* (Washington, D.C., Carnegie Institution, 1904), 7.

11. R. S. Neighbors, "The Na-u-ni or Comanches of Texas," in Henry R. Schoolcraft, *Historical and Statistical Information Respecting the History, Condition and Prospects of the Indian Tribes of the United States,* vol. 2 (Philadelphia, 1852), 132.

12. W. Bollaert, "Observations of the Indian Tribes of Texas," *London Ethnological Society Journal* 2 (1850): 277.

13. T. C. Pease and R. C. Werner, eds., *Memoir of De Gannes concerning the Illinois Country,* Collections of the Illinois State Historical Library, vol. 23, French series, vol. 1 (Springfield, 1934), 375–88.

14. John C. Ewers, *The Horse in Blackfoot Indian Culture,* Bureau of American Ethnology Bulletin no. 159 (Washington, D.C., 1955), 311.

15. P. J. de T. La Jonquire, Letter September 25, 1751, to French Minister in the French Regime in Wisconsin, Wisconsin Historical Collections, vol. 10, p. 88.

16. John R. Bell, *Journal of Captain John R. Bell,* ed. H. M. Fuller and L. R. Hafen (Glendale, Calif., 1957), 207–10, 221–22, 224–25.

17. Annie Heloise Abel, ed., *Chardon's Journal of Fort Clark, 1834–39* (Pierre, S.D., 1932), 193.

18. Wilbur S. Nye, *Bad Medicine and Good: Tales of the Kiowas* (Norman, Okla., 1962), 95, 227.

19. Powell, *People of the Sacred Mountain,* 2: 964.

20. Nicholas Point, *Wilderness Kingdom: Indian Life in the Rocky Mountains, 1840–1847,* trans. J. P. Donnelly (New York, 1967), 158.

21 Ibid., fig. 156.

22. Benjamin Capps, *Woman Chief* (Garden City, N.Y., 1979).

23. J. Willard Schultz, *Running Eagle, The Warrior Girl* (Boston: Houghton Mifflin, 1919).

24. Edwin T. Denig, *Five Indian Tribes of the Upper Missouri: Sioux, Arickaras, Assiniboines, Crees, Crows,* ed. John C. Ewers (Norman, Okla., 1961), 195–200.

25. John C. Ewers, Field notes, 1941–44.

26. Capps, *Woman Chief,* vii.

27. Patricia Albers and Beatrice Medicine, *The Hidden Half-Studies of Plains Indian Women* (Washington, D.C., 1983), 274–75.

28. Ewers, *The Horse in Blackfoot Indian Culture,* 191–93.

29. Alexander Philip Maximilian, Prince of Wied-Neuwied, "Travels in the Interior of North America," in *Early Western Travels, 1748–1846,*

ed. Reuben Gold Thwaites (Cleveland, 1906), 23: 149.

30. Douglas R. Parks, ed., *A Fur Trader on the Upper Missouri: The "Journals" and "Description" of Jean-Baptiste Truteau, 1794–96*, trans. Mildred Mott Wedel (Lincoln, Neb., in press).

31. Powell, *People of the Sacred Mountain*, 2: 981.

32. Ewers, Field notes, 1941–44.

33. Ibid.

34. Ibid.

35. Parks, *Fur Trader on the Upper Missouri*, n.p.

CHAPTER TWELVE

1. Meriwether Lewis, *The Lewis and Clark Expedition*, 3 vols. (Philadelphia, 1961).

2. Ibid., 1: 121.

3. John C. Ewers, *The Horse in Blackfoot Indian Culture, with Comparative Materials from Other Western Tribes*, Bureau of American Ethnology Bulletin no. 159 (Washington D.C., 1955), 291–98.

4. Ibid., 257–84.

5. Louise P. Kellogg, ed., *Early Narratives of the Northwest, 1634–1699* (New York, 1917), 73; Emma Helen Blair, ed., *The Indian Tribes of the Upper Mississippi Valley and Region of the Great Lakes* (Cleveland, 1911), 1: 163.

6. Kellogg, *Early Narratives*, 243.

7. Lawrence J. Burpee, ed., *Journal of Larocque from the Assiniboine to the Yellowstone, 1805*, Publication of the Canadian Archives no. 3, 31.

8. Alexander Philip Maximilian, Prince of Wied–Neuwied, "Travels in the Interior of North America, 1832–1834," in *Early Western Travels, 1748–1846*, ed. Reuben Gold Thwaites (Cleveland, 1906), 23: 342–43.

9. George Catlin, letter dated Mandan Village, Upper Missouri, August 5th, 1832, in New York *Commercial Advertiser*, November 13, 1932.

10. Maximilian, "Travels," 23: 152.

11. J. N. B. Hewitt, ed., *Journal of Rudolph Friederich Kurz, 1846–1852*, Bureau of American Ethnology Bulletin no. 115 (Washington, D.C., 1937), 98–107, 144, 215.

12. Henry A. Boller, *Among the Indians: Eight Years in the Far West, 1858–1866*, ed. Milo M. Quaife (Chicago, 1959), 290–91.

13. Maximilian, "Travels," 23: 136.

14. Edwin T. Denig, *Indian Tribes of the Upper Missouri*, Forthy-sixth Annual Report of the Bureau of American Ethnology (Washington, D.C., 1930), 496.

15. Ray H. Matteson, ed., "Henry A. Boller, Missouri River Fur Trader," *North Dakota History* 33, no. 2 (1966): 160.

16. Edwin T. Denig, *Five Indian Tribes of the Upper Missouri: Sioux, Arickaras, Assiniboines, Crees, Crows*, ed. John C. Ewers (Norman, Okla., 1961), xxxvii.

17. John C. Ewers, *Hair Pipes in Plains Indian Adornment; A Study in Indian and White Ingenuity*, Bureau of American Ethnology Anthropological Papers no. 50 (Washington, D.C., 1957).

18. John Francis McDermott, "Museums in Early St. Louis," *Missouri Historical Society Bulletin*, 4, no. 3 (April 1940); "William Clark's Museum Once More," ibid., 16, no. 2, (January 1960).

×▬×▬×

References

Unpublished Material

The British Museum. Ethnography Department.

Manuscript notes accompanying the William Bragge Collection of Tobacco Pipes.

Hudson's Bay Company Archives. Winnipeg, Manitoba.

Manchester House Journal, 1786–87. Manuscript B.121a1, fos. 28, 33, 99.

Peter Fidler's Journal of a Journey Overland from Buckingham House to the Rocky Mountains in 1792 and 3. Manuscript E.3/2.

National Archives, Washington, D.C.

Jean Baptiste Moncravie. In Registers of Enlistments in the United States Army, 1794–1914. Records of the Adjutant Generals Office. Record Group 94.

Office Purveyor of Public Supplies. Letters Sent, April 1805 to July 1807. Book 16. Pp. 233–34.

Letters Received Regarding Fort Pierre, 1855. In Records of the Office of Quartermaster General. Record Group 92.

Correspondence Blackfeet Agency, winter 1874–75. Indian Office Records. Record Group 75.

Missouri Historical Society, St. Louis, Mo.

American Fur Company Ledger Books.

Pierre Chouteau, Jr., and Company Records.

Published Material

Abel, Annie Heloise, ed.

1932 *Chardon's Journal of Fort Clark, 1834–39*. Pierre, S.D.: Lawrence

K. Frost, Superintedent, Department of History.

1939 *Tabeau's Narrative of Loisel's Expedition to the Upper Missouri.* Norman: University of Oklahoma Press.

Abert, Lt. James W.

1970 *Through the Country of the Comanche Indians in the Fall of the Year 1845.* Edited by John Galven. San Francisco: John Howell Books.

Ahlborn, Richard C.

1972 "European Dress in Texas, 1830: As Rendered by Lino Sánchez y Tapia." *American Scene* 12 (4):1–20. Tulsa: Thomas Gilcrease Institute of American History and Art.

Albers, Patricia, and Beatrice Medicine

1983 *The Hidden Half-Studies of Plains Indian Women.* Washington, D.C.: University Press of America.

Audubon, Maria R.

1897 *Audubon and His Journals.* Edited by Elliot Coues. New York: Charles Scribner's sons.

Bad Heart Bull, Amos

1967 *A Pictographic History of the Oglala Sioux.* Text by Helen H. Blish. Lincoln: University of Nebraska Press.

Baldwin, Gordon C.

1965 *The Warrior Apaches.* Tucson: Dale Stuart King.

Bandelier, Fanny, ed.

1905 *The Journey of Alvar Nuñez Cabeza de Vaca.* New York: A. S. Barnes.

Beals, Ralph L.

1932 "The Comparative Ethnology of Northern Mexico before 1750." *Ibero-Americana* 2:93–225. Berkeley: University of California Press.

Bell, John R.

1957 *Journal of Captain John R. Bell.* Edited by H. M. Fuller and L. R. Hafen. Glendale, Calif.: Arthur H. Clark.

Bell, Robert E., Edward B. Jelks, and W. W. Newcomb

1967 *A Pilot Study of Wichita Indian Archeology and Ethnology.* n.p.

Beltrami, Giacomo C.

1828 *A Pilgrimage in Europe and America.* 2 vols. London: Hunt and Clarke.

Berlandier, Jean Louis

1969 *The Indians of Texas in 1830*. Translated by Patricia Reading LeClercq. Edited and introduced by John C. Ewers. Washington, D.C.: Smithsonian Institution Press.

Blair, Emma Helen, ed.

1911 *The Indian Tribes of the Upper Mississippi Valley and Region of the Great Lakes*. 2 vols. Cleveland: Arthur H. Clark.

Bollaert, W.

1850 "Observations of the Indian Tribes of Texas." *London Ethnological Society Journal* 2. London, England.

Boller, Henry A.

1959 *Among the Indians: Eight Years in the Far West, 1858–1866*. Edited by Milo M. Quaife. Chicago: Lakeside Press.

Bolton, Herbert E.

1908 "The Native Tribes about the East Texas Missions." *Texas State Historical Association Quarterly* 11, no. 4.

1915 *Texas in the Middle Eighteenth Century*. University of California Publications in History, vol. 3. Berkeley.

1916 *Spanish Exploration in the Southwest, 1542–1706*. New York: Charles Scribner's Sons.

Bolton, Herbert E., ed.

1914a *Athanase de Mézières and the Louisiana-Texas Frontier, 1768–1780*. 2 vols. Cleveland: Arthur H. Clark.

1914b "The Founding of the Missions on the San Gabriel River, 1745–1749." *Southwestern Historical Quarterly* 17, no. 4.

Bourke, Capt. John G.

1892 *The Medicine-Man of the Apache*. Ninth Annual Report of the Bureau of American Ethnology, 443–603. Washington, D.C.: Smithsonian Institution.

Bradbury, John

"Travels in the Interior of America, in the years 1809, 1810, and 1811." In *Early Western Travels 1748–1846*, vol. 5. Edited by Reuben Gold Thwaites. Cleveland: Arthur H. Clark.

Bradley, James H.

1923 *Characteristics, Habits, and Customs of the Blackfoot Indians*. Montana Historical Society Contributions, vol. 9. Helena.

Brown, Dee
1971 *Bury My Heart at Wounded Knee.* New York: Holt, Rinehart & Winston.
Buckley, Eleanor Claire, ed.
1898 "The Aguayo Expedition into Texas and Louisiana, 1719–1722." *Texas Historical Association Quarterly* 1, no. 4.
Burbank, John A.
1870 Report Number 67 of John A. Burbank, Governor and ex officio Superintendent of Indian Affairs, Dakota Territory." *Annual Report, Commissioner of Indian Affairs for 1870.* Washington, D.C.
Burnet, David G.
1851 "The Comanches and Other Tribes of Texas and the Policy to be Pursued Respecting Them." In *Historical and Statistical Information Respecting the History and Prospects of the Indian Tribes of the United States*, edited by Henry R. Schoolcraft, 1:229–41. Philadelphia: Lippincott, Granbo.
Burpee, Lawrence, J., ed.
1907 "York Factory to the Blackfeet Country: The Journal of Anthony Hendry, 1754–55." *Transactions of the Royal Society of Canada*, ser. 3, vol. 1. Toronto.
1908 "An Adventurer from Hudson Bay: Journal of Mathew Cocking from York Factory to the Blackfeet Country, 1772–1773." *Transactions of the Royal Society of Canada*, ser. 3, vol. 2.
1910 *Journal of Larocque from the Assiniboine to the Yellowstone*, 1805. Publications of the Canadian Archives no. 3. Ottawa.
1927 *Journals and Letters of Pierre Gaultier de Varennes de la Vérendrye and His Sons.* Champlain Society Publications, vol. 16. Toronto.
Capps, Benjamin
1979 *Woman Chief.* Garden City, N.Y.: Doubleday.
Carroll, H. Bailey, and J. Villasana Haggard, eds.
1942 *Three New Mexico Chronicles.* Albuquerque: Quivera Society.
Casañas de Jesus Maria, Fray Francisco
1927 "Fray Francisco Casañas de Jesus Maria to the Viceroy of Mexico, August 15, 1691." *Southwestern Historical Quarterly* 30, nos. 3–4.

Castañeda, Carlos E.

1936 *Our Catholic Heritage in Texas*, 1519–1936. 7 Vols. Austin: Von Boeckman-Jones.

Catlin, George

1832 Letter dated "Mandan Village, Upper Missouri, August 5th, 1832." In *New York Commercial Advertiser*, November 13, 1932.

1832 Letter. *New York Commercial Advertiser*, November 23.

1841 *Letters and Notes on the Manners, Customs, and Condition of the North American Indian*. 2 vols. London: Published by the author at Egyptian Hall.

1848 *Catlin's Notes of Eight Years Travels and Residence in Europe with His North American Indian Collection*. 2 vols. London: The author.

Chittenden, Hiram M.

1902 *The American Fur Trade of the Far West*, 2d ed. 3 vols. New York: F. P. Harper.

Clark, William Philo

1885 *The Indian Sign Language*. Philadelphia: L. R. Hammersly.

Clifford, W,

1870 Report of Capt. W. Clifford, U.S.A., Indian Agent, Fort Berthold, Sept. 1, 1869. Annual Report, Commissioner of Indian Affairs for 1869. Washington, D.C.

Cohen, Felix S.

1942 *Handbook of Federal Indian Law*, with Reference Tables and Index. Washington, D.C.: Government Printing Office.

Collins, Dabney Otis

1969 "A Happening at Oglala." *American West Magazine* 6: 15–19.

Commissioner of Indian Affairs

Annual Reports 1849, 1850, 1853, 1862, 1864, 1867, 1877, 1883, 1890, 1892. Washington, D.C.

Cordry, Donald, and Dorothy Cordry

1968 *Mexican Indian Costumes*. Austin: University of Texas Press.

Cox, Isaac Joslin, ed.

1905 *The Journeys of Rene Robert Cavelier, Sieur de La Salle*. 2 vols. New York: A.S. Barnes.

Culbertson, Thaddeus

1952 *Journal of an Expedition to the Mauvaises Terres and the Upper*

Missouri in 1850. Edited by John Francis McDermott. Bureau of American Ethnology Bulletin no. 147. Washington, D.C.: Smithsonian Institution.

Curtis, Edward S.

1930 *The North American Indian*. Vol. 19. Norwood: Plimpton Press.

Denig, Edwin T.

1930 *Indian Tribes of the Upper Missouri*. Edited by J. N. B. Hewitt. Forty-sixth Annual Report of the Bureau of American Ethnology, 1928–29, 375–628. Washington, D.C.: Smithsonian Institution.

1961 *Five Indian Tribes of the Upper Missouri: Sioux, Arickaras, Assiniboines, Crees, Crows*. Edited by John C. Ewers. Norman: University of Oklahoma Press.

Denny, Sir Cecil Edward

1939 *The Law Marches West*. Toronto: J. M. Dent and Sons.

De Smet, Pierre-Jean

1862 *Western Missions and Missionaries*. New York: J. B. Kirker.

1905 *Life, Letters, and Travels of Father Pierre-Jean De Smet, S.J.* Edited by Hiram M. Chittenden and A. T. Richardson. 4 vols. New York: F. P. Harper.

1906 "Oregon Missions and Travels over the Rocky Mountains in 1846–7." In *Early Western Travels, 1748–1846*, vol. 29. Edited by Reuben Gold Thwaites. Cleveland: Arthur H. Clark.

Dodge, Col. Richard I.

1882 *Our Wild Indians*. Hartford, Conn.: A. D. Worthington.

Donnelly, Joseph, ed.

1967 *Wilderness Kingdom: The Journals and Paintings of Father Nicholas Point*. New York: Holt, Rinehart and Winston.

Dorsey, George A.

1995 *The Mythology of the Wichita*. Norman: University of Oklahoma Press.

1934 "Caddo Customs of Childhood." *Journal of American Folklore Society* 18.

Driver, Harold E.

1961 *Indians of North America*. Chicago: University of Chicago Press.

Dusenberry, Verne

1958 "Waiting for a Day that Never Comes: Story of the Dispossessed Métis of Montana." *Montana: The Magazine of Western History*

8 (2):26–39.

Ellis, R., and C. Steen

1974 "An Indian Delegation in France, 1725." *Journal of the Illinois State Historical Society* 64 (4):384–405.

Evans, Hugh

1925 "The Journal of Hugh Evans, 1834–1845." Edited by Fred S. Perine and Grant Foreman. *Chronicles of Oklahoma* 3 (3): 175–215.

Ewers, John C.

1938 *Teton Dakota Ethnology and History.* Western Museum Laboratories, National Park Service. Berkeley.

1943 "Primitive American Commandos." *Masterkey* 17 (July): 117–25. Los Angeles: Southwest Museum.

1954 "The Indian Trade of the Upper Missouri before Lewis and Clark: An Interpretation." *Bulletin of the Missouri Historical Society* 10, no. 4.

1955 *The Horse in Blackfoot Indian Culture, with Comparative Materials from Other Western Tribes.* Bureau of American Ethnology Bulletin no. 159. Washington, D.C.: Smithsonian Institution.

1956 "The Gun of Sitting Bull." *The Beaver,* Outfit 287: 20–23.

1957 *Hair Pipes in Plains Indian Adornment: A Study in Indian and White Ingenuity.* Bureau of American Ethnology Anthropological Papers no. 50. Washington, D.C.: Smithsonian Institution.

1958 *The Blackfeet: Raiders on the Northwestern Plains.* Norman: University of Oklahoma Press.

1962 "Mothers of the Mixed-Bloods: The Marginal Woman in the History of the Upper Missouri." In *Probing the American West,* 62–70. Santa Fe: Museum of New Mexico Press.

1967 "The White Man's Strongest Medicine." *Bulletin of the Missouri Historical Society* 24: 36–46.

1967 "William Clark's Indian Museum in St. Louis, 1816–1832." In *A Cabinet of Curiosities: Five Episodes in the Evolution of American Museums.* Edited by Walter M. Whitehill, 49–72. Charlottesville: University of Virginia Press.

1968 *Indian Life on the Upper Missouri.* Norman: University of Oklahoma Press.

1968 "Plains Indian Painting: The History and Development of an American Art Form." *American West Magazine* 5, no. 2 (March):

4–15, 74–76.

1971 "A Crow Chief's Tribute to the Unknown Soldier." *American West Magazine* 8 (6): 30–35.

1971 "When Red and White Men Met." *Western Historical Quarterly* 2, no. 2 (April): 133–50.

1972a "Folk Art in the Fur Trade of the Upper Missouri." *Prologue: The Journal of the National Archives* 4 (2): 99–108.

1972b "The Influence of the Fur Trade upon the Indians of the Northern Plains." *In People and Pelts: Selected Papers from the North American Fur Trade Conference*. Edited by Malvina Bolus, 1–26. Winnipeg, Manitoba: Peguis.

1973 "The Influence of Epidemics on the Indian Populations and Cultures of Texas." *Plains Anthropologist*, n.s. vol 98: 104–115.

1974 "Symbols of Chiefly Authority in Spanish Louisiana." In *The Spanish in the Mississippi Valley, 1762–1804*, edited by John Frances McDermott, 272–84. Urbana: University of Illinois Press.

1974 "Ethnological Report on the Blackfeet and Gros Ventres Tribes of Indians." In *American Indian Ethnohistory: Plains Indians— Blackfeet Indians*, edited by David A. Horr, 23–202. New York: Garland.

1975 "Intertribal Warfare as the Precursor of Indian-White Warfare on the Northern Great Plains." *Western Historical Quarterly* 4(4): 397–410.

1976 "Indian Views of the White Man Prior to 1850: An Interpretation." In *Red Men and Hat Wearers: Viewpoints in Indian History*, edited by Daniel Tyler, 7–23. Boulder: Pruett.

1977 "The Making and Uses of Maps by Plains Indian Warriors." *By Valor and Arms* 3 (1): 36–43.

1978 "Three Effigy Pipes by an Eastern Dakota Master Carver." *American Indian Art Magazine* 3 (4): 51–55, 74.

1979a "Images of the White Man in 19th-Century Plains Indian Art." In *The Visual Arts, Plastic and Graphic*, edited by Justin M. Cordwell, 411–29. The Hague: Mouton.

1979a *Indian Art in Pipestone: George Catlin's Portfolio in the British Museum*. London: British Museum Publications; Washington, D.C.: Smithsonian Institution Press.

1980 "Climate, Acculturation, and Costume: A History of Women's

Clothing among the Indians of the Southern Plains." *Plains Anthropologist*, n.s. vol. 25 (87): 63–82.

1981 "The Use of Artifacts and Pictures in the Study of Plains Indian History, Art and Religion." In *The Research Potential of Anthropological Museum Collections*, ed. Anne-Marie E. Cantwell, James B. Griffin, and Nan A. Rothschild, Annals of the New York Academy of Sciences. vol 376: 247–66.

1994 "Women's Roles in Plains Indian Warfare." In *Skeletal Biology in the Great Plains*, edited by Douglas W. Owsley and Richard L. Jantz, 325–32. Washington, D.C.: Smithsonian Institution Press.

Ewers, John C., and William Wildschut

1959 "Crow Indian Beadwork: A Descriptive and Historical Study." *Contributions* 16. New York: Museum of the American Indian Heye Foundation.

Garcia, Andrew

1967 *Tough Trip Through Paradise*. Edited by Bennett H. Stern. Boston: Houghton Mifflin.

Garry, Nicholas

1900 "Diary of Nicholas Garry, Deputy-Governor of the Hudson's Bay Company," *Proceedings and Transactions, Royal Society of Canada*, 2d ser. vol. 6. Toronto.

Gilmore, Melvin R.

1911 *Uses of Plants by the Indians of the Missouri River Region*, Thirty-third Annual Report of the Bureau of American Ethnology, 43–154. Washington, D.C.: Smithsonian Institution.

Goldstein, Marcus A.

1934 "Anthropology of the Comanches." *American Journal of Physical Anthropology* 19 (2): 289–319.

Gregg, Josiah

1954 *Commerce of the Prairies*. Edited by Max L. Moorhead. Reprint. Norman: University of Oklahoma Press.

Grinnell, George B.

1923 *The Cheyenne Indians: Their History and Ways of Life*. 2 vols. New Haven: Yale University Press.

Hammond, George P., and Agapita Rey, eds.

1953 *Don Juan de Oñate, Colonizer of New Mexico, 1595–1628*. Albuquerque: University of New Mexico Press.

1966 *The Rediscovery of New Mexico*. Albuquerque: University of New Mexico Press.

Hanson, Charles E., Jr.

1955 "The Northwest Gun." *Publications in Anthropology* no. 2. Lincoln: Nebraska State Historical Society.

1972 "J. B. Moncravie." In *The Mountain Men and the Fur Trade of the Far West*, edited by Le Roy Hafen, vol. 9: 289–98. Glendale, Calif.: Arthur H. Clark.

Harper, J. Russell, ed.

1971 *Paul Kane's Frontier*. Austin: University of Texas Press.

Hatcher, Mattie Austen, trans. and ed.

1927 "Description of the Tejas or Asinai Indians, 1671 to 1722." *Southwestern Historical Quarterly*. 31(2): 50–52. Austin: Texas State Historical Association.

Hatt, Gudmund

1969 "Arctic Skin Clothing in Eurasia and America: An Ethnographic Study." *Arctic Anthropology*. 5(2)1–148. Madison: University of Wisconsin Press.

Hayden, F. Y.

1860 *Contributions to the Ethnography and Philology of the Indian Tribes of the Missouri Valley*. Transactions American Philosophical Society, no. 12. Philadelphia.

Hennepin, Louis

1903 *A New Discovery of the Vast Country in America*. Edited by Reuben Gold Thwaites. 2 vols. Chicago: A. C. McClurg.

Henry, Alexander

1809 *Travels and Adventures in Canada, and in the Indian Territories Between the Years 1760 and 1776*. New York: I. Riley.

Henry, Alexander, and David Thompson

1897 *New Light on the Early History of the Greater Northwest*. Edited by Elliot Coues. 3 vols. New York: F. P. Harper.

Hewitt, J. N. B., ed.

1937 *Journal of Rudolph Friederich Kurz . . . 1846–1852*. Translated by Myrtis Jarrell. Bureau of American Ethnology Bulletin no. 115. Washington, D.C.: Smithsonian Institution.

Hodge, F. W., ed.

1910 *Handbook of American Indians North of Mexico*. Bureau of

American Ethnology Bulletin no. 30. 2 vols. Washington, D.C.: Smithsonian Institution.

Hornaday, William T.

1889 "The Extermination of the American Bison." *U.S. National Museum Annual Report for 1886–1887*. Washington, D.C.: Smithsonian Institution.

Houck, Louis, ed.

1909 *The Spanish Régime in Missouri*. 2 vols. Chicago: R. R. Donnelley & Sons.

Howard, Joseph Kinsey

1952 *Strange Empire*. Westport, Conn.: Greenwood Press.

James, Edwin

1823 *Account of an Expedition from Pittsburgh to the Rocky Mountains, Performed in the Years 1819 and 1820*. 2 vols. London: Longman, Hurst, Rees, Orme and Brown.

Johnson, A. M.

1956 "Mons. Maugenest Suggests," *The Beaver*, (Summer 1956): 49–53. Winnipeg.

Josephy, Alvin M., Jr.

1969 *The American Indian and the Bureau of Indian Affairs—1969*. Hearings, Subcommittee on Indian Education, Committee on Labor and Public Welfare, U.S. Senate, 91st Cong., 1st sess., pt. 2, app. Washington, D.C.

Josephy, Alvin M., Jr., ed.

1961 *American Heritage Book of Indians*. New York: American Heritage.

Kane, Paul

1925 *Wanderings of an Artist Among the Indians of North America from Canada to Vancouver's Island and Oregon, Through the Hudson's Bay Company's Territory and Back Again*. Toronto: Radisson Society of Canada.

Kappler, Charles J., comp. and ed.

1904 *Indian Affairs, Laws and Treaties*. Vol. 2. *Treaties*. Washington, D.C.: Government Printing Office.

Kellogg, Louise Phelps, ed.

1917 *Early Narratives of the Northwest, 1634–1699*. New York: Charles Scribner's Sons.

Kelsey, Henry

1929 The Kelsey Papers. Edited by A. G. Doughty and Chester Martin. Ottawa: Public Archives of Canada.

Kinnaird, Lawrence, ed.

1946–49 *Spain in the Mississippi Valley, 1765–1794*. 3 vols. American Historical Association Annual Report. Washington, D.C.

Kroeber, Alfred L.

1908 *Ethnology of the Gros Ventres*. American Museum of Natural History. Anthropological Papers, no. 1. New York.

1939 *Cultural and Natural Areas of Native North America*. Berkeley: University of California Press.

La Jonquire, P. J. de T.

1908 Letter, September 25, 1751, to French Minister in The French Regime in Wisconsin. Wisconsin Historical Society Collections, vol. 10.

Larpenteur, Charles

1933 *Forty Years a Trader on the Upper Missouri*. Edited by Milo M. Quaife. Chicago: Lakeside Press.

Le Sueur, Pierre-Charles

1902 *Le Sueur's Voyage up the Mississippi*. Collections of the State Historical Society of Wisconsin, vol. 16. Madison.

Lehmer, Donald J.

1971 *Introduction to Middle Missouri Archeology*. National Park Service Anthropological Papers no. 1. Washington, D.C.

Lewis, Meriwether

1961 *The Lewis and Clark Expedition*. 3 vols. Philadelphia: Lippincott.

Ludlow, Fitz Hugh

1870 *The Heart of the Continent*. New York: Hurd and Houghton.

McDermott, John Francis

1940 "Museums in Early St. Louis." *Missouri Historical Society Bulletin*, vol. 4, no. 3 (April). St. Louis.

1960 "William Clark's Museum Once More." *Missouri Historical Society Bulletin*, 16, no. 2 (January). St. Louis.

Mackenzie, Charles

1889–90 "The Missouri Indians, 1804–1805." In Louis R. Masson, Les bourgeois de la Compagnie du Nord-Ouest. 2 vols. Quebec: Générale A. Coté.

Mallery, Garrick

1881 *Sign Language among North American Indians*. First Annual Report of the Bureau of American Ethnology, 263–552. Washington, D.C.: Smithsonian Institution.

1886 *Pictographs of the North American Indians*. Fourth Annual Report of the Bureau of American Ethnology. 3–256. Washington, D.C.: Smithsonian Institution.

1893 *Picture-Writing of the American Indians*. Tenth Annual Report of the Bureau of American Ethnology, 1888–89. Washington, D.C.: Smithsonian Institution.

Mandelbaum, David G.

1940 *The Plains Cree*. American Museum of Natural History Anthropological Papers, vol. 37, pt. 2. New York.

Matthews, Washington

1877 *Ethnography and Philology of the Hidatsa Indians*. U.S. Geological and Geographical Survey Miscellaneous Publication no. 7, 1–239. Washington, D.C.

1883 *Navaho Silversmiths*. Second Annual Report, Bureau of American Ethnology, 167–79. Washington, D.C.

1884 *Navaho Weavers*. Third Annual Report, Bureau of American Ethnology, 371–91. Washington, D.C.

1887 *The Mountain Chant*. Fifth Annual Report Bureau of American Ethnology, 379–467. Washington, D.C.

Matteson, Ray H., ed.

1966 "Henry A. Boller, Missouri River Fur Trader." *North Dakota History* 33(2).

Maximilian, Alexander Philip, Prince of Wied-Neuwied

1906 "Travels in the Interior of North America, 1832–1834." In *Early Western Travels, 1748–1846*, edited by Reuben Gold Thwaites. Vols. 22–24. Cleveland: Arthur H. Clark.

Mooney, James

1898 *Calendar History of the Kiowa Indians*. Seventeenth Annual Report of the Bureau of American Ethnology, 129–445. Washington, D.C.: Smithsonian Institution.

1928 *The Aboriginal Population of America North of Mexico*. Smithsonian Miscellaneous Collections, vol. 80, no. 7. Washington, D.C.

Morgan, Thisba H.

1958 "Reminiscences of My Days in the Land of the Ogallala Sioux." *Report and Historical Collections of the South Dakota State Historical Society*, 29: 32.

Morse, Jedidiah

1822 *A Report to the Secretary of War of the United States on Indian Affairs*. New Haven: S. Converse.

Morton, Arthur S., ed.

1929 *The Journal of Duncan M'Gillivray of the Northwest Company at Fort George of the Saskatchewan, 1794–1795*. Toronto: Macmillan of Canada Ltd.

Mulloy, William

1958 *A Preliminary Historical Outline for the Northwestern Plains*. University of Wyoming Publications, vol. 22, nos 1–2. Laramie.

Murray, Alexander H.

1910 *Journal of the Yukon, 1847–48*. Edited by Lawrence J. Burpee. Publications of the Canadian Archives no. 4. Ottawa.

Nasatir, Abraham P., ed.

1952 *Before Lewis and Clark: Documents Illustrating the History of the Missouri, 1785–1804*. 2 vols. St. Louis: St. Louis Historical Documents Foundation.

Neighbors, R. S.

1852 "The Na-u-ni or Comanches of Texas." In *Historical and Statistical Information Respecting the History, Condition and Prospects of the Indian Tribes of the United States*, edited by Henry R. Schoolcraft, vol. 2: 125–34. Philadelphia.

Newcomb, William W., Jr.

1961 *The Indians of Texas, from Prehistoric to Modern Times*. Austin: University of Texas Press.

1978 *German Artist on the Texas Frontier: Friedrich Richard Petri*. Austin: University of Texas Press.

Nixon, Pat Ireland

1946 *The Medical Story of Early Texas, 1528–1853*. Lancaster, Pa.: Lancaster, Pennsylvania Press, Inc.

Nye, Wilbur S.

1962 *Bad Medicine and Good: Tales of the Kiowas*. Norman: University of Oklahoma Press.

1978 *Plains Indian Raiders*. Norman: University of Oklahoma Press.

Opler, Morris E.

1941 *An Apache Life-Way: The Economic, Social, and Religious Institutions of the Chiricahua Indians*. Chicago: University of Chicago Press.

Parker, W. B.

1856 *Notes Taken during the Expedition Commanded by Captain R. B. Marcy through Unexplored Texas, in the Summer and Fall of 1854*. Philadelphia: Hayes and Zeil.

Parks, Douglas R., ed.

in press *A Fur Trader on the Upper Missouri: The "Journals" and "Description" of Jean-Baptiste Truteau, 1794–96*. Trans. Mildred Mott Wedel. Lincoln: University of Nebraska Press.

Pease, T. C., and R. C. Werner, eds.

1934 *Memoir of De Gannes concerning the Illinois Country*. Collections of the Illinois State Historical Library, vol. 23. French Series, vol. 1. Springfield.

Petersen, Karen Daniels

1968 *Howling Wolf: A Cheyenne Warrior's Graphic Interpretation of His People*. Palo Alto, Calif.: American West.

1971 *Plains Indian Art from Fort Marion*. Norman: University of Oklahoma Press.

Pinckney, Pauline

1967 *Painting in Texas: The Nineteenth Century*. Austin: University of Texas Press.

Pino, Pedro Bautista

1942 *Three New Mexico Chronicles: The Exposicion of Don Pedro Bautista Pino, 1832*. Edited by H. Bailey Carroll and J. Villasana Haggard. Albuquerque: University of New Mexico Press.

Point, Nicholas

1967 *Wilderness Kingdom: Indian Life in the Rocky Mountains, 1840–1847*. Translated by J. P. Donnelly. New York: Holt, Rinehart and Winston.

Pope, Alexander

1824 *An Essay on Man*. New York: Clark and Maynard.

Powell, Peter John

1969 *Sweet Medicine: The Continuing Role of the Sacred Arrows, the*

257

Sun Dance, and the Sacred Buffalo Hat in Northern Cheyenne History. 2 vols. Norman: University of Oklahoma Press.

1981 *People of the Sacred Mountain.* 2 vols. New York: Harper and Row.

Quaife, Milo M., ed.

1916 *Sergeant Ordway's Journal.* Publication of the State Historical Society of Wisconsin. Madison.

Red, William S., ed.

1914 "Extracts from the Diary of W. Y. Allen, 1838–39." *Southwestern Historical Quarterly* 17, no. 1 (1914): 53. Austin: Texas State Historical Society.

Riggs, Thomas L.

1958 "Sunset to Sunset." *Report and Historical Collections of the South Dakota State Historical Society* 29: 256. Pierre.

Robinson, Doane

1904 *A History of the Dakota or Sioux Indians from Their Earliest Traditions.* South Dakota Historical Society Collections, vol. 2, pt. 2. Aberdeen.

Rodnick, David

1938 *The Fort Belknap Assiniboine of Montana.* Philadelphia: Published by the author.

Ross, Alexander

1856 *The Red River Settlement, Its Rise, Progress, and Present State.* London: Smith, Elder and Co.

Ruíz, Jose Francisco

1972 *Report on the Indian Tribes of Texas.* Translated by Georgette Dorn. Edited by John C. Ewers. New Haven: Yale University Press.

Sánchez y Tapia, José Maria

1926 "A Trip to Texas in 1828." Translated by Carlos E. Castañeda. *Southwestern Historical Quarterly.* 29(4): 249–88. Austin: Texas Historical Society.

Santa Maria, Fray Vicente

1930 *Relácion historica de la Colonia del Nuevo Santander y costa del San Mexicano.* Publicaciones del Archivo General de la Nación, vol. 4. Mexico City.

Schultz, J. Willard

1919 *Running Eagle, the Warrior Girl.* Boston: Houghton Mifflin.

Schultz, James W., and Jessie L. Donaldson

1930 *The Sun God's Children.* Boston: Houghton Mifflin.

Scott, Hugh L.

1911 "Notes on the Kado, or Sun Dance of the Kiowa Indians." *American Anthropologist,* n.s., 13(3): 345–79.

Sibley, John

1832 Historical Sketches of Several Indian Tribes in Louisiana, South of the Arkansas River, and between the Mississippi and Rio Grande. American State Papers, Class. 11, Indian Affairs. Vol. 1.

Smithwick, Noah

1900 *The Evolution of a State or Recollections of Old Texas Days.* Austin: Gammel Book Co.

Stearn, E. M., and A. E. Stearn

1945 *The Effect of Smallpox on the Destiny of the Amerindian.* Boston: B. Humphries.

Sunder, John C.

1964 *The Fur Trade of the Upper Missouri, 1840–1865.* Norman: University of Oklahoma Press.

Swanton, John R.

1996 *Source Material on the History and Ethnology of the Caddo Indians.* Norman: University of Oklahoma Press.

1952 *The Indian Tribes of North America.* Bureau of American Ethnology Bulletin no. 145. Washington, D.C.: Smithsonian Institution.

Taylor, Joseph Henry

1897 *Sketches of Frontier Life.* Bismarck: The Author.

Thomas, Alfred Barnaby, ed.

1932 *Forgotten Frontiers: A Study of the Spanish Indian Policy of Don Juan Bautista de Anza, Governor of New Mexico, 1777–1778.* Norman: University of Oklahoma Press.

Thompson, Erwin N.

1968 "Fort Union Trading Post." *Historic Structures Report, Part II.* Historical Data Section, National Park Service. Washington, D.C.

Thwaites, Reuben Gold, ed.

1902 *The French Regime in Wisconsin . . . 1634–1748.* 3 vols. Madison:

State Historical Society of Wisconsin.

1904–5 *Original Journals of the Lewis and Clark Expedition.* 4 vols. New York: Dodd Mead.

1904–7 *Early Western Travels, 1748–1846.* 32 vols. Cleveland: Arthur H. Clark.

Tixier, Victor

1940 *Tixier's Travels on the Osage Prairies.* Edited by John Francis McDermott. Norman: University of Oklahoma Press.

Tunnell, C. D., and W. W. Newcomb

1969 *A Lipan Apache Mission: San Lorenzo de la Santa Cruz, 1762–1771.* Texas Memorial Museum Bulletin no. 14. Austin.

Tyrrell, J. B., ed.

1916 *David Thompson's Narrative of His Explorations in Western America, 1784–1812.* Champlain Society Publications, vol. 12. Toronto.

U.S. Census Office, 11th U.S. Census, 1890

1894 Report of Indians Taxed and Indians Not Taxed in the United States. Washington, D.C.: U.S. Government Printing Office.

U.S. Department of Agriculture

1936 *Atlas of American Agriculture.* Washington, D.C.: Government Printing Office.

Vogel, Virgil J.

1970 *American Indian Medicine.* Norman: University of Oklahoma Press.

Wallace, Ernest, and E. A. Hoebel

1952 *The Comanche, Lords of the South Plains.* Norman: University of Oklahoma Press.

Wallace, W. S.

1952 "Notes of an 18th-Century Northerner." *The Beaver*, Outfit 283. Winnipeg.

Wedel, Mildred Mott

1974 "Le Sueur and the Dakota Sioux." In *Aspects of Upper Great Lakes Anthropology: Papers in Honor of Lloyd A. Wilford.* St. Paul: Minnesota Historical Society.

1988 *The Wichita Indians, 1541–1750.* Ethnohistorical Essays, Reprints in Anthropology, no. 38. Lincoln, Neb.: J. & L. Reprint.

Wedel, Waldo R.
1961 *Prehistoric Man on the Great Plains*. Norman: University of Oklahoma Press.

Wellman, Paul I.
1934 *Death on the Prairie*. London: W. Foolstian.

Wheelock, Lt. T. R.
1860 *Journal of Colonel Dodge's Expedition from Fort Gibson to Pawnee Pic Village (1834)*. American State Papers, Military Affairs, vol 5: 373–82. Washington, D.C.: Gales and Seaton.

Wilkinson, Mahlon
1864 Report Number 117 of Indian Agent M. Wilkinson in Report of the Commissioner of Indian Affairs. Washington, D.C.

Wilson, Thomas
1901 "Arrow Wounds." *American Anthropologist*, n.s. 3 (July–September): 517–31.

Williams, Glyndwr, ed.
1969 *Andrew Graham's Observations on Hudson's Bay, 1767–91*. Hudson's Bay Record Society, vol. 27. London.

Winship, George Parker, ed.
1896 *The Coronado Expedition, 1540 1542*. Fourteenth Annual Report of the Bureau of American Ethnology, part 1: 329–613. Washington, D.C.

Wissler, Clark
1912 *Ceremonial Bundles of the Blackfoot Indians*. American Museum of Natural History, Anthropological Papers, vol. 7, pt. 2. New York.

1915 *Costumes of the Plains Indians*. American Museum of Natural History, Anthropological Papers, vol. 17, pt. 2: 39–91. New York.

Wood, W. Raymond
1967 *An Interpretation of Mandan Culture History*. Bureau of American Ethnology Bulletin no. 198. Washington, D.C.: Smithsonian Institution.

1974 "Northern Plains Village Cultures Internal Stability and External Relationships." *Journal of Anthropological Research* 30, no. 1 (spring): 1–16. Albuquerque: University of New Mexico.

Wright, Muriel H.
1951 *A Guide to the Indian Tribes of Oklahoma*. Norman: University

of Oklahoma Press.

Yarrow, H. C.

1881 *A Further Contribution to the Study of the Mortuary Customs of the North American Indians.* First Annual Report of the Bureau of American Ethnology. Washington, D.C.: Smithsonian Institution.

Index